Library of
Davidson College

Dragmalogia de Eligibili Vite Genere

Paris, Bibliothèque Nationale, MS Latin 6694, fol. lr. Giovanni di Conversino da Ravenna, Dragmalogia, *Speech V–1 to second sentence of P–4, with illuminated initial.*

Giovanni di Conversino da Ravenna

Dragmalogia de Eligibili Vite Genere

Edited and Translated by
Helen Lanneau Eaker

With Introduction and Notes by
Benjamin G. Kohl

The Renaissance Society of America

Lewisburg
Bucknell University Press
London Associated University Presses

© 1980 by Associated University Presses, Inc.

Associated University Presses, Inc.
Cranbury, New Jersey 08512

Associated University Presses
Magdalen House
136–148 Tooley Street
London SE1 2TT, England

Library of Congress Cataloguing in Publication Data

Giovanni da Ravenna, 1343–1408.
Dragmalogia de eligibili vite genere.

(Bucknell Renaissance texts in translation)
Bibliography: p.
Includes index.
1. Ethics.   2. Political science—Early works to 1700.
3. Italy—Politics and government—1268–1599.   4. Giovanni da Ravenna, 1343–1408.
I. Eaker, Helen Lanneau, 1922–   II. Title.   III. Series.
BJ1131.G5613 1978   170   75–3911
ISBN 0-8387-1897-3

PRINTED IN THE UNITED STATES OF AMERICA

To Frederic Chapin Lane

and

To the Memory of Berthold Louis Ullman

Contents

Acknowledgments	9
Introduction by BENJAMIN G. KOHL	13
1. Life and Works of Giovanni da Ravenna	13
2. The Argument of the *Dragmalogia*	31
3. Manuscripts Used in This Edition	39
Dragmalogia Johannis de Ravenna de Eligibili Vite Genere	50
Dragmalogia of Giovanni da Ravenna on the Preferable Way of Life	51
1. The Troubled State of Italy	51
2. Why the Ravennate [i.e., Giovanni] Left the Court of Carrara	67
3. Courtly Arts	83
4. Relative Merits of a Monarchy and a Republic	107
5. Relative Merits of a Master and a Lord	141
6. The Good Life	165
7. Country versus City Life	169
8. Vices as Sources of Virtues	195
9. Value of the Seven Deadly Sins	203
10. Criticisms of Venice	225
11. The Nature of Liberty	243
12. Status of the Religious Vocation	257
Notes to the *Dragmalogia*	273
Selected Bibliography	285
Index	289

Acknowledgments

Two collaborators working for the most part on the western side of the Atlantic have, in the course of editing and introducing the text of a humanist whose writings exist mainly in widely scattered manuscripts in European libraries, incurred an unconscionable number of debts. First of all, we wish to acknowledge the very existence of this volume to Professor Kristine Gilmartin Wallace of Rice University, who brought us together in what has been, we hope, a profitable collaboration. For permission to publish their respective manuscripts used in this edition, we thank the directing bodies of the Bibliothèque Nationale, Paris, and the Fondazione Querini-Stampalia, Venice. For aid in procuring microfilms of or information about manuscripts used in the edition and introduction, we wish to thank Professor Emeritus Frederic C. Lane of the Johns Hopkins University, Professor Paul Oskar Kristeller of Columbia University, Professor Reinhold C. Mueller of the University of Arizona, and Professor Rhoda Rappaport of Vassar College. Financial support for the purchase of microfilms and the preparation of the typescript was generously provided by the Research Committee of Vassar College and by Rice University. We are grateful also to Professor George B. Parks, former chairman of the publication board of the Renaissance Society of America, for his interest and help in making our publication a reality. We are much in the debt of the Society's Executive Secretary, Professor Eugene Rice, for his interest in including this edition in the Text Series of the Society. Finally, we wish to express

our appreciation to the staff of Associated University Presses, Inc., and especially to Mrs. Mathilde E. Finch, Editor in Chief, for the expert care they have given in seeing our volume through the press.

Mr. Kohl wishes to thank the American Academy in Rome for the award of a fellowship in Post-Classical Humanistic Studies that enabled him to complete the introduction and notes. He is much in the debt of Dr. Hans Baron for a precise and penetrating reading of the introduction, which permitted him to eliminate many errors and ambiguities. For those errors of fact and interpretation which remain, Mr. Kohl is of course fully responsible. Finally, he wishes to express his gratitude to his wife and family, who have lived with this project longer than they could be expected to and who have borne cheerfully with its many vicissitudes.

Mrs. Eaker would like to thank Professor Konrad Gries of Queens College for many suggested improvements in interpretation and wording of the text. Her greatest debt is to Professor Guido Guarino of Rutgers University, the editor of the Bucknell Renaissance Series, who reviewed her entire manuscript, emending errors of translation and many infelicitous turns of phrase. To her husband, Professor Emeritus J. Gordon Eaker of the University of Houston, she is grateful for both professional and personal help, given abundantly.

Finally, we wish to assert that, although we have never met, our collaboration has been closer than the division of labor stated on the title page might suggest. Mr. Kohl made a rough transcription of the Venice manuscript that was of some use in Mrs. Eaker's edition. He has also made many suggestions for improvements in earlier versions of both the Latin text and the English translation. For her part, in addition to bearing the responsibility for both text and translation, Mrs. Eaker has contributed several of the notes and materially improved the wording of the introduction. The conventional confession that whatever errors of fact or interpretation remaining are the author's own therefore weighs equally upon us both.

In our dedication we seek to acknowledge, however inadequately, our profound debt to our former mentors, two fine

American scholars who, in quite different ways, have contributed so enormously to the study of the Italian Renaissance.

        Benjamin G. Kohl
        Poughkeepsie, New York
        Helen Lanneau Eaker
        Houston, Texas

Introduction

1. Life and Works of Giovanni da Ravenna

Early in the fourteenth century on the northern slopes of the Apennines in the region above Modena, three brothers were born into the local feudal family of the da Frignano.[1] One brother, Bonetto, studied surgery at Bologna and remained in that city to practice his profession for the rest of his life. Another brother, Tommaso, was called to the priesthood as a religious in the Franciscan Order, and rose to become Provincial of the Order at Bologna in 1354, Minister-General at Assisi in 1367, Patriarch of Grado in 1372, and Cardinal of the Church from September 1378 until his death a little more than three years later. The third brother, Conversino, chose the profession of medicine, obtained his doctorate at Bologna, and received a chair in medicine at the University of Siena some time after 1321. In 1342 Conversino met the young King Louis of Hungary and accepted his invitation to become a physician at the Hungarian court in Buda, where he remained the rest of his life. A year after Conversino and his wife arrived in the capital city, their only son, Giovanni, was born. The stay in Hungary of the infant Giovanni di Conversino da Ravenna, as he came to be known, was brief; soon after the death of his mother, the two-year-old infant was sent back

to Italy with his tutor, Michele da Zagrabia, to be entrusted to the care of his uncle Tommaso.

Giovanni's early years were spent in households and schools, under the supervision of a variety of teachers. First he lived in Ferrara, then at Bologna under the tutelage of two harsh teachers whose treatment caused him to run away. Finally, Uncle Tommaso placed him under the nuns of S. Paolo in Ravenna, and the next year he entered the grammar school of Donato Albanzani in the same city. For all his early migrations and indifferent treatment, Giovanni received a sound elementary Latin education. Like most boys of that period, he began with the study of the Psalter; he moved on to reading the works of Prudentius and the *Disticha Catonis;* he studied a rhymed version of St. Augustine's *Sententiae,* and ended with Boethius's *Consolation of Philosophy.*

At the age of ten Giovanni's life changed radically; he was betrothed to be married. To free himself from the cares of guardianship, to place Giovanni near a small patrimony inherited from his recently deceased father, and to give the boy a normal home life, Tommaso arranged the engagement of his nephew in 1353 to a somewhat older child in Ravenna, Margherita Furlan, the daughter of a local physician. Giovanni was sent to live in the home of his prospective in-laws, and two years later the two were married. But the early death of both of Margherita's parents deprived the youngsters of any close adult supervision. Since Giovanni found his bride frivolous, feckless, lazy, and completely incapable of running the household, the young couple soon quarreled. Tommaso found it necessary to send Giovanni to study under the Franciscans in Ferrara.

Giovanni's departure from his wife in 1355 set the pattern for his wanderings during the rest of their marriage. The next fifteen years were spent in peregrinations between the cities of north-central Italy and his nominal home in Ravenna. The year 1357 found Giovanni employed for a few months as a waiter and clerk in the household of Michele di Lapo de' Medici in Florence. He returned to Ravenna to find Margherita expecting their only child (Conversino, named after his grand-

father), but promptly departed for Bologna to further his studies in the Trivium. In the spring of 1359, having completed the first two parts on grammar and dialectic, Giovanni enrolled in courses in rhetoric. The first section, the exposition of the famous textbook of Giovanni di Bonandrea, the *Bononianatus*, lasted until Easter; in the early summer Giovanni followed the subsequent course on the pseudo-Cicero *Ad Herennium*. Partly in response to the financial exigencies at Ravenna, for the next two years Giovanni attended a more practical course at the notary school in Bologna, and in 1363 he became a full-fledged notary. But the attraction of literary studies was strong. As a member of the household of the grammarian Pietro da Moglio, Giovanni followed the master to Padua in the fall of 1363 and briefly studied at the university there. His nostalgia for the student life at Bologna was compelling, however, and the following spring he returned to the more famous university city. Giovanni's reputation as a student of literature preceded him, and at Bologna he gave a series of lectures commenting on the *Factorum ac Dictorum Memorabilium libri IX* of the Roman historian Valerius Maximus.

This first teaching experience, though brief, marked the end of his formal education. Giovanni now entered into the Goliardic world of a former student and not-yet-scholar in Bologna. After several years of this life, Giovanni left the university city (perhaps because of his scrapes with local authorities) to serve as tutor in Ferrara in the household of a courtier of the *signore* of the city, Niccolò II d'Este. At the urging of an old Bolognese schoolmate, Niccolò Boschetti, he soon traveled to Treviso and accepted a position as a teacher of Latin grammar in the school there.[2] At Treviso also he met a local notary and scholar, Paolo Rugolo, who was to become his closest intellectual companion, recipient of some of his more thoughtful letters and tracts, and his lifelong friend.

His Trevisan sojourn was cut short in 1367 by news of a disaster in Ravenna. His son, Conversino, had been blinded in one eye in a playground accident. Giovanni left his teaching position and returned to his home. His fame as a teacher and scholar preceded him at Ravenna; shortly after he arrived in

his adopted city the *signore* Guido II da Polenta appointed Giovanni as one of the Ravennates who served as foreign notaries at the *podestà's* court in Florence. In July 1368 Giovanni took office in Florence, but after a few months he tired of the exacting and arduous task of a court notary. He happily accepted an appointment as a lecturer at the University of Florence. There, making good use of the training he had received at Bologna, Giovanni commented on Vergil's *Georgics* and the rhetorical text *Ad Herennium*. According to his own testimony, the students asked him to stay on to lecture in other courses in the arts, but perhaps because of his youth (he was only twenty-five at the time) or his feeling of inadequate preparation, Giovanni chose to resign his post in the University.[3] Shortly after his resignation, at the invitation of the Bishop Pietro da Barone, Giovanni returned to a teaching post at Treviso and to a life of amorous adventures.

Since Giovanni's life of adventure and wandering had consumed his small patrimony, his wife and son in Ravenna began to suffer deprivation.[4] Soon after he returned to Treviso, he was joined by Margherita and Conversino. Both were gravely ill as a result of the poverty and neglect that Giovanni's itinerant life had caused. A few weeks after reaching Treviso, Margherita died and Conversino only narrowly escaped death. Giovanni felt enormous responsibility for the death of his wife, whom he knew he had mistreated. In the retrospect of his autobiography written nearly thirty years after the event, the self-recrimination and agony that her death caused is apparent.

> Into this situation entered my wife and son, sadder than whom I have never seen. Through the change of regions and because of the better quality of the air, my son was just able to overcome his illness. But, then, my wife, soon after taking sick, died because of my neglect and my guilt.[5]

Shortly after this family tragedy, Giovanni's friend Paolo Rugolo procured for him a teaching post in the small Veneto hill town of Conegliano. In July 1372, when newly installed there, Giovanni was visited by one of his deceased wife's relatives, Luigi da Ravenna. Probably in a quest for vengeance,

Luigi tried to poison Giovanni several times with arsenic. The attempts were not fatal, but Giovanni was severely weakened and remained bedridden for more than half a year. In this enforced period of convalescence, Giovanni had an opportunity for perhaps the first time to take stock of himself and to consider the future course of his life. Soon after recovering from his illness, Giovanni visited Uncle Tommaso, who had recently been installed in Venice as Patriarch of Grado. Unable to find suitable employment in Venice, Giovanni agreed to accept a teaching position in Belluno and early in 1374 he reached his new home, located in the northern Veneto in the foothills of the Italian Alps. At the age of thirty, his life as a Goliard was over, his career as a teacher, author, and courtier lay ahead.

Giovanni's five years in Belluno saw the establishment of a new family and first attempts at the literary expression of his moral and philosophical ideas. In 1375 he married a wealthy Bellunese widow, Benasuda, and the next year their only child, a son Israele, was born. Within his new domestic situation, Giovanni took charge of the local grammar school and began to compose short tracts and polished, thematic letters. The death of Petrarch in the summer of 1374 prompted one of his first literary efforts, a letter of consolation addressed to his former teacher Donato Albanzani. Giovanni had met the famed humanist through an introduction from Donato in 1363, and he had renewed his acquaintance with a visit to Petrarch at his house in Arquà at Christmas in 1373. His personal acquaintance with Petrarch, added to his sincere concern for Donato's grief, gives the letter poignancy and authority.[6]

Other works of this period, *De fato, De miseria humane vite,* and the fragmentary *De Christi conceptu,* show a Stoic-Christian outlook and concern with moral philosophy.[7] In the two shorter tracts Giovanni treated in cursory fashion the nature and purpose of the incarnation and of the origins of human suffering, which he posited as beginning even before birth. In the *De fato* Giovanni turned to one of the perennial philosophic problems of early Italian humanist thought—the question of free will and determinism. In this tract Giovanni

argued against the concept of blind fate that the ancients had accepted, and for the utility of the human will in shaping an individual's own destiny. The treatise, which took the form of a letter addressed to Paolo Rugolo, begins with a condemnation of the ancients' belief in fate and an attack on astrological determinism as held by both the contemporary astronomer Marco Trevisan and the ninth-century Arabian scientist Abū Ma'shar. Giovanni used St. Augustine's arguments against the power of fate, except when it is identified with the Christian concept of divine providence.[8] Similarly, Giovanni followed St. Augustine in at once admitting the power of divine providence and asserting the freedom of man to will moral ends. In support of God's omnipotence, Giovanni foreshadows the argument of the *Dragmalogia,* that good often proceeds from apparent evil, and indeed he tells the anecdote of St. Bernard of Clairvaux and the thief that he also used in the late dialogue to prove this point. At the same time, Giovanni combines, as did many of his contemporary humanists, a belief in God's providence with an assertion of the individual's freedom to determine his own goals and actions. In these earliest of his inquiries into matters of moral philosophy, Giovanni broached one of the commonplace themes of early Renaissance thought, the grandeur and misery of man.[9]

During the years at Belluno, Giovanni's relations with his uncle seem to have mellowed. In 1378 he received as a belated wedding present part of his inheritance in the form of three crates of books from his father's estate. Partially as a result of this new closeness, Giovanni wrote a long dialogue dedicated to his uncle on the occasion of his elevation to the cardinalate. In this *Dialogus inter Johannem et Literam* another commonplace theme, the status of the religious, was treated in some detail. As in his other dialogues, one interlocutor, in this case the author of the letter being sent to his Uncle Tommaso, Johannes, does most of the talking, while the other, here Litera, or the letter being sent, usually only asks questions or makes short responses. Since the dialogue shows many of Giovanni's concerns of this period and anticipates some of the arguments of the *Dragmalogia,* it may be worthwhile to treat

it extensively here, particularly since it has never before been analyzed.[10]

The dialogue begins with a consideration of the qualities of Tommaso that earned him the cardinalate and then moves on to discussions of the calling of the religious life, the duties of prelates, the demands of chastity, and the qualities of leadership expected of churchmen. These discussions of the demands of virtue in the religious vocation next entail a consideration of the role of fortune in determining the success of any career. In this context the Johannes of the *Dialogus* describes the duel between *fortuna* and *virtus,* in which the exercise of the individual will is the major cause of the success of virtue. Hence Giovanni here reasserts his belief that adverse fortune can be overcome through the exercise of virtue, and more generally, that the religious life, if properly practiced, can lead to salvation. Next, in a series of questions from Litera, the events of Tommaso's life and examples from contemporary affairs figure prominently. In this section Giovanni touches on the character of Pope Urban VI, who appointed Tommaso cardinal, the need for a united Italy to end the internecine warfare among the city-states, and Tommaso's role in negotiating several peace treaties.

In the second half of the dialogue Giovanni alternates his discussion of Tommaso's qualities and his own personal experiences with a consideration of the vocation of the religious and the morally good life in general. Here Giovanni treats the need for bravery in facing death, the questions of clerical celibacy and Christian marriage, and the relationship between the study of the liberal arts and the understanding of Christian truth. In several contexts Giovanni draws upon autobiographical data: the question of patronage and just rulership includes a discussion of his father, Conversino, and his patron King Louis of Hungary; the problem of immoderation and lust is based on personal memories; and a consideration of the status of women is founded on his own marital experiences. Finally Giovanni praises the itinerant life, with justifications for it adduced not only from his own past history but from the travels of St. Paul and the example of St. Paula, who journeyed

to the Holy Land in order to study under St. Jerome.

In a personal passage Giovanni thanks his uncle for his care and interest in his nephew's career and attempts to justify the need for such patronage with the ancient example of Horace and Maecenas, and the contemporary examples of Dante and Guido da Polenta, and Petrarch and the Carrara lords in Padua. In the concluding section the author touches on several topics that he later develops more fully in the *Dragmalogia*. Here he treats the frailty and ignorance of the human state, the need to love God and to trust in His inscrutable will for salvation, and the superiority of the contemplative over the active life. The final argument, bolstered by quotations from Horace's *Epodes* and Seneca's *Phaedra*, concludes in a virtual paean to the rural, contemplative life and the religious vocation and status.[11]

In 1379 the commune of Belluno did not renew Giovanni's contract as schoolmaster, and he took the enforced leisure as an opportunity to visit Rome for the first time and to see his Uncle Tommaso, who was living at the papal court. In his reminiscences of his Roman sojourn recorded in his autobiography, Giovanni reveals himself as a typical pilgrim of the Trecento.[12] He was interested only in visiting the shrines of the Christian martyrs and saints; he had no eyes for the ruins of classical Rome, which had so moved Petrarch and which would become the principal attraction of the city for humanists, such as Francesco da Fiano, who served in the papal curia early in the next century. Rather, it was the Rome of the tombs of St. Jerome and St. Gregory the Great and the Rome of the Christian monuments and churches that evoked Giovanni's emotional response, just as the religious vocation provoked his most profound and sincere admiration both in the *Dialogus* of 1378 and the *Dragmalogia* of 1404.

Returning from Rome, Giovanni visited Padua at the request of his friends the physician Marsilio da Santasofia and the grammarian Carletto Galmarelli. Almost immediately Giovanni attracted the attention of the lord of the city, Francesco il Vecchio da Carrara, who asked him to serve at the signorial court. Giovanni soon became a favorite of the

Paduan lord, and his closeness to Francesco aroused the jealousy of the other courtiers. In order to avoid their enmity, Giovanni delayed the publication of the short tract on the noble origins of the ruling family, *Familie carrariensis natio*, which he had written soon after meeting Francesco. Later, in order to escape further mistreatment by the household staff, he gratefully accepted the use of a house in Padua granted him by Francesco. During his three years in Padua, Giovanni made acquaintances within the scholarly community; he numbered among his friends the jurists Baldus del Ubaldis and Arsendino Arsendi, and the learned recluse Lombardo della Seta, who was completing Petrarch's *De viris illustribus* in rustic retirement in the Paduan suburb of Sermeola. But the backbiting and hazing that he continued to suffer from his fellow courtiers outweighed the benefits of membership in the Carrara household. Soon after the death of his second wife late in 1382, Giovanni left the employ of the Carrara lord and went to Venice.

Giovanni's stay there, where he was employed as a schoolmaster and numbered the young Marco Giustinian among his pupils, lasted only about six months. Perhaps through the intercession of the recently widowed Queen Elizabeth of Hungary, Giovanni received an appointment as the principal notary of the aristocratic republic of Ragusa (the modern Dubrovnik), which since 1356 had been under Hungarian rule. Late in the summer of 1383, Giovanni with his young son Israele journeyed down the Adriatic coast to take up his new position. According to his own reports, the office of notary (which Giovanni calls chancellor) entailed onerous duties. He served as a witness to all sorts of notarial documents, was often a judge in civil cases, and oversaw the promulgation of new statutes. In general, Giovanni was the central official in the daily administration of the legal matters of the city.[13]

Despite the pressures of long hours and the exacting duties of this post, at Ragusa Giovanni was able to compose several long literary works. In the epistolary tract *De primo eius introitu ad aulam*, addressed to Marco Giustinian, he gives his first sustained exposition of what was to become one of

his favorite literary themes, the hazards and corruption of court life. In this largely autobiographical tract, Giovanni explains in detail how he came to settle in Padua, the character and friendship of Francesco il Vecchio, and the machinations and hazing of the jealous courtiers that finally forced him to leave Padua.[14] In another long letter to Marco, Giovanni reports on his situation in Ragusa and on the events of his past life in Belluno. A letter to Paolo Rugolo, written soon after his arrival in Ragusa, describes the strange customs of the region, his new duties as chief notary, and his domestic situation.

The most important work of these years spent outside Italy was the *Historia Ragusii*. This work, addressed to an anonymous Venetian, is even broader in concept than the word *historia* in the title might suggest. After a long introductory lament over his position in Ragusa, Giovanni describes the geographic situation of the region, the layout and architecture of the city, the social customs and form of government of the republic, and the barbaric customs of the city population and of the nomadic tribes of the hinterland. Then Giovanni, through an implicit comparison between Ragusa and his native Italy, returns to the theme of Italian patriotism, which had received treatment in the *Dialogus* and which was to inform much of the political attitude of the *Dragmalogia*.[15]

Giovanni's discontent with his lot in the backward city of Ragusa eventually resulted in a change of scene, and in early 1388, accompanied by Israele and his Slavic housekeeper, Giovanni had returned to Venice. Under the patronage of Marco Giustinian, he established a grammar school in the contrada di S. Patrignano and began to renew acquaintances in the Venetian intellectual community. But Giovanni's quiet seclusion in Venice did not pass unnoticed. The year after his return, the vicars of Visconti-occupied Padua offered him the chair of grammar and rhetoric in the Studium there, but out of loyalty for his former Carrara patrons he refused to serve the Visconti regime. His position in Venice was now becoming difficult. His son Conversino had moved there and a number of bitter quarrels arose between father and son. The result

was the legal emancipation of Conversino[16] and the eventual departure of Giovanni in October 1389 for the humble position of schoolmaster in the commune of Udine in Friuli. After nearly three years of teaching, Giovanni left, mainly because of difficulty in disciplining the children and frequent, often bitter, disputes with parents. In April 1392, more by accident than by design, Giovanni found himself in Padua. There he was to remain for the next twelve years.

Giovanni's return to Padua marked a period of broadening intellectual interests and scholarly contacts and his employment as a lecturer in the University. The Carrara family, in the person of the lord Francesco Novello, had returned to Padua in 1390, and soon the humanist was drawn into the circle of the court. But Giovanni's main occupation in his first year or so in Padua was as lecturer in grammar and rhetoric, in which capacity he taught such future humanists as Pier Paolo Vergerio, Sicco Polentons, and Guarino da Verona. This teaching made a profound impression upon the young Sicco, who later praised Giovanni's skill in the following fulsome and not quite accurate terms:

> As a beginner in the Latin poets and as a student of rhetoric I heard Giovanni da Ravenna, son of the grammarian Conversino. This man was both by the sanctity of his morals and from his learning in all that treats the humanistic and rhetorical arts the prince in lecturing of all those scholars who lived in Italy in his time.[17]

Even after Giovanni entered the service of the Carrara lord as chancellor after the death of the incumbent, Nicoletto d'Alessio, in 1393, he continued to offer private instruction to the best of the young scholars in Padua. In this context he taught Latin literature to the future educator Vittorino da Feltre as well as other, less well-known students.

Giovanni's steady employment as schoolmaster in Udine and Venice, and his even greater income from university teaching and employment as chancellor in Padua, permitted him to indulge in the passion of his life—the collecting of books. His interests were eclectic, as an examination of the residue of his library shows. In 1389 Giovanni exchanged several codices

with the Venetian notary Lorenzo de' Monaci in return for the Latin translation of Aratus by Germanicus, the first eight comedies of Plautus, the *Raptus Proserpinae* of Claudian, and the twelfth-century satirical poem *Architrenius* by Jean de Hanville.[18] In 1391 he acquired a copy of an anonymous twelfth-century dialogue, *Phylosophia*.[19] Later, in Padua in 1393, Giovanni added to his collection a Latin translation of Aristotle's *In Cognitione Naturarum Animalium;* a codex containing Cicero's *De Natura Deorum*, the pseudo-Sallust and Cicero *Invectivae,* and a curious medieval work in praise of monarchy entitled *De Principatu*, attributed to Apuleius.[20] It was probably also in the Paduan period that he acquired Gregory the Great's *Regulae Pastorales*.[21] By about 1400 he had added the Latin translation of Plato's *Phaedo* and *Timaeus* with Chalcidius's commentary, which he lent to Coluccio Salutati.[22] Another codex (later bought by Francesco Barbaro) verifies Giovanni's more-than-passing interest in medieval logical works and scholastic authors. This manuscript contains, in order: Aegidius Colonna's lecture on Aristotle's *De bona fortuna,* the *Philosophia naturalis* of Albertus Magnus, a logical work entitled *Dialectorum locorum tractatus,* an Italian oration by Giovanni Lottini, another logical work named *Fallaciarum sive figurarum tractatus,* a commentary of the *Aulularia* of Plautus, fragments of Quintilian's *De Institutione oratoria* and of an unidentified manual of rhetoric, a third logical work entitled *Suppositionum tractatus* and often attributed to Peter of Mantua, the *Expositio* on Aristotle's *Politica* by St. Thomas Aquinas, and a letter from Francesco Zabarella to Antonio ser Chelli of Florence.[23] For Trecento authors, he certainly possessed from 1378 onwards Boccaccio's *De casibus virorum illustrium*.[24] No doubt other untraceable works swelled Giovanni's collection so that it was, if not the massive library of a Salutati, a very respectable collection of books.[25]

In the first half of the 1390s, the duties of teacher and Carrara chancellor weighed heavily on Giovanni; only in 1396 was he able to return to writing.[26] In that year, in the tract *De fortuna aulica,* he resumed one of the constant themes of his writings—the nature of court life. Giovanni here describes

the hierarchy of the Carrara household and condemns the vices, especially the avarice that he found there. Giovanni next found time to compose two dialogues that narrated fictional tales. One, *Dolosi astus narratio,* written probably at the request of Francesco Novello, treats contemporary events at the Este court in Ferrara through the guise of Roman narrators. This device of ancient interlocutors, Galba and Cato, permitted Giovanni to treat frankly and openly the theme of court intrigue and princely cunning. The other dialogue, *Violate pudicicie narratio,* or the *Historia Elysia,* is a praise of conjugal fidelity. Set in medieval France, the beginning of the tale draws its inspiration from the story of Lucretia in Livy's account and later traditions, and the ending is inspired by the final scenes in Boccaccio's *Teseida.* Hence Giovanni was able to combine the heroism of wifely chastity with the opportune death of the transgressor and the happy reunion of the married couple.[27]

Other tracts composed during the last years of the Trecento drew extensively on Giovanni's personal experience of court life and his observation of local Paduan events. In his *Apologia,* which is dated May 15, 1399, Giovanni defends himself against the slander of other courtiers, who accused him of incompetence in his exercise of the chancellorship. In this reply Giovanni admits that he prefers scholarly leisure and country life to the duties of his office, but he also ironically asserts that he has practised many trades during his career, including cookery and the preparation of medicinal compounds. Hence the chancellorship posed no great problem. In a narrative, the *De lustro Alborum in urbe Padua,* addressed to his old friend Paolo Rugolo, Giovanni describes the visit of the Bianchi sect to Padua in 1399 and incidentally includes a valuable and detailed topography of the city. Another tract, *De dilectione regnantium,* completed in September 1399, anticipates some of the arguments on just rulership that are used in the *Dragmalogia.* This treatise, addressed to Francesco Novello, deals with the nature of the best relationship between the prince and his subjects. In order to gain the affection and esteem of the Paduan people, Francesco is advised through a number of contemporary examples to become friendly toward,

and intimate with, his subjects.

By 1400 Giovanni had become such a reliable member of the Carrara household government that Francesco Novello entrusted him with three delicate diplomatic missions. In January he left for Florence to enroll the mercenary captain Alberico da Barbiano in Paduan service and to warn the Florentine *signoria* of Visconti plans for the capture of Perugia. In an embassy to Bologna at the same time, he attempted to strengthen one of the principal Paduan allies through the mediation of the dispute for the lordship of that city between the factions led by Nanni Gozzadini and Giovanni Bentivoglio. The most difficult embassy, the one to Rome, was undertaken in the heat of summer, at a time of war and pestilence, and on roads crowded with pilgrims going to the Jubilee celebrated that year. Robbed as he neared Rome, Giovanni nonetheless proceeded on his mission to the camp of the *condottiere* Conte da Carrara, illegitimate son of Francesco il Vecchio, who was serving in the papal army. There he delivered a message from the Paduan lord to his half-brother, and then went on to an audience at the Vatican with Pope Boniface IX. To his disgust, Giovanni was met in the halls of the Vatican by a crowd of armed guards, and he had to conduct his interview with the Pope while mass was being celebrated. Such obvious abuses of the Christian religion made a deep impression on him and perhaps help to account for the diatribes against avaricious and hypocritical clergy recorded in the *Dragmalogia*.

Giovanni returned to Padua to be visited by domestic tragedy. His two illegitimate children, who had probably been born in Udine, died of the plague. The son who had been full of intellectual promise and the daughter who was already proficient in household chores had been objects of Giovanni's pride and hope.[28] Soon thereafter, in the conclusion to his autobiography, Giovanni turned his thoughts to the comforts of religion:

> Grant, therefore, Lord God, that Thou wilt complete what Thou hast wrought in us, as in Thy holy temple, so that whatever time may be left to me beyond this fifty-sixth year, I may place my whole self in Thee and may practice Thy commands in complete freedom and with my whole heart.[29]

This conclusion to the *Rationarium vite* was soon followed by the composition of Giovanni's sole poetic effort, a hymn to St. John the Evangelist, a rather confused summary of the saint's life in which the Evangelist is mistakenly identified with the nephew of the Virgin Mary, St. Simon, and with John the Presbyter. The same year saw another tragic family loss, the death of Israele at the age of twenty-five. Giovanni's gifted but troubled son had finally settled in Padua to study, only to be struck down by the plague in 1401. In order to assuage his grief, Giovanni composed a long dialogue between a "Mestus" and a "Consolator," which he addressed to his Trevisan friend, Paolo Rugolo. In the course of the dicussion, the consoler marshalls examples and evidence from both Christian and pagan sources to comfort his grief-stricken friend. The result is, as Sabbadini states, "the first example of a humanist consolatory tract of ample proportions where the author, however, consoles not others but himself."[30]

Throughout this difficult period Giovanni continued to serve as chancellor in the Carrara court, although he was clearly becoming increasingly dissatisfied with his position. The resumption of Francesco Novello's policy of territorial aggrandizement in northeast Italy after the death of Giangaleazzo Visconti in September 1402 earned Giovanni's condemnation in the opening section of the *Dragmalogia* and probably merited the humanist's disapproval when it occurred. In any case, Giovanni saw the Carrara policy of conquest as doomed to failure. When the Venetian Republic joined the regent of Lombardy, Caterina Visconti, against the Carrara early in 1404, Francesco Novello dismissed or reduced the salaries of the scholars in his household in an effort to divert all his resources to military needs. Sometime between March 27, when he witnessed a treaty with Guglielmo della Scala, and June 23, when Venice formally declared war, Giovanni left Padua and resettled in Venice.

Giovanni's first literary effort after his return to Venice was the *Familie carrariensis natio,* which had been drafted in 1379 and now was refurbished with a dedicatory preface to Rudolfo da Carrara, an illegitimate son of Francesco il Vecchio and half-brother to the ruling *signore*. Evidently Giovanni wanted to show that he still had affection for the family even

though he did not approve of the actions of Francesco Novello, an opinion echoed at length in the *Dragmalogia*. Next, Giovanni promptly turned to the composition of the *Dragmalogia* during the six months after he left Padua. At the same time he earned a living as a tutor and schoolmaster, numbering the future humanist Francesco Barbaro among his students and including among his friends the Giustinian brothers, Marco and Leonardo. But his sudden and unexpected departure from the Carrara court loomed large in his preoccupations during this period, as both contemporary letters and several passages in the *Dragmalogia* suggest. Early in 1405 Giovanni wrote letters to his successor as chancellor in Padua, Zilio Calvi, and to one of the chief officials of the Carrara household, Enrico Gallo, to thank them for continuing to provide a small stipend even after he had left the Carrara service. These letters are among the most bitter and abject Giovanni ever wrote; they show that his condemnation of Francesco Novello's character and policy in the *Dragmalogia* was not just a passing pique, but that he still harbored hopes of returning as chancellor to the Carrara court.[31] In these letters Giovanni complains, for virtually the first time, of physical pain—sciatica caused by the rigors of the Venetian winter and other signs of advancing old age. In fact, the Venetian climate was one of Giovanni's constant worries; in the summer of 1406 he decided to avoid it altogether by accepting the directorship of the public schools in Muggia, a small town situated to the south of Trieste on the Istrian coast.

When the fall of Padua to the Venetians in November 1405 made it apparent that Giovanni could never return to the Carrara household, several of his friends tried to help him find a better position than tutor to the children of Venetian patricians. Pier Paolo Vergerio, who had left the Carrara staff for service in the papal curia, sang Giovanni's praises to Pope Innocent VII. Moved by Vergerio's description of Giovanni's abilities and his reputation as an author, the Pope used such intermediaries as Vergerio and Simone Saltarelli, Bishop of Trieste, to include Giovanni to enter papal service. Vergerio wrote several letters designed to persuade Giovanni

to come to Rome; in one that reached Giovanni later in 1406, the younger humanist stresses Innocent's good character and qualities as a patron who chose men only on the basis of merit.[32] He further argues that, despite the long hours and exacting work of the curia, papal service was pleasant and rewarding, for the Pope was (to quote Vergerio) "not so much a prince as a companion, not so much a pontiff as a common father to everyone."[33] Finally, at the insistence of the Pope, Vergerio urged Giovanni to present a dedication copy of the *Dragmalogia* to Innocent VII, since so elegant and polished a work would be gratefully received by Innocent. Later, when Vergerio's efforts failed, the Pope through Simone Saltarelli asked Giovanni to collect his letters for him and again tried to induce him to accept a post in the curia.[34]

Giovanni would have nothing of these offers to go to Rome. In a letter to Vergerio, he describes himself as too old to move again.[35] Besides, he averred that he had composed the *Dragmalogia* not for wealth, position, or human plaudits, but rather to express the truth. Thus he explicitly refused to have a dedication copy made for Innocent, although he allowed the dialogue to circulate privately among his close friends. Similarly, with the project for collecting his letters, Giovanni responded that he had worked on the collection not to win fame but to preserve for posterity his correspondence with so many illustrious friends.[36] In any case, Innocent died on November 6, 1406, and with his demise any hope for Giovanni's employment in the papal curia came to an end.

At Muggia, Giovanni began the composition of what were to be his last two works: the *Conventio inter podagram et araneam,* dedicated to Fantin Dandolo, and the unfinished *Memorandarum rerum liber.* The *Conventio* tells the story of the exchange of residence between the gout and a spider. The spider goes from his normal rural habitat to the city, where his webs are constantly destroyed; the gout goes to the country, where he is unable to infect the hardy, healthy peasants. Only when the two return to their original homes are they happy and successful. The theme of comparing country and city life was not a new one, for it had been used in the *Dragmalogia,*

but in this story Giovanni's immediate inspiration was undoubtedly a letter on the subject in Petrarch's *Epistolae ad Familiares*.[37] Giovanni based his last work on the ancient treatise of Valerius Maximus, *Factorum ac Dictorum Memorabilium Libri IX*, on which he had lectured at Bologna nearly forty years before, and upon Petrarch's *Rerum memorandarum libri*.[38] But unlike Petrarch, Giovanni drew none of his examples from antiquity, using, rather, only anecdotes from contemporary history. This penchant for modern examples gives Giovanni's last work the quality of censuring or praising contemporaries that is also found in the *Dragmalogia*.

In failing health, Giovanni returned to Venice in 1408. There he continued to work on his memorabilia and the collection of his letters, and he composed a valedictory epistle to his lifelong friend Paolo Rugolo. The letter concludes as follows:

> Now, what would be sweeter than if the burden of old age embraced together those who as youths used to delight in brotherly zeal? As the poet says, "I remember that with you did I pass long days, with you did I pluck for feasting the early hours of the night." First from Florence, the place of Treviso welcomed me as a foolish youth and there you and many others have preserved with me the unbreakable bond of friendship. Let it be repeated; what could be sweeter? Only that the fatal circle, the uninterrupted course of my wanderings, would result so that after so many mistakes I might be carried back to that place where fortune had first so humbled my offspring and my family. But at last, Paolo, I have ceased to strive and to lust, since I have tried almost everything in vain. At one time it was fated where I am to rest my soul; in the meantime I have to use what is offered by chance. Yours everywhere. Farewell.[39]

A short time after this was written, and certainly before September 27, 1408, Giovanni di Conversino da Ravenna died in Venice.

2. The Argument of the Dragmalogia

Throughout his long literary career, Giovanni da Ravenna demonstrated a continuing affinity for the dialogue form. His first really substantial literary effort, the *Dialogus inter Johannem et Literam*, dedicated to his Uncle Tommaso da Frignano upon his elevation to the cardinalate in the autumn of 1378, was cast in the form of a series of discussions between Giovanni and the personification of an epistle that the young nephew was sending to his beloved uncle. Likewise, in the last decade of the Trecento, Giovanni employed the dialogue form as a means of telling stories and describing contemporary events. In both the *Violate pudicicie narratio* and the *Dolosi astus narratio*, Giovanni used ancient interlocutors as the means for presenting his tales. And in his mythical account of the origins of the Carrara family, which was drafted in about 1379 and finally published in 1404, Giovanni resorted to a series of dialogues to relate the story of the settlement of the young Landolfo da Carrara and his bride in the Euganean Hills back in the eleventh century. Hence, the choice of the form of dialogue was natural and perhaps inevitable when, in the autumn of 1404, Giovanni set about to record his ideas on the best way of life.

As the title *Dragmalogia* suggests,[1] Giovanni saw the dialogue as a staged piece of discussion between two interlocutors, rather than as the polished Ciceronian version that Leonardo Bruni was beginning to use in his *Dialogi* written in Florence at about the same time. For the Ravennate, debate on a wide range of subjects took the form of *interrogatio* and *responsio*, which was nearer to the catechism than to a freewheeling, open discussion. In this form, one interlocutor (the Paduan, in this case) made long speeches expounding his point of

view while the other character (the Venetian, in this instance) made only brief replies or asked appropriate leading questions. Such a form inevitably lacked the subtlety and drama of a philosophic dialogue, but it did ensure that a particular viewpoint was clearly and fully presented. The *Dragmalogia* was, then, cast in this rather heavy-handed form, which gave rise to rhetorical persuasion more than to philosophic demonstration.

In order to provide a basis for further discussion of the *Dragmalogia* and to give a preliminary notion of its contents, the following skeleton outline has been devised:[2]

V1–P6 : Meeting of Paduan and Venetian speakers and discussion of current politics in northern Italy; condemnation of wars waged by Francesco Novello da Carrara and the previous Venetian policy of neutrality.

V7–P17 : Discussion of the reasons why the Ravennate, i.e., the author Giovanni di Conversino da Ravenna, left the Carrara court in Padua.

V18–P24 : General discussion of the nature of service as a courtier, with most examples drawn from Giovanni's service for the Carrara lords.

V25–V33 : Discussion of the relative merits of monarchy and republic as the "best form of government," with examples drawn mainly from Padua and Venice.

P28 : On the benefits of princely patronage.

P31 : On the efficiency of princely rule.

P33–P40 : Discussion of the relative merits of the political leader (dominus), defended by the Venetian, and the schoolmaster (magister), praised by the Paduan; topic adumbrated in P23–P24.

V41–P44 : Introduction to a discussion of the "good life."

V44–V51 : Discussion of the relative merits of city life (favored by the Venetian) and country life (favored by the Paduan).

P51–V56 : Introduction to the discussion of virtues arising out of vice; topic anticipated in P48.

The Argument   33

P56–P60 : Discussion of the nature of each of the Seven Deadly
   Sins in the so-called Gregorian order—Pride, Envy,
   Anger, Sloth, Lust, Gluttony, and Greed.
V61–P66 : Condemnation by the Paduan of Venice's site,
   climate, lack of culture, and exclusive interest in profit-
   making.
V67–V76 : Discussion of the nature of liberty, with the Paduan
   providing examples mainly from Scripture and recent
   history.
P76–P80 : Praise of the status of the religious vocation.

As this outline suggests, Giovanni was able in the *Dragmalogia* to present fundamental differences between two ways of life and two systems of government. Even though Venice and its citizens are usually presented almost as caricatures and patently unequal to Padua in most spheres, the opposing views of the Paduan and Venetian can be expressed as a series of binary oppositions. These antitheses, which are as clear-cut as any in the literature of early Renaissance humanism, may be stated without respect to any levels of interpretation as follows :

Padua	Venice
rural life	urban existence
honest agricultural labor	deceitful commercial enterprise
monarchy	republic
piety	impiety
contemplative life	active life
princely efficiency	democratic inefficiency
scholarly leisure	trading activity
land	water
cleanliness, purity	filth, contamination
classical literature	*volgare* literature
primitivism, utopian view of past	modernism, hope for the present

At its most obvious level, the *Dragmalogia* is a record of

an imaginary conversation, or better, a series of conversations, between a Paduan and a Venetian as they walked from the inland town toward the city of the lagoon. The setting is vague and unobtrusive, and the pair turn to topics of mutual interest and concern. The two friends begin with a survey of current affairs, and soon move to the nature of the Carrara court in Padua. This subject permits the Paduan (who is virtually Giovanni's *persona*) to introduce the author of the dialogue as a subject for discussion. Thus, Giovanni is able to describe his own bad fortunes at court by having the omniscient Paduan detail Giovanni's own career through a series of flashbacks prompted by questions from the Venetian. At this level, the opening part of the dialogue becomes a piece of self-justification for the author. After the first seven pairs of speeches discussing the war that led to Giovanni's dismissal, the author himself is introduced into the discussion as the Ravennate friend of the Paduan. The story of his relations with the Carrara lords, both the admired father, Francesco il Vecchio, and the despised son, Franesco Novello, is told at some length. Blame is freely meted out by the Paduan to wicked courtiers, greedy soldiers, and especially the benighted Carrara lord who refused to follow his own best interests, which lay in preventing war and in fostering the patronage of letters and learning. In this context, at least the first third of the dialogue may be viewed as therapeutic for the bruised ego of a once-loyal man of the court. As is apparent from letters sent to Zilio Calvi early in 1405, a man of Giovanni's temperament required a rationale for the misfortunes that had been visited upon him and an explanation for his declassed position as a schoolmaster in Venice after so many years of loyal service to the Carrara family.[3] (In fact, at least three times during the year following his dismissal, he averred that he had served the family for forty years, instead of the fifteen years he actually gave.) With this opening to the *Dragmalogia*, Giovanni was able to assuage his anguish, present his version of his life in Padua, and justify his misfortunes through a series of diatribes against the war, the stupidity of rulers—especially Francesco Novello's—and the hazards and meanness of court life.

The remainder of the dialogue is precisely what it has been interpreted as by Hans Baron and other commentators—a series of connected discussions on the theme of the superiority of one way of life over another.[4] With the twenty-fifth set of speeches, the subject moves naturally from a discussion of Giovanni's recent life to a more general consideration of the superiority of the quiet life of the scholar over the active life of the political leader: "the pen is mightier than the sword." This discussion leads logically into a consideration of the best surroundings for the practice of the good life, or a description of the reasons for the superiority of country over urban living. From a consideration of the benefits of rural labor, the argument for the arising of good from apparent evil is broached. This topic, which treats the question of God's will, leads in turn to the final section on the best kinds of life in God's vision—an argument for the religious calling.

In the topics of the latter part of the dialogue, Giovanni's solipsism no doubt also played a role in the choice of themes and the preferences stated and argued for by the Paduan. The principal speaker's basic desires for a well-governed monarchical state, the leisure worthy of a scholar, and the praise of a life of Vergilian labor and of the nobility of literature and learning were doubtless shared by Giovanni himself. For example, in the discussion of the virtues of monarchy over republicanism, the Paduan is at once realistic and theoretical. His realism derives from his ready admission that the office of monarch is not always well practiced. From the experiences of the courtier Giovanni da Ravenna, it is shown that the older Carrara lord understood the function of patronage, curbed the excesses of his courtiers, and resorted to war as little as possible, while the son Francesco Novello ruled badly, patronized mercenaries and cutthroats rather than scholars and artists, and found delight only in war and bloodshed. One of Francesco's principal allies, Rupert of Habsburg, showed still other defects with his weakness for wine and women and his ineffectiveness on the field of battle. But the Paduan argues that, when properly practiced, monarchy can accomplish great things; the wise ruler can bring prosperity to his subjects and

beauty to his city through patronage of industry and a program of public works. Moreover, he can, as did King Robert of Naples, create a brilliant court culture that not only adds luster to his name, but also aids worthy scholars and artists. The Venetian is forced to admit that his republic cares very little for the arts, prefers the use of the vernacular over Latin, often promotes war by its erratic policies, and lacks the sense of direction and purpose that a single head of government can give. But it is worth noting that the Paduan makes no more than a conventional appeal to divine sanction of monarchical rule, nor does he justify one-man rule on the basis of "mysteries of state"; monarchy is best because of the practical benefits that it affords, not because of any supernatural sanction it might have received.[5]

The transition from the discussion of political forms to the argument on the best way of life brings Giovanni to another of the *topoi* mentioned earlier: the superiority of the life of the mind over that of action. The interlocutors discuss this question in terms of the superiority of the calling of *magister* (teacher) over that of *dominus* (political leader). Through a series of rather long speeches, the Paduan piles up example after example from Scripture, history, and contemporary life of the superiority of the scholar over the man of action, of the *vita contemplativa* over the *vita activa*. From this the dialogue moves to a discussion of where best to follow the contemplative life, that is, to a discussion of the relative merits of rural and urban living.

Giovanni's discussion of the joys of country life obviously derives some of its intellectual inspiration from the author's early and repeated reading of the works of Horace and Vergil, especially the *Georgics*. At the same time, contemporary personal examples show how much the author valued country living; so here, as elsewhere in the dialogue, there are both learned and personal sources for the ideas presented. The passages on the chores and benefits of farm life are frequently almost lyrical; Giovanni obviously worked at the composition of these passages, which stood above the conversational tone of most other parts of the dialogue. In these speeches the

Paduan is able to tie in the need for peace with the wholesomeness of rural life and to condemn the hectic pace and unhappy existence of those who have sought to become rich through trade. Thus the section becomes a praise of peace, poverty, labor, and happiness as against war, riches, frantic city commotion, and dissatisfaction. The praise of conditions, such as poverty, that many considered to be hindrances to happiness, leads naturally to the next section, the nature of good arising from apparent evils.

In this highly original and certainly ironic part of the dialogue, the Paduan speaker overturns the conventional view of the Seven Deadly Sins and shows that out of evil a greater good can arise.[6] The Paduan observes that a number of psychological incentives that are usually held as sins—envy, greed, pride—can cause and have caused nations and individuals to rise to great heights. More mundanely, he shows that the greedy man fills the pocket of the hunter or fisherman or that the less bellicose, more slothful leader usually turns his attention to public works and his subjects' happiness. But the majority of the examples are drawn from antiquity or Scripture, so that Giovanni is able to utilize his study of Roman historians and thinkers that went back to his student days and corroborate the divine nature of moral laws with biblical *exempla*. The precise source of Giovanni's dissatisfaction and ironic treatment of the deadly sins is not clear; it seems probable that his views were not unrelated to the current nominalist doctrines of the inscrutability of God's will. Although he probably did not know the works of William Ockham and his followers directly, Giovanni's argument at the beginning of the section does parallel Ockham's view that "the source of moral obligation is the absolute freedom of God."[7] Hence, what God, with His absolute power and will, orders must be good, and therefore in the final analysis moral laws are based not so much on the nature of things or ethical precepts as upon God's will. This voluntaristic approach to ethics, coupled with a growing skepticism toward the conventional medieval system of the Seven Deadly Sins, gives Giovanni's treatment a novelty that is unique in all of early Italian human-

ist literature. Here is probably the earliest Italian example of an ironic treatment of the category of deadly sins.

In its concluding section, the dialogue functions at its most philosophic and profound level in the discussion of the nature of freedom and of man's highest calling. Here Giovanni the courtier, diplomat, and pious Christian is clearly more concerned with providing contemporary political examples of the lack of freedom and the ultimate religious nature of liberty than with producing philosophical abstractions. For example, in the beginning of the discussion Giovanni indulges in another anti-Florentine diatribe by making an allusion to the War of the Eight Saints (1375-1378) against the papacy, to which he ascribes only a propaganda value to Florence's claim to act as a guardian of Tuscany. Moreover, the term *libertas* is seldom discussed in a purely moral or secular context, but mainly through scriptural quotations and allusions. Giovanni felt increasingly in his later years that true freedom was to be found in the service of God. In his efforts to identify a practitioner of the good life, Giovanni turned to the spiritual hero of his early manhood, his uncle the Cardinal Tommaso da Frignano, who had died more than twenty years before. The dialogue ends with a virtual paean to Tommaso's virtues and rather smug praise for the religious calling. A figure saturated with many of the nostrums of Trecento religious life, Giovanni has not progressed much beyond the position that Petrarch had taken on the status of religious life nearly half a century earlier. Like Salutati, Giovanni da Ravenna was nearly unaffected by the growing ambiguity of attitude toward the life of asceticism, withdrawal, and religious vocation. In the end, there is a consistency in Giovanni's view on religion, politics, history, and culture; he remained true to the values of the monastic calling, the signorial regime, the glories of the Roman Empire, and a classicism based on such medieval favorites as Vergil, Horace, Cicero, Valerius Maximus, and on Scripture.

It was probably this allegiance to the values of a "Gothic" world that made Giovanni (like Salutati) less than fully admired by the next generation of humanists, many of whom he had

taught and trained. The more thoroughly secular and militant classicism of such men as Vittorino da Feltre, Guarino da Verona, and Sicco Polenton closely paralleled the new humanistic views of Leonardo Bruni south of the Appenines. In the years of rapidly changing literary and intellectual fashion of the early Quattrocento, it is remarkable that Giovanni's works were copied and read at all; even more significant is the fact that several exist in two or more copies.[8] Despite his ugly Latin, curious concern with the then defunct Carrara family, and lack of cosmopolitan spirit, Giovanni's works were probably read by a circle of Venetian humanists and statesmen that included the Giustinian brothers, Marco and Leonardo, and by Francesco Barbaro. Along with his younger friend Vergerio, Giovanni was one of the two most important humanists in the Carrara court in the years immediately preceding the debacle of 1405, and along with *De ingenuis moribus*, the *Dragmalogia* is the most significant product of that period of Paduan humanism. Now that it has received a complete edition, perhaps the ideas and philosophy of Giovanni da Ravenna, largely neglected because of the change in fashion of the fifteenth century, will receive the close and ample study that they so manifestly merit.

3. *Manuscripts Used in This Edition*

The present edition of the *Dragmalogia* is founded upon a collation of the texts of the two extant manuscript witnesses (referred to as V and P; see below). Neither manuscript is an autograph and it is difficult to establish the relationship between them and the parent manuscript (or manuscripts).

However, it seems certain that P, which was copied in the early fifteenth century by a Dutch scholar residing in northern Italy, is the less corrupt version of the two. Manuscript V dates probably from the middle years of the fifteenth century and was copied in northeastern Italy by an Italian scribe, probably in Padua or Venice. The two manuscripts provide a good, if not impeccable, basis for the edition in which the reading in P has usually been given preference over that of the less reliable V. In this edition all variants, as well as all emendations and editorial additions, have been noted at the bottom of the Latin page. The resulting text, it is hoped, is as reliable as possible, although the corrupt state of the witnesses may have necessitated some questionable reconstructions.

In the brief description of the codices given below, the contents of both V and P are noted in full. In addition, the manuscript of Giovanni's letter-book is described, since its contents have been used considerably in the introduction. All other manuscripts are fully cited at first instance in the notes.

V   Venice. Biblioteca Querini-Stampalia, Classe IX, no. 11. Parchment, early s. XV. 86 fols. 28 x 21 cm., 2 cols., written in two hands, fols. 1–64v in a somewhat notarial Italian hand in 52 lines, fols. 65–86v in a Gothic German hand in 36 lines. The copyists doubtless worked consecutively, since the German hand begins in the middle of one of the gatherings. At the beginning of each tract there are initial letters in gold, blue, red, and green, and initials in red and blue alternately begin each paragraph. See V. Zaccaria, "Il *Memorandarum Rerum Liber* di Giovanni di Conversino da Ravenna," *Atti dell'Istituto Veneto, Classe di scienze morali et lettere* 106, pt. 2 (1947–1948): 231, and P. O. Kristeller, *Iter Italicum,* 2 vols. (Leiden, 1963–1967), 2 : 280.

The codex contains the following works:

Ad Iustinianum Venetum, fols. 1–6/b.
Familie Carrariensis natio, fols. 6/b–10v/b.
Dragmalogia de eligibili vite genere, fols. 10v/b–34v/a.
Conventio inter podagram et araneam, fols. 34v/a–46v/b.
Memorandarum rerum liber, fols. 46v/b–55v/a.
De miseria humane vite, fols. 55v/a–57v/b.
De Christi conceptu, fols. 57v/b–58/a.
De fato, fols. 58v/a–64v/b.
Historia Ragusii, fols. 65/a–86v/b.

P   Paris, Bibliothèque Nationale. Lat. 6494. Parchment, early s. XV. 109 fols. with 109r–v blank, 31 x 22 cm., 2 cols. written in hand of Jacobus Witte in 36 lines. Initial letter at the beginning of each tract in gold, red, blue, and green. The initial letters V and P are red and blue respectively in the *Dragmalogia* and the same colors appear as paragraph initials in the other tracts. See V. Zaccaria, "Il *Memorandarum* . . . ," p. 232, who claims that the hand is Italian rather than German, and the *Catalogus Codicum manuscriptorum Bibliothecae Regiae*, Book 4, Pt. 3 (Paris, 1744), p. 249, which states that the manuscript is derived from the collection of Le Tellier.

The codex contains the following tracts:
Dragmalogia de eligibili vite genere, fols. 1v/a–40v/a.
Conventio inter podagram et araneam, fols. 40v/a–62/a.
Memorandarum rerum liber, fols. 62/b–78/a.
Historia Ragusii, fols. 78/a–100v/a.
Familie Carrariensis natio, fols. 100v/a–108v/b.

Z   Zagrab. Knjižnica Jugoslavenske Akademije Znanosti i Umjetnosti. Codex II c 61. Parchment, s. XV, 180 fols., 30 x 22.2 cm., 2 cols, of 35 lines probably written in the hand of Jacobus Witte with colored initial letters. On fol. 1/a entitled: *Epistole Johannis de Ravenna*. See D. Kniewald, "Ioannes Conversini," pp. 87–88, for a description of the codex.

Notes to
1. Life and Works of Giovanni da Ravenna

1. Unless otherwise indicated, this biographical sketch is based upon R. Sabbadini's nearly exhaustive biography, *Giovanni da Ravenna, insigne figura d'umanista (1343–1408)* (Como, 1924), and the extracts drawn from Giovanni's works, especially from his autobiography, *Rationarium vite,* published in the second half of that book. However, wherever I have had access to works of Giovanni or studies and editions unknown to Sabbadini, I have given these more extensive coverage; the result is, I hope, an adequate sketch of Giovanni's life and works combined with a detailed discussion of events and works not treated by Sabbadini and of all factors in Giovanni's experience that might contribute to a better understanding of the *Dragmalogia.* On the feudal origins of the Da Frignano family, see G. Pistoni, "Un modenese amico del Petrarca, il cardinal Tommaso Frignani," *Atti e Memorie dell' Accademia di scienze, lettere, ed arti di Modena,* 5th ser. 12 (1954): 83–84.

2. For an informative account of Giovanni's stay in Treviso, see L. Gargan, "Giovanni Conversini e la cultura letteraria a Treviso nella seconda metà del Trecento," *Italia medioevale e umanistica* 8 (1965): 85–159, esp. 85–86, 95–97, 125–28.

3. See Sabbadini, p. 148, for Giovanni's own testimony.

4. In December 1368 and in April 1369, Giovanni and Margherita sold what was probably nearly all their real property in Ravenna. See S. Bernicoli, "Maestri e scuole letterarie in Ravenna nel secolo XIV," *Felix Ravenna* 32 (Dec. 1927): 61–69, at 65.

5. Sabbadini, p. 150, from the *Rationarium vite.*

6. This letter has been edited with an introduction and notes by B. G. Kohl and J. Day in *Studies in the Renaissance* 21 (1974): 9–30.

7. The following discussion is based on my reading of the texts in MS V. fols. 55v/a–64v/b (described below in Part 3).

8. He quotes St. Augustine, *De Civitate Dei* 5.9.

9. For an informative discussion of other Italian humanists on this topic, see Charles Trinkaus, *In Our Own Image and Likeness, Humanity and Divinity in Italian Humanist Thought,* 2 vols. (Chicago, 1970), 1: 171–99.

10. Although Sabbadini knew from references in the autobiography that Giovanni had written such a work (p. 49), he did not have a text nor know of the existence of the two MSS, which were discovered later. I have used Oxford, Bodleian Library, New College D 155, fols. 1–40, which is the dedication copy presented to Tommaso and dated January 5, 1379.

11. Giovanni is quoting *Epodes* 2.1–4:

Happy the man who, far from town's affairs,
The life of old-world mortals shares,
With his own oxen tills his forbears' fields
Nor thinks of usury and its yields.

(trans. John Marshall); also Seneca, *Phaedra* 483–93:

There is no life so free and innocent, none which better cherishes the ancients ways, than that which, forsaking cities, loves the woods. His heart is inflamed by no mad greed of gain who has devoted himself to harmless ranging on the mountain-tops; here is no shouting populace, no mob, faithless to good men, no poisonous hate, no brittle favor. No slave is he of kings, nor in quest of kingship does he chase empty honors or elusive wealth, free alike from hope and fear; him venomous spite assails not with the bite of base-born tooth.

12. See Sabbadini, pp. 50–51, 159; and, for a discussion of Francesco da Fiano's quite different reaction, Hans Baron, *Crisis of the Early Italian Renaissance,* 2 vols. (Princeton, 1955), 1: 282–83.

13. For a full account of Giovanni's tenure at Ragusa, see F.. Rački, "Prilozi za poviest humanisma i renaissance u Dubrovniku, Dalmaciji i Hrvatskoj; I. Ivan Ravenjanin učenik Petrarkin dubrivički kancelar (1384–1387)," *Rad Jugoslavenske Akademije znanosti i umjetnosti* 74 (1885): 135–91, at 162–74; and D. Kniewald, "Ioannes Conversini de Ravenna dubrovački notar, 1384–1387," *Glas srpske akademije nauka i umjetnosti* 229, Odeljenje literature i jezita 3 (Belgrade, 1957): 39–160, at 60–72. I wish to thank Miss Maja Basioli for aid in translating these essays from the Serbo-Croat.

14. I have used the text in Oxford, Balliol College, MS 288, fols. 85v/b–93v/b.

15. This is based on the description in Sabbadini, pp. 62–66, and in Kniewald, pp. 118 ff.

16. For the record of Conversino's legal emancipation from his father, see E. Bertanza and G. Dalla Santa, *Documenti per la storia della coltura in Venezia: I. Maestri, scuole, e scolari in Venezia fino al 1500,* Monumenti storici pubblicati dalla R. Deputazione Veneta di Storia Patria, Ser. I. Documenti, vol. 12 (Venice, 1907): 190–91.

17. Sicco Polentone, *Scriptorum Illustrium Latinae Linguae Libri XVIII,* ed. B. L. Ullman, Papers and Monographs of the American Academy in Rome 6 (Rome, 1928): 166.

18. See Sabbadini, pp. 67, 212.

19. The codex is to be found in Florence, Biblioteca Laurenziana, Ashburnham 98, and is described in C. Paoli, *I codici Ashburnhamiani della R. Biblioteca Medicei-Laurenziani di Firenze,* Ministero dell'Istruzione Publica, *Indici e Cataloghi, VIII* (Rome, 1928): 166.

20. See P. O. Kristeller, *Iter Italicum,* 2 vols. (London and Leiden, 1962–1965): 2: 495, 590. The codices are: Belluno, Seminario Gregoriano, Lolliniana 7, aud Vatican City, Biblioteca Apostolica Vaticana, Vat. Pal. lat. 1520, respectively. I am currently writing an article on the pseudo-Apuleius *De principatu,* which will deal with some of the questions on the provenance and meaning of this tract.

21. See I. P. Tommasino, *Bibliothecae Patavinae Manuscriptae Publicae et Privatae* (Udine, 1639), p. 59.

22. In a letter of June 1401, Coluccio Salutati asked Giovanni for the loan of his codex of these Platonic works for the purpose of having them copied. See C. Salutati, *Epistolario,* ed. F. Novati, 4 vols. (Rome, 1891–1911), 3: 515, for the text, and B. L. Ullman, *The Humanism of Coluccio Salutati* (Padua, 1963), pp. 245–46, and Hans Baron, *Humanistic and Political Literature in Florence and Venice at the Beginning of the Quattrocento* (Cambridge, Mass., 1955), pp.119–21, for the significance of the request.

23. This MS, now Venice, Biblioteca Nazionale Marciana, Lat. XIV, 129 (4334), was formerly Codex 136 in the library of the monastery of S. Michele, Murano, and its contents are described in G. B. Mittarelli, *Bibliotheca codicum manuscriptorum Monasterii S. Michaelis Venetiarum prope Murianum* (Venice, 1779), cols. 9, 14–15, 324, 383–84, 693, 911, 982, 1012, 1098, 1123, 1125–27, 1230. I am indebted to Professor Paul Oskar Kristeller for pointing out to me that Giovanni once owned this codex and for providing me with a list of the columns of Mittarelli's catalogue in which the contents are described.

24. Vatican City. Biblioteca Apostolica Vaticana. Vat. Pal. lat. 970, which contains Giovanni's own copy of the *Dialogus inter Johannem et Literam* as well as Boccaccio's work. See Ullman, *Salutati,* p. 200.

25. This attempt at a reconstruction of Giovanni's library on the basis of a description of codices that it is certain he owned is only partial and provisional. Any definitive study of the sources of Giovanni's thought and the contents of his library must await the complete editing of his works.

26. Giovanni voiced complaints on the difficulties of being chancellor to both Desiderato Lucio, chancellor of Venice, and to Salutati; see Sabbadini, pp. 217–18, no. 69, and Salutati *Epistolario,* 4: 307, respectively.

27. For this dialogue I have used the text published in M. Korelin, *Rannii ital'ianskii Gumanizm i ego istoriografiia* [Early Italian Humanism and Its Historiography]. Moskovski Universitet, Uceniya Zapiski, Otdyel Istoriko-filologiceskii, 14–15 (Moscow, 1892), Appendix, pp. 16–26.

28. The mother of these two children is unknown; she was probably not the coarse Slavic housekeeper whom Giovanni describes only in derogatory terms. They were born, however, either in Ragusa or Udine, at a time when the Slavic woman was a constant member of the household.

29. Sabbadini, p. 173, no. 42.
30. Ibid., p. 87.
31. See the excerpts in ibid., p. 226.
32. The letter is published in Vergerio, *Epistolario,* ed. L. Smith (Rome, 1934), pp. 283–92, no. 109.
33. Ibid., p. 291.
34. See Sabbadini, pp. 113, 235.
35. The text of Giovanni's reply is in Vergerio, *Epistolario,* pp 293–96, no. 110.
36. See Sabbadini, pp. 113, 235–36.
37. The text of Petrarch's letter is in *Le Famaliari,* ed. V. Rossi (Florence, 1933–1942), 1: 131–33, Liber 3, no. 13.
38. For a discussion of Giovanni's debt to Valerius Maximus, see T. Kardos, "Magyar Tárgyú Fejezetek Giovanni da Ravenna Emlékeratában [Hungarian Anecdotes in the *Memorandarum rerum liber* of Giovanni da Ravenna]," *Egyetemes Philologiai Közlöny (Archivum Philologicum)* 40 (1936): 286–87; for his debt to Petrarch, see G. Billanovich, *Petrarca Letterato, I. Lo Scrittoio del Petrarca* (Rome, 1947), p. 341. An edition of most of the treatise is available in V. Zaccaria, "Il *Memorandarum Rerum Liber* di Giovanni di Conversino da Ravenna," *Atti dell'Istituto Veneto,* Classe di Scienze morali e lettere 106, pt. 2 (1947–1948): 221–50.
39. Sabbadini, p. 239. The quotation is from Persius, *Satirae* 5.41–43.

Notes to
2. The Argument of the Dragmologia

1. The strange Greek derivation of the title is discussed in H. Baron, *Crisis* (1955 ed.), 2: 489–90.
2. The best discussion of the *Dragmalogia* is in ibid. (1966 ed.), pp. 134–45; I have also found useful the discussion in M. Korelin's work on early Italian humanism (cited in n. 27, above), I wish to thank the Misses Hannah and Jitka Umlauf for providing me with an English translation of the apposite pages. The number of the speeches and grouping into chapters does not appear in Giovanni's text, but is an editorial addition done by the present editor for the convenience of the reader.
3. For a discussion of Giovanni's dissatisfaction with court life, see G. Calò, "Nota Vergeriana," *La Rinascita* 2 (1939): 226–52, esp. 236, 246–48.
4. Baron, *Crisis* (1966 ed.), pp. 134–45, and Sabbadini, pp. 106–7.

5. In its lack of appeal to divine sanction, the *Dragmalogia* contrasts with Petrarch's tract on princely rule written for Francesco il Vecchio da Carrara in 1373 and edited by V. Ussani (Padua, 1922). I realize that a passing allusion to the divine sanctioning of monarchy is emphasized in Baron, *Crisis* (1966 ed.), p. 144, but I do not think it is a significant argument taken within the context of the entire dialogue.

6. On the growth of "dissatisfaction" with the Deadly Sins at the end of the fourteenth century, see S. Wenzel, "The Seven Deadly Sins: Some Problems of Research," *Speculum* 43 (1968): 1–22, esp, 21–22. From the fact that no other work on the benefits of the Seven Sins is listed in either Wenzel's article or Morton Bloomfield, *The Seven Deadly Sins* (East Lansing, Mich., 1952), I surmise that Giovanni was original in his ironic treatment. For a famous example of virtue arising from vice known throughout the Middle Ages, see St. Augustine's account of the Romans achieving greatness through love of praise in *De civitate Dei*, 5.13.

7. See D. W. Clark, "Voluntarism and Rationalism in the Ethics of Ockham," *Franciscan Studies* 31 (1971): 72 ff.

8. Even the *Dragmalogia* once existed in three copies; see A. Battistella, "Un inventario di libri e oggetti domestici d'un maestro friulano del Quattrocento," *Memorie Storiche Forogiulesi* 21 (1925): 137–59 at p. 152, where is listed "Item *Dragmalogia* Johannis da Ravenna *De elegibili vite genere collocutores,* in membranis coopertum corio rubeo." This is clearly neither MS V nor MS P (described below), but a third copy now lost. Similarly, the *De dilectione regnantium,* written in 1399, exists in three copies and perhaps a fourth, now lost. See my paper "The Manuscript Tradition of the Works of Giovanni da Ravenna," to be published in the *Acta* of the Second International Congress for Neo-Latin Studies.

Dragmalogia Johannis de Ravenna de Eligibili Vite Genere

Dragmalogia of Giovanni da Ravenna on the Preferable Way of Life

Contents

1. The Troubled State of Italy — 51
2. Why the Ravennate [i.e., Giovanni] Left the Court of Carrara — 67
3. Courtly Arts — 83
4. Relative Merits of a Monarchy and a Republic — 107
5. Relative Merits of a Master and a Lord. — 141
6. The Good Life — 165
7. Country versus City Life — 169
8. Vices as Sources of Virtues — 195
9. Value of the Seven Deadly Sins — 203
10. Criticisms of Venice — 225
11. The Nature of Liberty — 243
12. Status of the Religious Vocation — 257

Dragmalogia[1] *Johannis de Ravenna de Eligibili Vite Genere*

Collocutores: Venetus et Paduanus

V-1.   Advenire te sospitem, Paduane exoptate dudum atque amate, plurimum grator.

P-1.   Quin vicissim desiderio te ingenti, Venetice, adesse integrum conspicor. Sed quid necessarii, quid denique rerum fortuna? Sospesne ac felix?

V-2.   Usque huc incolumi numero, sed haud usquequaque periucunda. Quenam enim esse mera iocunditas, bellis estuantibus, potest? Quae nimirum nos exhauriunt, vos funditus perdunt. Mali causa, Euganeus ductor, acceptam sortem mestius[2] pati.

P-2.   Quicumque culpe obvius obstare, cum valet, parcit aut dissimulat sic iuxta[3] delinquit. Veneto noxa potius inuri debet.

---

1. Dracmologia V.
2. nescius PV.
3. si iusta PV.

Dragmalogia of Giovanni da Ravenna on the Preferable Way of Life

Speakers: a Venetian and a Paduan

1. The Troubled State of Italy

V-1.   I am delighted that you have arrived safely, my long-awaited Paduan friend.

P-1.   And on my part, I am very happy to see you are well, my dear Venetian. How are your family and your personal affairs? All safe and sound?

V-2.   Until now still intact, but not in all respects very pleasant. For what real pleasure can there be when there are wars raging that in truth are exhausting us, but are utterly destroying you. The Paduan leader,[1] who is the cause of the trouble, is sorrowfully suffering the fate that has befallen him.

P-2.   Whoever refuses to prevent wrongdoing when he can, or ignores it, is in either case equally guilty. It is rather the Venetian leader who must be branded with this offense. For

Erat enim illius urbis autoritas quam veneranda tam imperiosa finitimis, cuiusque nutu pax bellumque imminerent. Que si manus opposuisset, et Gallicana pridem et nunc strages abstitisset Euganea.
V–3. Quo pacto? Quisnam coercuisset[4] Ligurum ducis insolentiam, cunctis paulo ante intentatis, arma cunctis horrendi?
P–3. Erras opido. Homo erat ad omnia maxime quam natus ad bella, delicias omnifariam voluptatesque operoso queritans studio. Porro, qui Martiis gloriam artibus expetunt corporis illecebras contemnere, commoda calcare, prebere sese negotiis, discrimina haud magnopere[5] formidare, animos militum presentia erigere, augere, audacie exemplum esse. Sed aversis[6] studiis omnia[7] agebat, aspectu et eloquio plus quam vir, audacia minus quam femina. Cumque tot populi, tot parerent exercitus, paucissimis notus, nemini prope adibilis erat. Quo factum est ut quam paucis communis, tam carus paucis, et quoniam eo ipso multis dispendio, multis etiam exosus foret. Quod si nostri ducis magnitudine animi invaluisset militarique audacia, que menia, quos populos sue terrore presentie non concussisset, non stravisset! Absente nimirum imperatore[8] tepent, presente exercitus fervent. Cumque illum chori puellarum conclavisque potissimum vindicaret, pro illo stetit magis fortuna quam virtus.
V–4. Unde nam, ergo, bella, ipso superstite, semper tamquam Ydre capita rediviva?
P–4. Quo altius montium iuga ornique[9] tolluntur, hoc flatibus quatiuntur. Vicinam magnitudinem populi horrebant nec minus invidebant, ferocia precipue Tusca, que discidiis[10] efflagrans

---

4. coercuisset *om.* V.
5. magno opere V.
6. versis V.
7. omnia studiis PV.
8. imparatore P.
9. ortuque P.
10. dissidiis P.

the influence of that city was as respected as it was powerful in the eyes of its neighbors, and either peace or war depended upon its whim. If it had displayed its strength in opposition, both the former Gallic disaster and the present Paduan one would have been avoided.[2]

V-3. How so? Who on earth could have restrained the insolence of the leader of the Ligurians[3] when he had shortly before menaced everyone; and who could have stopped the weapons of the man dreaded by all!

P-3. You are quite mistaken. He was a man born assuredly for all things rather than waging wars, pursuing enthusiastically every sort of delights and pleasures.[4] Now those who seek glory through the arts of Mars scorn the enticements of the body, disdain comforts, devote themselves to their duties, and have little fear of dangers. They arouse and increase the courage of their soldiers by their presence, and furnish an example of boldness. But in his diverse interests he engaged in all things, being in appearance and eloquence more than a man, in boldness less than a woman. And although so many people, so many armies obeyed him, he was known to very few and accessible to almost no one. As a result, he was not only friendly to few, but also beloved of few; and because by this very fact he brought harm to many, he was even hated by many. But if he had had the strength of our leader's great courage and military boldness, what walls, what peoples would he not have shaken and destroyed by the terror of his presence! Naturally, when the general is absent, armies are lukewarm; when he is present, they burn with eagerness. And so, since numerous young women and the dining hall were his chief occupations, fortune, rather than his personal worth, was his mainstay.

V-4. Then why on earth, while he was living, were wars constantly springing back to life like the heads of the Hydra?

P-4. The higher the ridges and the ash trees on mountains rise up, the more they are shaken by the winds. The people feared their neighbor's greatness and yet their envy equaled their fear, particularly savage Florence, which, ablaze with internal and foreign dissensions on every side, pursues wars

intestinis, ascitis, undequaque, seu veris seu causis[11] ex composito simulatis bella venatur. Pelagariarum more navium turbine procelloso fruitur, mari sedato contorpet.[12] Ardescentibus itaque nixibus, cum undique tiranno infesta esse moliretur, ad repellendum[13] structa bella aut ultro inferendum ne struerentur,[14] illum vigilare compellebat. Inde evenit ut qua depressum iri hostem arbitraretur, nonnumquam eius augeret imperium.

Inter invidiam ergo vimque geminorum, hinc Tusci, inde principis Longobardorum, si Venetus intentasset ponique arma simili attestatione iussisset quisquis pacem turbaret Italicam vires et subsidia partem in contrariam relaturum, quis contramoliri, quis arma exuscitare ausus fuisset, veritus opes tantas adversariis affuturas? Verumtamen prudentes scientesque, dum partium favorem adeptum iri autumant, amborum perdunt.

Silere preterita libet. Mantuanum, seris pene subsidiis, de victoris manu vix erutum,[15] minore certe mortalium iactura furorum initiis valuit obstari. Pridem sane Robertum Bavarie ducem non ausim pronuntiare imperatorem;[16] quid enim ignominiosius Cesaree[17] maiestati quam si mercenarius imperator agnoscitur? Hunc, inquam,[18] elatio Florentina[19] stipendio pellexit in Latium—et quanta spe, Deus bone, quantis sponsionibus, quanto laudum[20] incremento! Et quo cuncta, nisi[21] propter vicina odia? Que si demas, laudes, sponsiones, dona, pretiaque prorsus arescant. Pudor Italice probitatis accire barbaros, quo preda barbaris pateat Italia. Usque adeo urunt odia!

Cumque nemo principum Latiorum Florentinatium votis hostilibus ab Euganeo alius consonaret, ut dici solet scutum sibi et lanceam constituerunt. Inde, pronus ad arma parique morbo deflagrans, tot laboribus, periculis, sumptibus, rerumque suarum

---

11. seu ex causis V.
12. cum torpet V.
13. repellendam V.
14. strueretur V.
15. eruptum V.
16. imparatorem P.
17. *ex* cesare *corr.* P².
18. nonquam V.
19. Florentia V.
20. laudium V.
21. tusci V.

The Troubled State of Italy 55

for reasons either real or feigned. Like deep-sea ships she enjoys a gusty storm, but she grows bored when the sea is calm. Therefore, when the struggles grew fierce, since Florence was endeavoring to threaten the tyrant from all sides, she forced him to be vigilant either in defending himself against attacks or in instigating wars himself to prevent attacks. Thus it happened that where she thought the enemy would be checked, sometimes she strengthened his power.

So if the Venetian had interposed himself between the envy and strength of the two, the Florentine leader on one side and the Lombard prince[5] on the other, and had threatened them and had ordered them to lay down their arms, making it clear that if either one disturbed the peace of Italy, he would bring troops and aid to the other side, who would have dared to attack or to brandish arms, fearing the great resources that would be available to his adversaries? However, even prudent and knowledgeable men, when they believe they are going to acquire the favor of both sides, lose that of both.

It is better to keep silent about past events. In the beginning of the madness the Mantuan[6] could have been withstood, certainly with less loss of human life, when his auxiliary troops were nearly too late and he was just barely rescued from the grasp of the victor. In past times, indeed, I would not have dared to proclaim as emperor Rupert, Duke of Bavaria,[7] for what is more disgraceful to the majesty of Caesar than for a mercenary soldier to be acknowledged as emperor? This man, I say, the pride of Florence enticed into Italy with a salary—and with what expectations, good God, what promises, what an allotment of honors! And for what reason did Florence do all this if not because of hatred for her neighbors? If you were to take that hatred away, the honors, promises, gifts, and rewards would immediately run dry. It is a disgrace to Italian honor to call in the barbarians, leaving Italy an open prey to them. So hot do hatreds burn!

And since none of the Italian princes except the Paduan was in sympathy with the warlike aims of the Florentines, they, as is customarily said, set up shield and lance for themselves. Then Rupert, eager to fight and burning with the same

ingenti iactura Robertus[22] maturavit. Imo, adeo stimulavit adventum ut Paduana regio nepotum quoque etate demolumenta[23] commemoret. At qui applausu ingenti speque plurimorum adventaverat eatenus moram traxit quatenus edaces Padua valuit explere, devorataque soli feracis pinguedine, spe irritos lusosque dimisit.

Potare et cum uxore Schachis ludere Cesari iuge negotium erat. Nempe qui subigere Italos vino et otio putant virtutem Italicam nesciunt aut insaniunt! Discant ac memorent, quemadmodum sapientia barbari, ita armorum magnificentia ab Italis anteiri. In quibus unanimitas si vigeret, omne genus externum vano[24] fabe grano prorsus non licerentur. Verum discissi odiis alliciunt hostes et nutriunt. Quanto igitur sanctius atque fructuosius fastigium Venetorum exordiis autoritatem obiecisset[25]: "Quid, Florentinas, tibi cum barbaris? Tuo num[26] patiar odio gentem feram, avaram, exlegem, improbam in Latium trahi? Non annuam, non feram, non sinam! Si minus quiescet odium vestrum,[27] at quiescant arma. Quisquis exercitum parabit, exercitum et omnes copias contraponam. Dominantem Ligurum metuis? Tecum, si insurget, insurgam. Si vero inquies bella insuscitaveris,[28] Liguri partes communiam." Huiusmodi sane protestationis tonitruo nec Bavaria foret accita nec Gallia bellis lacerata. Verum dum somniculosis vicinos furores oculis intuentur, communi plerumque alluvione exundantur.

V-5. Vere assertionis seriem infitiari nequeo. Sed quid? Inviti[29] rebus exteris immiscemur, negotio nostro vacamus, suorum aliis curam omittimus. Merces quoque nos et lucri estus, fateor, vindicat.

---

22. Roberti PV.
23. demolumenta: apparently coined. Cf note 713.
24. intervano PV.
25. obiectisset V.
26. non V.
27. si minus ... vestrum *om.* V.
28. inscuscitaveris V.
29. intuiti V.

The Troubled State of Italy 57

fever, with many difficulties, dangers, expenses, and a great outlay of his resources, rushed in. In fact, he so hurried his arrival that the Paduan region will remember the destruction even in the time of its grandchildren. This man who had come with the enthusiastic approval and hope of most of the people protracted his stay as long as Padua was able to satisfy his greedy retinue. Then, when the richness of the fertile soil had been devoured, he abandoned them, cheated of their vain hopes.

It was the constant occupation of the emperor to drink[8] and to play chess with his wife. Surely those who expect to subdue Italians while indulging in wine and idleness are ignorant of Italian virtue or are mad! Let them learn and remember that just as the Italians surpass the barbarians in wisdom, so do they surpass them in strength of arms. If unanimity flourished among the people of Italy, they would not think any foreign race worth a hollow bean seed! But since they are split by hatreds, they call in our enemies and sustain them. With how much more honor and success could the powerful Venetians have interposed their influence at the beginning: "Why, oh Florentine, are you dealing with barbarians? Shall I allow a fierce, greedy, lawless, and wicked race to be drawn into Italy because of your hatred? I will not assent to it, nor endure it, nor permit it. If your hatred does not rest, at least let your arms be at rest. Against whoever prepares an army I shall oppose my army and all my resources. Do you fear the lord of the Ligurians? If he rises up, I shall rise up with you. But if you in your restlessness stir up wars, I shall take up arms on the side of the Ligurian." Indeed, with such a thunderous proclamation, Bavaria would not have been summoned and Gaul would not have been ravaged by wars. But since the Venetians gaze with drowsy eye upon the madness of their neighbors, they are very often overwhelmed by the common flood.[9]

V–5. I cannot, of course, deny your facts. But consider our point of view. We Venetians are unwilling to become involved with foreign affairs. We attend to our own business, we leave to others concern for theirs. Also, commercial interests and a great desire for money, I admit, have a hold on us! Further-

Paci rursum ita studemus ut quamvis irritati semel et iterum ad ferrum prorsus lenti surgamus. Nequaquam dissidio proximorum sed concordia letamur[30] fecundique sumus. Hanc ultro et vocati libenter inserimus et fovemus. Namque, sublato[31] Mediolani duce, inter eius superstites Euganeumque pacem legibus equis pepigimus. Captivi Padue ex primatibus restituti; sanctum utrinque vulgatumque fedus.

Sed mox hostico Paduanus annixu Mediolanensi hostes omnifariam solicitat, excitat, contrahit. Necdum mense exacto, calcata pace, neglectis autoribus pacis, federeque contempto, Guelforum ope Brixiam, Insubrium primam[32] caputque, occupat; qua cede Ghibelinorum virorum, senum, feminarum, puerorum notum est, diffamatum est,[33] et apud superos conclamatum. Sed quam, averso[34] numine, civitate potitus[35] est, tam exitu indecoro deseruit qui, velut exitio Ghibelinis accessit, tam infaustus[36] decessit et Guelfis, miro Dei iudicio, ut civitas impatiens unitatis civili vicissim dissidio repente concideret. Ad has nempe victimas nuntiatum iter temere nimis annuimus, nam si stare contentumque suis esse finibus Paduanum senatus censuisset, nec miserabili cruenta suorum cede Brixia nec suborta mala sequentia. Quippe ferox animus armis abstinuisset nec spem invadendi vicinas urbes nec manum erexisset. Ceterum dum secura post tergum omnia iudicat,[37] sponte obvios impetit, usque adeo preceps dum nos quoque tandem experrectos[38] ad intercipiendum improbos conatus impelleret.

P-5. Que Venetos ratio in iram succendit? Nec invadebantur nec petebantur. Sua omnia illis pacata, tuta omnia. Nec rebus nec hostile finibus quicquam[39] intentabatur. Quid ad eos si qua

---

30. lectamur V.
31. in sublacto V.
32. om. V.
33. om. V.
34. adverso V.
35. cecitate pocius V.
36. infaustis V.
37. indicat P.
38. expectos P. om. V.
39. quicquam finibus V.

The Troubled State of Italy 59

more, we are so desirous of peace that, although angered time and again, we are slow to rise to the sword. We do not at all enjoy dissension with our neighbors, but concord, and we have this in plenty. When called upon, we willingly and gladly instill and encourage harmony. When the Duke of Milan died, we arranged a peace with just laws between his successors and the Paduan.[10] Captives from among the chief citizens of Padua were restored; a treaty was ratified by both sides and published.

But soon the Paduan in a hostile struggle with Milan roused up the enemy in all sorts of ways, antagonized them, united them. Scarely a month had passed when the peace was trodden underfoot. Ignoring the authors of the peace and scorning the treaty, with the help of the Guelphs the Paduan seized Brescia, chief city and capital of the Lombards; and because of the slaughter of the Ghibellines, men and women, old and young, Brescia has become famous, spoken of far and wide, wept for in Heaven. But just as he seized the city against divine will, so did he leave it ignominiously. Even as his coming brought destruction to the Ghibellines, in the same way his leaving was so disastrous for the Guelphs, by the marvelous decision of God, that the city, impatient of unity, fell suddenly in its turn into civil dissent. To be sure, we acquiesced too carelessly when he proposed his campaign against these victims; for if our senate had decreed that the Paduan should stop and be content with his own lands, Brescia would not have suffered the cruel, bloody slaughter of its people, nor would the other evils have followed. Surely the Paduan's fierce mind would have refrained from war, and he would have neither hoped nor attempted to invade the neighboring cities. But since he judged all things secure to the rear, he willingly attacked those before him, being exceedingly headstrong, until he compelled even us at last to rise up and oppose his wicked onslaughts.[11]

P–5. What cause inflamed the Venetians' anger? They were being neither invaded nor attacked. All their territories were at peace, everything was safe. Nothing hostile threatened either their belongings or their territory. What was it to them if the

vocaret fortuna secundo flatu decurreret, nisi forte, quod[40] assolet, premit successus invidia?

V–6. Haud hec aberit causa, semperque prosperitatis livor incrementa morsabit; verum alia vel maxima aderat. Namque dialetice rationis lex admonet : qui in mediocri superbus fortuna extra mensuram insolenter egreditur, in maxima cohiberi non poterit. Si favilla tamen inferatur[41] incendii, quidnam erit si in flammam excreverit peritura? Cum autem imperandi libidine et una urbe impotentiores subicere insolens decertet, renuat pace componi, sed usquequaque bella potius estuet,[42] struat, cogitet, credo etiam somniet, quanta superbia, quanto item vicinarum rerum exitio Verona ceterisque urbibus Cispadanis potiatur?

Quare sperata illa magnitudo Veneto bellum ac turbinem in tempore minabatur, qui nequaquam quod in Paduanum acies struxit sed magnopere arguendus quod sero oculos aperuit. Interest enim rei publice non quod obest modo in presenti, sed quod posset obesse, repulsare;[43] riteque[44] per vim coerceri ad quietem convenit qui nequitia quieti aliene degrassari non desinit. Iustoque iudicio datum celitus reor[45] ut qui tantopere armis ceteros perturbasset adversis idem armis fatigetur.

P–6. Falleris. Minime fatigatur, quin suo nunc tempore fruitur, experiri se suasque artes iuvat. Omnes[46] enim ad que bene didicere voluptate trahuntur. Quis porro instantius bella studuit[47] in pace? Quis providit exactius? Quis uberius[48] instruxit? Ei pax theorica bellorum est, bella vero sunt pratica. Tanta siquidem bellandi subiciendique proximos fines libido incessit, ne occasioni usquam deesset, ut cetaras studiis curas Martiis supponeret. Primum

---

40. quid P.
41. inferat PV.
42. estuat V.
43. impulsare V.
44. ricteque V.
45. reo V.
46. omnis V.
47. studivit V.
48. liberius V.

The Troubled State of Italy

Paduan sailed with a favoring breeze where fortune called him—unless perhaps, as is common, envy treads on the heels of success!

V-6. One cause will scarcely ever fail: envy will always gnaw at increased prosperity. But there was another reason, a very important one. For the law of dialectic science[12] teaches that the man who is haughty when his fortune is modest, going insolently beyond all measure, cannot be restrained when his fortune is very great. If from a mere glowing ember a fire can be ignited, why indeed will it perish when it has grown into a flame? If in his lust for ruling and for one city he insolently strives to overthrow those less powerful, refuses terms of peace, and everywhere prefers to brew wars, and plans, thinks, and I believe, even dreams of them — with what arrogance, then, and with what destruction to his neighbors' possessions as well, would he seize Verona and the other cities on the northern side of the Po!

Hence, that anticipated power was threatening war and eventually stormy times for the Venetian leader, who is not at all to be blamed because he went to battle against the Paduan, but rather because he opened his eyes too late. For it is to the interest of the commonwealth to repel not only what can hurt it right now, but what has the potential to hurt it. And it is duly fitting to force peace on one who through his wickedness does not cease to attack the peace of others. And with just judgment, I believe, Heaven has granted that the man who has greatly harassed others by arms should himself be wearied by opposing arms.[13]

P-6. You are mistaken: the Paduan is not at all wearied, but is now taking advantage of time and is pleased to test himself and his skills. All men turn with pleasure to the things that they have learned well. Besides, who has more eagerly made a study of wars during peacetime? Who has prepared for them more carefully? Who has planned them in fuller detail? For him peace is a philosophical speculation about war, and war is the practical application. Indeed, so great a passion for fighting and conquering nearby territory has seized him that he has subjected all other interests to

nempe, quod preteritorum nemo principum sue[49] gentis, longe quamquam sapientie rerumque ac civium gloria venia dixerim precellentium, umquam attentavit, urbem validissimis tutam menibus muris recinxit; turribus auxibus fornicalia intercolumnia, supervacuum opus, implevit; pontes abscidit; portas deformavit angustiis. Edes, insuper, amplissimo urbanorum detrimento, contiguas menibus demoliri iussit, signa prorsus timeri quam diligi studentis omniaque struentis ut subditos infrenaret.

Ad hec litterarum studia, decus, et gloriam[50] urbis hactenus nostre posthabuit; litteratos omnifariam contempsit stataque omnibus stipendia interdixit. Nam quicquid ex vectigalibus, tributo, exactionibus, rapinis, coentionibus congeri valebat, in usus bellicos servabatur. Cunctis preter armigeros, qui velut in sentinam facinorum ex omni alluvione confluebant, tenacissimus; his liberalis et[51] indulgens, his blandus erat. Nemo felicius Paduam accessit, presentius nemo receptus est, quam qui vel gliscere bella vel nosset.[52] Studiorum autem studiosorumve sapientie iactura omnino nulla. Inde pater et patronus Saccomanorum et Saccardorum (ita enim abiectissimus quisque turbe castrensis nominatur) unus ipse predicari. Quo dempto usus horum nullus ac iners vita contemptaque prorsus iaceret. Iactari el ipse tali predicatione letari atque apud hec monstra in pretio et admiratione haberi glorie ascribere. Verum sperare eiuscemodi hominibus qui nullis laudibus fulcirentur grandescere[53] claritudine insani est, optare improbi. Quanto illustrius philosophorum, poetarum, ceterarumque precellentium[54] dignitate scientie personarum susceptor amatorque audiretur! Ob istos quidem amari et honorari, ob illos dumtaxat metui odirique contingat.

49. sive V.
50. gloria PV.
51. *inser. supra* V.
52. noscet V.
53. grande scelere V.
54. precelletium P.

camp of soldiers. No culture, no appearance of civil modesty, exists among the citizens. Even more, the professors of learning, having cast aside the insignia of their wisdom in order to gain access and favor, have disgraced themselves by assuming the ways of mercenaries. Concerning these persons, the Ravennate, formerly chancellor, was accustomed to repeat a humorous but true saying that they had learned in order to unlearn.[14]

2. Why the Ravennate [i.e., Giovanni] Left the Court of Carrara

V-7. I keep hearing much praise of this Ravennate, not only because of his knowledge but because of his virtue. Do you know him? Is he like this?

P-7. I know the facts well, for the proof is clear and has been spread abroad through his deeds and words. When he was in the service of Francesco il Vecchio, and also of his son, what commonwealth, what prince, what city did not speak highly of his performance as ambassador? Therefore, though you and other peoples near this shore hold him in esteem, only a small part of his reputation is due to you. As regards us, who have long approved his life and character, he lived without envy (a rare accomplishment) in the midst of courtiers and citizens, a very solitary man and a lover of the just and true, an encourager of peace and the good arts. In the entire city you could not easily find anyone who refrained from praising him or who did not regret his departure. It was the man's constant occupation to discuss or to meditate on what he would dictate, or to read the things he was going to say.

V-8. How long did the Paduan court avail itself of his services?

P-8. He remained there until he was old, without complaint or faultfinding, living justly and uprightly. As he was about to leave, he bore eloquent witness to this when, in the presence of Carrara himself and with the prince's sons and a group of public servants standing by, he said, "I leave, oh prince,

lustris tuo et genitoris obsequio famulatus. Nichil infestum, nichil arguendum in me censuistis. Grator nimirum[66] quod tua et cunctorum dilectione ac laude discedo." Quas penitus[67] voces prefectis aule, qui domini consilium appellantur, cum valefaceret impressit. Querentibus namque et egre se eius recessum asserentibus ferre, "Sic," inquit, "inter vos[68] agens, semper annixus sum meam uti absentiam mesti acciperetis." O paucos de se idem proferre valuisse!

V-9. Cur ille dominus virum adeo predicatum et expertum decedere sit passus opido miror!

P-9. Nemo in tanta[69] civitate non miratur. Sed admiratio procul absistat si quisque[70] hunc et huiusmodi professionis homines quam flocci fecerit Euganeus norit. Quem quo[71] pectore gestaret hinc licebit advertas. Cum per Henricum Gallum et Michaelem de Rabata, quibus internuntiis Carriger pene singula digerebat, deposci Ravennas veniam abeundi mandasset, ultro hac assertione concessit: "Utinam sic omnes alii facerent!" Vox ista nimirum palam fecit, et, si in posteros evasura sit, faciet nec animo complexum esse diuturnum servitorem nec liceri studiosos litterarum.

V-10. Indigna, mehercule, principe qui suos amet inexcusabilis[72] adeo licentia! Sed edisseri efflagito parabolam, quid sibi velit, "Utinam sic omnes alii facerent!"

P-10. Siccine hebes ut pronam adeo licentiam improbes et verborum sensum minime attingas? Is prorsus est sensus, ut omnes sapientie intentos, inertes ad ferrum, insolentesque facinorum, quoniam quicquid eiuscemodi personis impenderetur dispendio[73] ascriberet, cupiat absistere, tamquam[74] onere solvendus inutili.

---

66. nimium P.
67. pene PV.
68. nos P.
69. in quanta est PV.
70. quis V.
71. quo *ex* quocum *corr.* V.
72. inexcussa PV.
73. impederetur stipendio V.
74. tamque P.

taking with me the glory of knowing that I have obediently served you and your father for almost forty years.[15] You have found in me nothing troublesome, nothing reprehensible. I am indeed gratified because I depart with your love and praise and that of all men." These words deeply impressed the prefects of the court, who are called the lord's council, when he made his farewell. When they protested and asserted that they took his departure very hard, he said, "I have always tried to act in such a way among you that you should be sad at my leave-taking." Few men could have said the same about themselves!

V-9. I surely wonder why that lord permitted so praiseworthy and experienced a man to leave.

P-9. There is no one in this great city who does not wonder. But there would be no bewilderment if every one knew how little value the Paduan placed on him and those of his profession. What sort of feeling Francesco had toward him you can observe from this: when through the agency of Enrico Gallo and Michele da Rabatta, whom Carrara used as intermediaries in arranging nearly all matters, the Ravennate had requested the privilege of leaving,[16] Carrara willingly granted it, adding, "I wish that all the others would do the same!" That statement, if made public and if it should come down to our descendants, will make known to posterity the fact that he had no affection for this man who had served him so long, and that he did not value those who devote themselves to the study of literature.

V-10. Such an inexcusable dismissal is unworthy, by heaven, of a prince who loves his people! But I would like an explanation of what he meant by his statement: "I wish that all the others would do the same."

P-10. Are you so slow-witted that you disapprove of his granting permission to leave so readily and yet do not at all grasp the meaning of his words? He means, of course, that he wishes all who pursue knowledge, and who are unskilled with the sword and unaccustomed to crimes, to depart, as if freeing him from a useless burden, since he counted as a loss anything paid to persons of this sort.

V–11. Itane vita homo ille[75] sumptuosus extat, eoque degere apparatu deposcit ut regiis opibus gravis sarcina videretur? Diuturna precipue fide genitori, mox deinde sibi famulatus.

P–11. Quod ceteri admirarentur[76] atque magnopere in primis senior Franciscus, tam diu favore aulico circumfusus, nullum traxit ab aula contagium elationis, iactantie, vanitatis; cumque secundo principe uteretur, nichil minus quam aule blandimentum duxit Dudum iussus ire Sermeolam, urbis Padue suburbanum, quo se Lombardus otio litterato contraxerat, puero comite, pedes iit.[77] Re profecta,[78] vesperi contantur confamuli ea luce ubinam abfuisset. Causa exposita, quo foret vectus equo rogitant. Ille "Fratrum Minorum," iocabundus respondit. Ilicet risare singuli, temnere, arguere quod pedes tantisper commeasset. Frugique hominis minime libertatem sed arrogantiam potius suam contractam ex aula mensi, factum improbabant et ad ipsum usque Franciscum principem detulere. Is, ut natura magnificus quique haberet in deliciis Ravennatem quod pedibus iter vasisset, familiari monitu increpuit. Tum ille, "Scio idque apprime gratissimum duco," inquit, "dominator optime, equos aulicos, ceu tantopere tua clementia semel et iterum largitur, obtulit, usu fore semper michi; ex arbitrioque[79] indulgentia tua opportunos exciperem. Verumtamen priore suetus fortuna pedare, nolim hisce consuescere deliciis quorum fieret absentia, si presens desereret condicio, difficilis." Ita respondit, ita fecit, ita vixit, ut afflante profectum nullum et reflante fortuna defectum nullum[80] sentire videretur. Ex quo satis animadverti licet quam erat tenui retinendus impendio, sed quorum virtus despicitur contingit ut persona etiam[81] contemnatur.

V–12. Infaustus nimium profecto huius hominis famulatus, qui,

---

75. ille homo vita V.
76. admirentur V.
77. pedes init P pedessiit V.
78. profectum PV.
79. arbitrio tuoque V.
80. nullum *addidi.*
81. et V.

the pursuits of Mars, in order not to miss an opportunity anywhere. First, then, he did what no one of the past princes of his family ever attempted, although I would say, with your permission, they were exceedingly outstanding in the glory of their wisdom and deeds and citizenry: he recircled with walls a city already protected by very strong ramparts; he filled with planks the impractical arched, intercolumnar spaces in the towers; he cut down bridges; he disfigured the gates with narrow passageways. Furthermore, he ordered the destruction of the buildings contiguous to the walls, with very great loss to the city's inhabitants. These are definitely signs of a man who desires to be feared rather than loved, contriving all things so as to hold a tight rein on his subjects.

He preferred such activities to the study of literature, once the honor and glory of our city. He contemned literary men in all respects and refused to pay the salaries agreed upon for them. Whatever could be collected from taxes, tribute, fees, plunder, and fines was kept for war. He was very niggardly to all except soldiers, men who came to him from everywhere, like floodwaters flowing into a cesspool of wickedness; but to these he was generous, indulgent, and agreeable. No one came to Padua under better auspices, no one was accepted more quickly, than the man who either greatly loved warfare or was experienced in it. But there was no expenditure at all for studies or for persons interested in knowledge. Therefore, Father and Patron of Saccomani and Saccardi (for these terms, meaning robbers and scoundrels, are applied to the most worthless of the military horde) was the title given to this man. Without him there would be no use for such wretched individuals, and their lives would be idle and contemptible. He himself boasted and rejoiced in this title and called it glory to be held in esteem and admiration by these monsters. But to hope to grow great in renown through men of this sort, who are supported by no merit, is insane; to wish for it, wicked. How much more illustrious it would be to be named patron and lover of philosophers, poets, and other persons excelling in the dignity of knowledge! With men like these, he would achieve love and honor; with the other sort, only fear and hatred.

In quo genere laudis Mediolani dux, Johannes Galeaz, magnifice se curavit. Nam quisquis singulari virtute scientiave prestaret, hunc ad se trahere iacturam, quantalibet summa, non duxerat. Ad Galeaz ergo undelibet quivis sapientie laude clari coibant. Huc[55] autem, premissa fama, quicquid undique nefariorum hominum qui patrie, qui parentibus, qui flagitio et cedibus invisi suis forent, qui denique legibus honestarumque artium institutis obstarent, quibus prorsus abuti vita voluptas foret, confluebant. Quibus nusquam alias salus securitasque pateret, premium et gratia presto erant. His festum se liberalemque agebat.

Quin etiam, ex agris iuventutem pellexit, facileque a glebe labore ad arma, ad cedes, tum spe predandi, tum adhortationibus, tum blando favore donatiumculisque impiavit. Ac brevi in otium et sevitiam pronos ex colonis vispiliones[56] sanguinarios et latrones, raptores, inque omne audaces nefas reddidit. Quo civitas infelicius nichil umquam vidit. Namque tot hostes quot agricolas habet; predia aut illaborata aut dominis, superbiente villico, infructuosa. Continuo preterea agrestes in armis aut fossis eruderandis aut vallandis castris aut aversa per itinera fluminibus alveandis esse urgebat, ita ut deserta cultoribus rura silvescant nec fecundent ubere solito civitatem. Atque ex hoc insolentia rurestribus tanta, licentiose presumptionis venia, incessit ut non exteris modo viatoribus sed ne patronis quidem urbanis spatiari per agros tuto satis liceret.

Atqui adeo mentes infecit[57] armorum studium placere tiranno ut urbs ipsa, honestissimis quondam celebris et populosa erudientium discentiumque choris, philosophorum, iuristarum, medicorum, facies manipulorum[58] castrensium appareret. Nullus cultus nullusve

---

55. hunc V.
56. vespiliones V.
57. infecit mentes V.
58. mapulorum PV.

The Troubled State of Italy 65

With praise of this better kind the Duke of Milan, Giangaleazzo, provided himself magnificently. For when a man excelled in singular virtue or knowledge, Galeazzo did not consider it an extravagance to attach him to himself, however great the cost. Therefore, men famous for the excellence of their wisdom came to him from all directions. To Francesco Novello, however, since his reputation had gone abroad, from every side came wicked men who were hateful to their country, their parents, and their people because of their crimes and murders, men who, in short, were opposed to law and the practice of honorable skills, men who truly took pleasure in misusing their lives—all these streamed in. For those to whom safety and security were available nowhere else, reward and favor were ready here. To them he showed himself pleasant and generous.

Furthermore, he easily enticed the youth from the fields and from the labor of the soil to arms and to slaughter, and corrupted them not only by the expectation of booty, but by encouragement, flattering favor, and small gifts. In a short time those prone to idleness and violence were changed from peasants to bloodthirsty grave-robbers, cutthroats, and thieves, emboldened for every crime. The city never saw a greater misfortune. For it has as many enemies as it has farmers; the farms are either unworked or unproductive for the owners because of insolent overseers. Furthermore, Francesco constantly urged the country people to take up arms, to clear ditches of rubbish, to fortify camps, or to dig out new river beds. Consequently, the countryside, bereft of cultivators, turns to woods and does not provide the city with its usual abundance. As a result of all this, such great insolence has come upon the country people, whose overwhelming audacity was looked upon with indulgence, that it is not possible for foreign travelers or even city landowners to walk with complete safety through the rural areas.

And people's minds have become so imbued with the idea that love of war pleases the tyrant, that the city itself, formerly famous for its honorable men and thronged with teachers and pupils, philosophers, jurists, and doctors, now looks like a

habitus civilis modestie civibus constitit; quin scientie professores, insignibus sapientie deiectis, quo aditum et gratiam sortirentur, stipendiario se habitu deformarent. De quibus ludicram sed veram Ravennas, olim cancellarius, solebat[59] ferre sententiam, quatenus dediscerent didicisse.

V-7. Ravennatis huius tum scientia tum virtute confertum laudibus nomen audio. Nostin? Itane est?

P-7. Probe[60] novi, nam vulgata passim in dictis factisque experientia patet. Et Francisco Seniore, nato quoque,[61] iubente, que res publica, quis princeps, que urbs ministerium huius legationis non probavit?[62] Si igitur apud vos ceterosque hanc prope oram populos extimatione licet, quantula vobis laudis portio contingit. Ad nos, qui vitam diu moresque probavimus,[63] sine invidia, quod rarum invenias, inter aulicos civesque versatus est, homo utique solitarius, iusti verique amans, pacis artiumque bonarum adhortator. In universa civitate nullum vel abstinere ab eius laudatione vel non queri de eius[64] abscessione facile reperias. Orare homini aut meditari que dictaret aut legere que memoraret iuge negotium erat.

V-8. Quam dudum aula famulatum Euganea produxit?

P-8. In senium usque, sine querela et reprensione, equus ac dexter vivens. Quod, abiturus,[65] magnifice in ipsius Carrigeri facie, natis apparitorumque manu astantibus, ultro testatus, ait: "Abeo, princeps, gloriam conscientie mecum ferens, quod octo prope

---

59. *om.* P.
60. prope V.
61. que V.
62. probauta V.
63. palpavimus P.
64. ab evis P.
65. abtrus V.

camp of soldiers. No culture, no appearance of civil modesty, exists among the citizens. Even more, the professors of learning, having cast aside the insignia of their wisdom in order to gain access and favor, have disgraced themselves by assuming the ways of mercenaries. Concerning these persons, the Ravennate, formerly chancellor, was accustomed to repeat a humorous but true saying that they had learned in order to unlearn.[14]

2. Why the Ravennate [i.e., Giovanni] Left the Court of Carrara

V-7. I keep hearing much praise of this Ravennate, not only because of his knowledge but because of his virtue. Do you know him? Is he like this?

P-7. I know the facts well, for the proof is clear and has been spread abroad through his deeds and words. When he was in the service of Francesco il Vecchio, and also of his son, what commonwealth, what prince, what city did not speak highly of his performance as ambassador? Therefore, though you and other peoples near this shore hold him in esteem, only a small part of his reputation is due to you. As regards us, who have long approved his life and character, he lived without envy (a rare accomplishment) in the midst of courtiers and citizens, a very solitary man and a lover of the just and true, an encourager of peace and the good arts. In the entire city you could not easily find anyone who refrained from praising him or who did not regret his departure. It was the man's constant occupation to discuss or to meditate on what he would dictate, or to read the things he was going to say.

V-8. How long did the Paduan court avail itself of his services?

P-8. He remained there until he was old, without complaint or faultfinding, living justly and uprightly. As he was about to leave, he bore eloquent witness to this when, in the presence of Carrara himself and with the prince's sons and a group of public servants standing by, he said, "I leave, oh prince,

lustris tuo et genitoris obsequio famulatus. Nichil infestum, nichil arguendum in me censuistis. Grator nimirum[66] quod tua et cunctorum dilectione ac laude discedo." Quas penitus[67] voces prefectis aule, qui domini consilium appellantur, cum valefaceret impressit. Querentibus namque et egre se eius recessum asserentibus ferre, "Sic," inquit, "inter vos[68] agens, semper annixus sum meam uti absentiam mesti acciperetis." O paucos de se idem proferre valuisse!

V–9. Cur ille dominus virum adeo predicatum et expertum decedere sit passus opido miror!

P–9. Nemo in tanta[69] civitate non miratur. Sed admiratio procul absistat si quisque[70] hunc et huiusmodi professionis homines quam flocci fecerit Euganeus norit. Quem quo[71] pectore gestaret hinc licebit advertas. Cum per Henricum Gallum et Michaelem de Rabata, quibus internuntiis Carriger pene singula digerebat, deposci Ravennas veniam abeundi mandasset, ultro hac assertione concessit: "Utinam sic omnes alii facerent!" Vox ista nimirum palam fecit, et, si in posteros evasura sit, faciet nec animo complexum esse diuturnum servitorem nec liceri studiosos litterarum.

V–10. Indigna, mehercule, principe qui suos amet inexcusabilis[72] adeo licentia! Sed edisseri efflagito parabolam, quid sibi velit, "Utinam sic omnes alii facerent!"

P–10. Siccine hebes ut pronam adeo licentiam improbes et verborum sensum minime attingas? Is prorsus est sensus, ut omnes sapientie intentos, inertes ad ferrum, insolentesque facinorum, quoniam quicquid eiuscemodi personis impenderetur dispendio[73] ascriberet, cupiat absistere, tamquam[74] onere solvendus inutili.

---

66. nimium P.
67. pene PV.
68. nos P.
69. in quanta est PV.
70. quis V.
71. quo *ex* quocum *corr.* V.
72. inexcussa PV.
73. impederetur stipendio V.
74. tamque P.

Why the Ravennate Left the Carrara 69

taking with me the glory of knowing that I have obediently served you and your father for almost forty years.[15] You have found in me nothing troublesome, nothing reprehensible. I am indeed gratified because I depart with your love and praise and that of all men." These words deeply impressed the prefects of the court, who are called the lord's council, when he made his farewell. When they protested and asserted that they took his departure very hard, he said, "I have always tried to act in such a way among you that you should be sad at my leave-taking." Few men could have said the same about themselves!

V-9. I surely wonder why that lord permitted so praiseworthy and experienced a man to leave.

P-9. There is no one in this great city who does not wonder. But there would be no bewilderment if every one knew how little value the Paduan placed on him and those of his profession. What sort of feeling Francesco had toward him you can observe from this: when through the agency of Enrico Gallo and Michele da Rabatta, whom Carrara used as intermediaries in arranging nearly all matters, the Ravennate had requested the privilege of leaving,[16] Carrara willingly granted it, adding, "I wish that all the others would do the same!" That statement, if made public and if it should come down to our descendants, will make known to posterity the fact that he had no affection for this man who had served him so long, and that he did not value those who devote themselves to the study of literature.

V-10. Such an inexcusable dismissal is unworthy, by heaven, of a prince who loves his people! But I would like an explanation of what he meant by his statement: "I wish that all the others would do the same."

P-10. Are you so slow-witted that you disapprove of his granting permission to leave so readily and yet do not at all grasp the meaning of his words? He means, of course, that he wishes all who pursue knowledge, and who are unskilled with the sword and unaccustomed to crimes, to depart, as if freeing him from a useless burden, since he counted as a loss anything paid to persons of this sort.

V–11. Itane vita homo ille[75] sumptuosus extat, eoque degere apparatu deposcit ut regiis opibus gravis sarcina videretur? Diuturna precipue fide genitori, mox deinde sibi famulatus.

P–11. Quod ceteri admirarentur[76] atque magnopere in primis senior Franciscus, tam diu favore aulico circumfusus, nullum traxit ab aula contagium elationis, iactantie, vanitatis; cumque secundo principe uteretur, nichil minus quam aule blandimentum duxit Dudum iussus ire Sermeolam, urbis Padue suburbanum, quo se Lombardus otio litterato contraxerat, puero comite, pedes iit.[77] Re profecta,[78] vesperi contantur confamuli ea luce ubinam abfuisset. Causa exposita, quo foret vectus equo rogitant. Ille "Fratrum Minorum," iocabundus respondit. Ilicet risare singuli, temnere, arguere quod pedes tantisper commeasset. Frugique hominis minime libertatem sed arrogantiam potius suam contractam ex aula mensi, factum improbabant et ad ipsum usque Franciscum principem detulere. Is, ut natura magnificus quique haberet in deliciis Ravennatem quod pedibus iter vasisset, familiari monitu increpuit. Tum ille, "Scio idque apprime gratissimum duco," inquit, "dominator optime, equos aulicos, ceu tantopere tua clementia semel et iterum largitur, obtulit, usu fore semper michi; ex arbitrioque[79] indulgentia tua opportunos exciperem. Verumtamen priore suetus fortuna pedare, nolim hisce consuescere deliciis quorum fieret absentia, si presens desereret condicio, difficilis." Ita respondit, ita fecit, ita vixit, ut afflante profectum nullum et reflante fortuna defectum nullum[80] sentire videretur. Ex quo satis animadverti licet quam erat tenui retinendus impendio, sed quorum virtus despicitur contingit ut persona etiam[81] contemnatur.

V–12. Infaustus nimium profecto huius hominis famulatus, qui,

---

75. ille homo vita V.
76. admirentur V.
77. pedes init P pedessiit V.
78. profectum PV.
79. arbitrio tuoque V.
80. nullum *addidi*.
81. et V.

V-11. Is the Ravennate so extravagant, and does he insist upon living with so much splendor that he seems a heavy burden to the royal treasury? He did serve the father with extraordinarily long-lasting fidelity, and then afterwards the son.
P-11. A fact that others marveled at, and especially the elder Francesco, is that although he was so long surrounded by court favor, he contracted from the court no touch of arrogance, boastfulness, or vanity; and when he was enjoying the friendship of the succeeding prince, he valued nothing less than the flattery of the court. Once when ordered to go to Sermeola, a suburb of Padua, where Lombardo della Seta[17] had retired for his literary leisure, he went on foot accompanied by a boy. That evening, after his business had been accomplished, his fellow courtiers asked where he had been that morning. When he explained, they asked what horse he had ridden. He jokingly responded, "The Franciscans' horse." Immediately they all made fun of him, derided him, and found fault with him because he had made such a long journey on foot. They did not consider it as a sign of an honorable man's independence but of arrogance contracted from the court; consequently they disapproved of his act and reported it to prince Francesco himself. He, being noble in nature and pleased with the Ravennate because he had made the journey on foot, chided him with a friendly admonition. Then the Ravennate said, "I realize, and consider it a very gratifying thing, my excellent lord, that the horses of the court are always at my disposal, since time and again your kindness has bestowed or offered them; and I would have accepted them in deference to your judgment and generosity as very useful. However, being accustomed by my previous fortune to go on foot, I would not wish to grow used to these luxuries whose absence would be a hardship if my present condition should change." Thus he answered, acted, and lived, so that he seemed to notice no profit when fortune blew his way and no loss when it blew the other way. From this, one can sufficiently perceive at how small an expense he could have been retained; but it turns out that even the person is scorned of one whose virtue is despised.
V-12. This man was certainly very unfortunate in serving

si in equissimum virtutis interpretem incidisset, nequaquam hasce pateretur angustias.

P–12. Minime falleris. Si enim qua erat apud genitorem et genitum omnesque pariter aulicos ea extimatio insignem ad aliquem principum detulisset, qui pacis mallet quam belli artibus inclarescere, esset pro voto rei familiaris instrumenta sortitus. Sed, quod solet, in maligno aere cum floreret, exaruit. Nam preter multiplicem corporis servitutem cum familiam Carrigeram ingenii opibus multifariam exornaverit, laudabilis tamen officii ab his quibus debuit cura nequaquam perpensa est.

V–13. Licet nunc princeps torpeat[82] ad virtutes, tamen, diuturna radicatus mora et compositus ac senex, quamobrem decesserit, ratio haud[83] satis patens linguas solvit. Nam si fortuna aberat quam meruisset, nichilominus equanimiter que aderat frueretur.

P–13. Tibi quoque, quod solet inscios ac de rebus temere iudicantes ad verberandum[84] excitare, admirationem peperit ignorantia. Ceterum qui[85] aule conditio quam ex olim augusta in angustum et in[86] dedecus ex decora variaverit, et in deterius quoque variatura videtur, intelliget, nequaquam unde tute miraris hunc emigravisse mirabitur, sed diuturnam potius moram extendisse culpabit. Enim vero primum liberalitas omnis exclusa, sine qua nec aula claritudinem nec servare frequentiam ac per hoc nec hominum fidem valet. Quippe, ubi nemo fructum sperat, nemo diligit. Ita enim providentia superior instituit ut qui virtute[87] non mereatur emere pretio amorem conveniat. Favor hominum prodiens[88] ex virtute constantior, mercenarius autem fugax. Quod vere tragicus monuit : "Pretio parta pretio vincitur fides."

Atqui, avaritia coartante, illo ignominie ventum ut atria illa, litteratissimis quondam ac militaribus viris imaginumque domesticarum gloria splendidissimis celeberrime frequentata et celebrata

---

82. principes torpeant P.
83. aut V.
84. verpandum PV.
85. quibus PV.
86. in *om.* V.
87. virtutem V.
88. *ex* exprodiens *corr.* V.

such lords. If he had happened upon a just judge of his virtue, he would never have suffered these straits.

P–12. You are not mistaken. For if that reputation which he had equally with the father and the son and all the courtiers had presented him to some distinguished prince who preferred to be famous for the arts of peace rather than those of war, he would have received what he wished for his personal needs. But, as is usual, since he flowered in bad air, he withered. For although he adorned the Carrara family with the wealth of his genius in many ways in addition to the manifold services he performed, his praiseworthy attention to duty was not at all recompensed by those who should have rewarded it.

V–13. Although now the prince is lukewarm toward virtues, still, since the Ravennate was an old man, rooted in and suited to court life because of his long stay, the reason why he left is not adequately clear and causes tongues to wag. For even if the fortune which he had deserved was lacking, he could still enjoy in tranquillity what he had.

P–13. You, too, are bewildered for the same reason that usually causes criticism from people who do not understand and are careless in their judgments—that is, ignorance. But the man who knows how status at court can change from excellent to difficult and from honorable to dishonorable and may seem on the point of changing for even worse, will not wonder at all, as you do, that this man left, but rather will blame him for having stayed so long. For first all generosity was shut off, without which the court can preserve neither fame nor courtiers, nor, as a result, the good faith of men. Surely where no one expects gain, no one loves. For providence has so arranged matters that if a man does not earn love through his virtue, he must buy it for a price. The affection of men that arises from virtue is enduring, while that which is bought is fleeting. This truly the tragic writer has given warning of: "The trust born of money is overcome by money."[18]

And yet, because of the constraints of avarice, such a point of ignominy has been reached that those halls, formerly thronged by literary and military men and persons most splendid in the glory of their family's ancestral images, now have yielded to

frequenter, lixarum nunc ac villanorum imperio cesserunt.[89] Muneraque aulica, a prestantibus solita dudum ex urbe civibus laudabiliter ministrari, servi ac serviles turpiter occupant, collata nimirum concubinarum maritis. Quis impresentiarum expensis dispensandis, thesauro quis cogendo, quis stipendiis exolvendis, quis obeundis muneribus, quis negotiis imperandis[90] nunc prefectus? O pudenda temporum ratio! O iactura preterite maiestatis!

Qui porro muneribus gerendis a principibus destinatur, decet ante omnia, quo admirabilior adeunti compareat, forma prestare, quatenus rursum autoritatem pretiumque honori suscepto vindicet. Fama clarus[91] haberi et nomine integer debet; ut autem postremo accipiendis aptius reddendisque responsis satisfaciat,[92] facundie elegantia prepollere.

At isti contra, pene pueri et pridem omnes aut rustici aut turbe forensis rudes incultique,[93] sermone tardicordes,[94] virtutis inopes, nequitie divites, morum civilium ignari, contemptibiles vita preterita odibilesque presenti, accepta autoritate superbiunt et reverentia atque honore dignissimos calcant. Condiunt cuncta mendacio, arrogantia depravant. Quid concipiat mente qui ei quem merito contemnit supplicare compellitur? Assueti honoribus, magistratibus functi, cives quantopere[95] venerari coguntur impurissimum ephebum qui paulo ante concubinus, mox emissarius concubine, primatu collatisque privatum supra modum opibus antecellit et omnia sub se videt. Quis ferat? Quis non rubeat? Quis non indignetur et inardescat per eiusmodi monstra substerni, stipendia item, provisiones, ac premia supplex postulare?

V–14. Ede, queso, quamobrem eiusmodi utatur prepositis. Nam pars optima glorie principantis de prefectorum virtute sintillat,

---

89. cesserit PV.
90. imparandis P.
91. fama et clarus V.
92. satisfiat PV.
93. rudes et incultique V.
94. tradicordes V.
95. quantabile PV.

the rule of camp followers and peasants. Court offices, previously filled through an excellent custom by outstanding inhabitants of the city, are being basely grasped by servants and servile men and are even conferred upon the husbands of concubines. Who now has been put in charge of dispensing payments, who of controlling the treasury, who of paying salaries, who of attending to functions, who of managing business? Oh, the shameful custom of the times! Oh, the loss of past majesty!

In addition, it is proper that the man who is designated by a prince for filling an office be before all things outstanding in appearance, so that he may look more worthy of admiration to anyone approaching him and thus acquire influence and success in the office he has undertaken. He ought to be of excellent reputation and unblemished name. Finally, so that he may suitably give and receive responses, he must excel in the elegance of fluent speech.

But on the contrary, those people, mere boys and formerly all either rustics or rude and uncivilized members of the marketplace mob, slow of speech, poor in virtue but rich in wickedness, ignorant of civil manners, contemptible for their past life and hateful for their present — those men flaunt themselves with their acquired authority and tread under their feet persons most worthy of honor and reverence. They flavor all things with falsehood, pervert all with arrogance. What can a man think when he is compelled to ask for something from one whom he rightly despises? Citizens accustomed to honors, having served as magistrates, are compelled to do honor to a vile youth who shortly before was a male concubine, then the emissary of a female concubine, and who now exceeds them in eminence and in wealth collected beyond the means of a private citizen and sees all things beneath himself. Who could bear it? Who would not blush for shame? Who would not be indignant and wrathful to be held in subjection by such monsters and, as a suppliant, to beseech them for salaries, provisions, and payments?

V-14. Please explain why Francesco makes use of functionaries like these! For the best part of the glory of a ruler shines

velut ignominia fuscatur. Qui enim ministerii pondus ignorant ipsa que tractantur damnabiliter maculant, quosque mereri gratia debuit, alienant.

P–14. Avaritia primum. Hoc namque genus hominum, ceu nullo dignum est, sic nullo pretio famulatur. Adde quod licentius obsequiis utitur, imo vero abutitur, quoniam quicquid libet in eos licet quos ab imis sordibus erexisset. Concubinarum quoque[96] thoris federatos et collato autoratos honore sibi tenacius astringit, paraphernalisque[97] instar ipse honos adiungitur.

V–15. Quid igitur? Gerant impii vices suas. Quid cancellariatum, quid aulicum primatum, quid locorum hominumque deseruit consuetudinem?

P–15. Numquam inter improbos probosque, omni licet occasione sublata, convenit. Quippe mali in bonos, minime quia[98] lacessiti, sed quoniam ultro mali sunt, degrassantur. Boni vero facinora nocentium equanimiter ferre valent, amare numquam valent.[99] Porro noster iste nec ius cancellarii nec meritum nec gradum sensit, elatis hominibus, quo ne exercita virtute claresceret, per diversa sese studia obicientibus. Quamobrem simul advertit perastutos[100] obstare provectibus periculosumque potentiori contendere, eo maxime quod qui imperaret hisce rebus indiscretus ac negligens foret, cessit arrogantibus. Mercenarias partes assumens, nichil preter quam quod iuberetur eniti. Quam reris onerosum, cum studiosi hominis dictata censerent, qui litteras nesciebant et sine dicendi lege dicendi legem prescribebant? Illius profecto imperii et aulice claritudinis nomen calamo exornavisset,[101] si emittenda[102] pro eloquentie arbitrio licuisset venustare. Sed, velut olim questus est Plinius, illitteratas litteras edere iubebatur.[103] Quamobrem

---

96. que V.
97. parafernique PV.
98. que V.
99. amare numquam valent *om.* V.
100. perastratas PV.
101. exornavisse V.
102. emittendi V.
103. iubebantur V.

forth from the virtue of his prefects, just as it is darkened by their ignominiousness.[19] Indeed, those who are ignorant of the dignity of their ministry taint shamefully the very things they handle, and alienate people whom they ought to win over with their favor.

P-14. In the first place, because of greed. For this class of men, worthy of no reward, serves for none. The ruler uses their services freely, or rather, abuses them, since he may do anything he wishes to those whom he has raised up from the lowest, most sordid depths. Also he binds more tightly to himself persons leagued to him by the couches of concubines and obligated by the office conferred upon them. The office itself is added like an extra piece of property.

V-15. What of it, then? Let the wicked have their turn. Why did the Ravennate desert the chancellorship, the highest place in the court, and the places and people he was accustomed to?

P-15. Never can wicked men and good get along, though every opportunity be offered. Evil men attack the good, not because they themselves have been injured, but because they are innately bad. And although good men can endure with equanimity the misdeeds of the wicked, they can never love them. Furthermore, our friend the Ravennate had neither the rights of a chancellor nor his rewards nor his high station, since arrogant men thrust themselves forward in diverse ways so that he might not grow famous through his customary virtue. Therefore, as soon as he realized that very crafty men were blocking his advancement and that it was dangerous to contend with one more powerful, particularly because the ruler was indiscreet and careless in these matters, he yielded to their arrogance. Assuming the role of a hired servant, he strove to do nothing except what he was ordered. How burdensome do you think it was when a man of letters had judgment passed on his words by those who were ignorant of literary accomplishments and who without knowledge of the rules of speaking yet prescribed those rules? Surely he would have ornamented the name of that reign and the fame of the court with his pen if he had been permitted to beautify his publications according to the dictates of eloquence. But as Pliny once

nuncupari cancellarius summopere vetuit; scriba uti erat concessit. Talis itaque forma talisve dignitas cancellariatus quem tu et nescii liceris extitit. Sub hac mole tamen equanimiter imperia tulit, donec preter illiuscemodi contemptum annonaria quoque pactio subducta et stipendia non soluta sunt.

V-16. Quod dedecus, quam indignitatem audio de aula Carrigera? Vile est, culpandum est. Quo maiorum constantia, quo fides, quo munificentia abiit? Quid enim referri turpius valet indigniusve de dominante cognosci quam sponsa dedicere et stata obsequiosis alimenta deducere? Vulgaris id de se exhorruisset audiri.

P-16. Regnantes[104] quemadmodum leges non verentur, ita que legibus constant minime reverentur. Hinc fides et constantia plebeis nunc cessere.[105] Potentes autem quam inferiorum vim, tam voces negligunt; quoniam simulac avaritia invaluit, viluit prorsus gloria, cuius desiderio sublato[106] fama non licet. Igitur cum diuturnam servitutem minime licere et sponsionem sepenumero cumulatam sanctaque scriptis ac sigillis pacta non constare conspicaretur, quid tum agat liber animi et secularium studiorum fugitans[107] homo? Indignam certe contumeliam et parasitis scurrisve supplicare non tulit, ac immerita exasperatus iniuria decessit. Quanam spe moraretur cum indignissimos quosque extolli et non nisi predonibus quique pacem odissent locum ac gratiam patere[108] cerneret? At conceptam penitus iram abiturus evomuit. Siquidem Micaelem Rabatam[109] et Henricum Gallum, primos in aula, libera palam indignatione, alloquens, "Silere nequeo," inquit. "Debitores michi estis, totiens promissa Francisci dominatoris propensius replicantes,

---

104. pregnantes P.
105. censere V.
106. sublacto V.
107. flagitans V.
108. patrie V.
109. rabata P

Why the Ravennate Left the Carrara 79

complained, he was ordered to publish unlettered letters, and for this reason he utterly refused to be entitled chancellor, conceding that he was only a clerk.[20] Such was the form, such the high honor of the chancellorship on which you and other ignorant men put such value! Yet under this burden he bore commands with equanimity, until, in addition to that contemptuous treatment, the yearly contract was withdrawn and the salaries were not paid.

V-16. What disgrace, what dishonor do I hear about the court of Carrara! This is vile, this is criminal. Where has the dependability of his ancestors gone, their trustworthiness, their generosity? For what baser thing can be said, or more dishonorable deed be learned, about a ruler than that he breaks his promises and takes away the support promised to obedient servants? Even a common man would shrink from hearing this said about himself.

P-16. Since rulers do not fear the laws, they do not respect anything that is based upon the laws. Hence dependability and good faith toward the common people have now vanished. Moreover, the powerful ignore not only the strength of their inferiors, but also what they say. For as soon as avarice grows strong, glory becomes valueless; and when desire for glory has fled, then a good reputation is not esteemed. Therefore when the Ravennate perceived that his long service was not valued and that a promise often made and agreements ratified by writings and seals did not hold, what then was he to do, being a man free in spirit, a shunner of secular pursuits? Certainly he could not endure the undeserved insults, nor bear to supplicate parasites and rascals; so, angered by the unmerited injustices, he departed. For with what hope could he remain when he realized that all the most unworthy individuals were exalted, and that position and favor lay open only to plunderers and to those who hated peace? But as he was leaving he poured forth the wrath he felt deep inside. Openly, and with unrestrained indignation addressing Michele Rabatta and Enrico Gallo,[21] the chief men of the court, he said, "I cannot keep silent. You owe me something, since you so many times eagerly repeated the promises of lord Francesco Novello,

mentiti vel quod non promisit, assentando vel maligni ut impleret quod spopondisset,[110] minime procurando." Abiit igitur, et sibi sero locorum et hominum consuetudine remoratus, quod inde licet advertas.

Nempe Udinatium populus, biennio ante exorationibus iteratis, ampla cum sponsione ut ad se transiret extorserunt. Ad quem comitandum educendumque Patavo honoratos ex civibus destinavere. Sed notorum preces et caritas loci utilitatem prolatam supergressa est, ut exoptatam occasionem prorsus omitteret.[111] Divinitus tandem evenisse arbitror ut homo pacificus et turbinis osor, ne ingruentibus obrueretur[112] procellis, absced‍eret. Quod ipse diu ante presa‍giit, asserens unde decessisset prolapsuram in deterius loci semper esse fortunam.

V-17. Seu temere seu mentis auspicio, verum protulit, verum vidit, secundumque numen habuit. Attamen nullus admirari nequit quod totenni famulatu sub Francisco Seniore, deinde sub genito, precipue carus utrique, nullas opes senecte solacia corrogavit. Et specto novitios acceptorum pompa diffluere.

P-17. Deus liberat et custodit ab omni malo quos elegit. Iste nequaquam inter optimos enumerari[113] valet, nec rursus inter malignos debet. Porro assertum illud, si cui rationarium olim vacet, evolvere ex ordine et minime casu reppererit[114] prodiisse. Non est autem quod pauperem admireris hominem, utique simplicem, astipulatum honestissimis studiis, nec simulare nec dissimulare patientem,[115] et quicquam ex alieno poscere ac de proprio negare iuxta verecundum. Ad hec artes omnino quibus crescitur metiturve fructus in aula semper exhorruit.

110. spopodisset V.
111. omittent V.
112. obruetur V.
113. numerari V.
114. reperit V.
115. patiens PV.

either lying about what he did not promise or maliciously assuring me that he would fulfill what he did promise, but not carrying it out." Then he left, having lingered too long for his own good because of his fond familiarity with the places and people, as you can see from this.

To be sure, the people of the Udine two years earlier repeatedly begged and insisted with generous promises that he come to them. To accompany and guide him from Padua, they selected highly honorable citizens.[22] But the entreaties of his friends and his affection for the city overcame the offered advantages, so that he let pass a desired opportunity. I think it came about at last by divine will that this peace-loving man, who abhorred trouble, departed lest he be overwhelmed by the approaching storms, which he himself long before had foreseen, asserting that the fortunes of the place from which he had departed would constantly deteriorate.

V-17. Whether by chance or by the guidance of his mind he foretold the truth, he saw the truth, and he had God on his side. Yet no one can fail to wonder that through so many years' service under Francesco il Vecchio and then under his son, being exceptionally dear to both, he collected no wealth as a comfort in his old age. And I see that the newcomers have acquired enormous wealth.

P-17. God sets free and protects from all evil those whom he has chosen. While the Ravennate cannot be counted among the best, on the other hand he should not be considered among the wicked. Furthermore, if ever his account book is available to anyone, it will be found that his prophecy came about rationally and not by chance.[23] However, there is no reason for you to wonder that a poor man, who is very sincere and devoted to honorable studies, does not patiently feign or dissemble, and is reluctant to ask for something from another's belongings while being equally reluctant to refuse to give from what is his own. In addition, he always avoided entirely the arts of sowing and reaping rewards in the court.

V-18. Vellem has ipsas nosse.[116] Quenam sint, edoce, rogo.
P-18. Series producta nimis, quam nec nosse[117] plenam nec explicare posse confidam.
V-19. Poteris qui conversatione didicisti. Vel saltem quorum meministi dum tantisper vicissim fruimur, absolve.
P-19. Quo tibi moriger obtemperem, minime quatenus tantam rem explicare sufficiam, que longa inter aulicos vita recensui ex multis pauca subiciam.

Primum namque omnium, aulicaturus in ipso tirocinii aditu patientia corpus atque animum communiat. Quicquid dicatur et iubeatur primus excipiat. Non laborem, non vigilias, non itinera, non obsequia, quamvis indecora, nefaria, ima, declinet, sed ubique gaudeat vel gaudere fingat. Quodque tolerantie affine est, ad convicia surdescat. Hic risabit obsequiosum, ille detractione mordebit; alius vera peccata, ficta alius obiciet. Mores alter et verba imitatione deludet. Omnes huiusmodi[118] culices nichil sentire vel equanimi alacritate perpeti, non autem despicere assimulet.
V-20. Cur non despicere?
P-20. Quoniam plerique insolentia magis quam nequitia infestant. Verum dum contemni se animadvertunt, quos irridere presumpserant odiunt ac hostes fiunt. At dum familiariter licentiosos excipiunt, ridentium[119] molestias sopiunt demumque favorem socium emerentur.

Porro quam surdus ad oblocutores, tam sit ad efferendum sese audendumque temerarius. Inter pares negotiis obeundis nulli pretium faciat, nullum respiciat, nulli deferat. Verecundia omnis

---

116. nosce V.
117. nosce V.
118. huiuscemodi V.
119. ridentius V.

3. Courtly Arts

V-18. I would like to know these arts. Please teach me what they are.
P-18. The discussion would be too lengthy, and I am not sure I know the subject fully or can explain it.
V-19. Yes, you can, because you have learned it from your way of life. Or at least relate what you remember, while in the meantime we enjoy each other's company.
P-19. In order to oblige and humor you, though without hoping to explain satisfactorily so great a subject, I shall mention a few things out of the many that I observed in my long life among courtiers.

Now first of all, one who wishes to be a courtier, as the very first step of his apprenticeship, must fortify his mind and body with patience. He must be the first to undertake whatever is mentioned or ordered. He must not refuse hard work, sleepless nights, journeys, or services, no matter how dishonorable, base, and low; he should always enjoy or pretend to enjoy them. And, something that is related to tolerance, let him become deaf to insults. One man will make fun of his obsequiousness, another will snap at him with detractions; one will cast in his teeth his real sins, another imaginary ones; and another will mock his habits and speech by imitation. All gnats of this sort he should pretend he does not feel or else endure them cheerfully; but he should not despise them.[24]
V-20. Why not despise them?
P-20. Because most people annoy others more from insolence than from malice. But when they perceive they are scorned, they hate those whom they have presumed to make fun of, and they become their enemies. However, if the ambitious courtiers accept their unrestrained behaviour in a friendly manner, they will stop their mocking and will finally accept them as comrades.

Now, let the courtier be as bold and daring in putting himself forward as he is deaf to his detractors. Among his peers let him have consideration for no one when accomplishing his ends, respect no one, defer to no one. All modesty and

et tepor[120] omnis abeat. Non preire socios, non se ultro ingerere, ministeria preoccupare, ulla mentis deiectio respectusve recellat. In aula temeritas verecundiam ablegat; inverecundia temeritati nutrit audaciam et sepenumero successum parit.

Magnum, mehercule, fructum etiam adulatio comparat;[121] consonet namque pro conversantium varietate ac vanitate, fronte secundus et ore. Idque perscite quippe haud minus est opere ficto placere quam vero. Quemadmodum enim vera laus nonnumquam indecenter exprimitur, sic sepenumero mentita contemnitur. Ille porro qui[122] dixit, "Aiunt, aio; negant, nego; persuasi michimet assentari[123] omnia," quibus servandum id foret premonuit.. Ceterum apud cordatos versutosque, qualibus hominibus plurimum aula fulcitur (nam vecordes segnesque eliminat), veritate ut hauriatur illinenda est. Successu carebit si patens nudave prodierit. Idcirco, ne ante deprendatur quam feriat, est fucanda; nam qui usquequaque assensionibus insinuare se nituntur, aliquando sensuri sunt illum Celii morsum, ut ait Anneus : "Dic aliquid contra ut duo simus." Nichil item assentari dominantibus pertinacie et presumptionis est, omnia vero vanissimi nebulonis. Que igitur quisque callebit, assentandi adulandique vicibus callidius utetur. Inde fructum et affectum leget. Adulator enim quidam velut aulicus ypocrita valet iure censeri. Nam sicut humane laudis favore Dei amor plerumque simulatur, sic amor hominum utilitatis intentione confingitur. Unde potest non ab iure adulator facetus, seductor, et auditorum auceps nuncupari. Est insuper adulatio falsa minoris assensio. Nempe aut virtus affirmatur[124] adesse que abest, aut vitium abesse quod adest. Grandificatur item quod exhile bonum est vel exiguum asseritur quod damnabile malum est.

Quo fit ut in adulatione ferme semper intercidat false

---

120. topor P.
121. comperat V.
122. qui porro V.
123. asentiri V.
124. firmatur V.

half-heartedness must be gone. No shyness or respect should cause him to recoil from outstripping his companions or to fail in putting himself forward voluntarily or in being first to assume duties. In the court, boldness banishes modesty; immodesty nourishes the courage for rash acts and often produces success.

Flattery also, by heaven, brings him much reward. He should be in harmony with the fickleness and vanity of his associates by showing himself agreeable in countenance and speech. And it is not less clever to please by a feigned act than by a sincere one; for just as true praise is sometimes expressed unbecomingly, so is the false often scorned as well. Moreover, the man who said, "They say yes, I say yes; they say no, I say no; I have convinced myself to agree in all things,"[25] advised by what means this should be observed. But among the wise and clever, the sort of men by whom the court is for the most part supported (for the silly and dull it eliminates), flattery must be daubed over with truth so that it may be accepted. It will not succeed if it goes forth exposed and bare. Therefore, lest it be caught before it can hit its mark, it must be painted up; for those who strive to insinuate themselves continually by flattery will eventually feel that bite of Celius, as Seneca says: "Contradict me, that there may be two of us!"[26] Not ever to agree with rulers is an act of obstinacy and presumption; but to assent in all things is the part of an empty-headed fool. Thus the cleverer a man is, the more cleverly will he make use of opportunities to agree and flatter, from which he will reap rewards and affection. Indeed, a sycophant can rightly be judged a court actor; for as love for God is usually feigned for the sake of human praise, so love for men is simulated in the interests of self-advantage. Hence not without reason can a flatterer be called witty, a deceiver, a snarer of his listeners. Flattery is moreover the false approval of an inferior. Either a virtue that is absent is claimed to be present, or a fault that is present is claimed to be absent. Sometimes a very small good is magnified, or a reprehensible evil is asserted to be unimportant.

Therefore in flattery there is nearly always a mixture of

enuntiationis assertio. Nec solum in assensione aut fictione continetur, sed plerumque etiam, dum probitas laudatur et vitium improbatur, ingeritur; quoniam sive laudes probanda seu detestanda improbes, placendi et minime veritatis studio adularis. Atqui circumstatur principibus terre, et vera aut mentita laude coram quas colunt persone predicantur, e regione insuper quas odere damnantur. Verum quia nequaquam id zelo veritatis effutis, adulantis vices[125] subis.

Rursus, haud modo bene fari de bono et male de malo, sed etiam arrisio, derisio, applausus, admiratio, fletus, comploratio, ipsa quoque salutatio assentatoris nonnumquam tela sunt, quibus superborum vanorumque pectora sauciantur. Pape, quanta verbulum plerumque illitum[126] adulatione perreptat! Communi usu compellando et respondendo "Domine" dicitur. Quid adulator nisi[127] semper adiecerit? Cum interim vel ab ipsis qui amare et[128] amari artius extimantur, talis adiectio in omni penitus sermone taceatur. Quemadmodum hec vocula, sic expressiores, innumere assentationes condimento saporantur.

Erat Antonius Meneghini, perfamiliaris seniori Francisco et ob facinora quoque percarus, vafer siquidem ac varius homo et qui scelus nullum perderet,[129] moliri ac referre mala iuxta[130] pronus. Hic Francisci dicta, levia licet interdum ac vana, quasi oracula rapere, admirari, stupere, referre, probare cunctis. Quid de homine facile adeo ad nutum, voces, sensumque flectente concipias? Profecto quam vultus volubilis est, tam fides extimari debet. Raro enim evenit ut qui mendaciter presentem laudet, idem absenti non detrahat.

Sed parum est voces, quin mores, cultus, studiaque adulantur. Cum enim placere certatur, eorum vitia student imitari quos colunt. Nam censetur quisque mores comprobare quos imitatur.

---

125. effictis vices adulantis V.
126. illicitum V.
127. mi PV.
128. vel V.
129. penderet V.
130. iusta V.

falsehood. Not only is falsehood used in agreeing and pretending, but most often it is also present when probity is praised and vice censured; whether you praise what is due approval or disapprove what is due disapproval, you flatter, since you are moved by a desire to please and not because you wish to speak the truth. And so men stand around the princes of the earth and in their presence laud with either true or false praises those persons whom the princes cherish, and damn those whom they hate. But because you pour out these things without any zeal for truth, you are playing the part of a flatterer.

Again, not only speaking well of the good and badly of the evil, but also mockery, derision, applause, admiration, weeping, lamentation, even the very title used in a greeting, are often the weapons of a sycophant, with which he smites the hearts of the haughty and vain. It is remarkable how heavy a coating of flattery a little word can carry along! By custom the word *lord* is used in addressing and replying. What does a sycophant do except constantly repeat this, although in the meantime even those who are known to love and be loved sincerely entirely omit this epithet in their conversation. Like this word, other countless agreeable expressions are flavored up with seasoning.

Antonio Meneghino, a close friend of Francesco il Vecchio and cherished also because of his crimes, a clever and versatile man who never missed an opportunity for evil, was wont both to contrive and to report mischief.[27] He would often seize on the words of Francesco, however light and frivolous they might occasionally be, as if they were oracles, marvel at them, gape in amazement, repeat them, speak approvingly of them to all. What would you think of a man bending so easily to a whim, a word, an emotion? Surely not only his countenance but his trustworthiness must be considered fickle. For rarely does it happen that one who falsely praises a man in his presence does not also disparage him in his absence.

But it is not sufficient merely to praise one's words; even character, manners, and interests are subject to flattery. In fact when men vie to please, they are eager to imitate the faults of those whom they are cultivating, for each man is assumed

Quo fit de presidentis morbo ut sumat civitas tota contagium, ut, verbi causa, bella regnantis,[131] studia, cultusque iuvabit armorum. E vestigio aurarii vota faciemque suscipiunt, et laudatur peccator[132] in desideriis anime sue. Bella probabunt, arma fervebunt, castrensium habitum capient, ac in ferrum pronum iter ostendent. Quocumque denique affectu[133] animus laborabit, impinguabitur[134] oleo peccatoris,[135] quod non est aliud quam evertentis et everse mentis assensio. Velut confessor Carrigeri huius qui stuprare puerum quam virginem perlaudavit[136] minime notitia caligante, verum curavit, quod animadvertit favorabilius auditum iri, calcata veritate sonare.

Porro, quemadmodum aulicus assentiri et assentari pronus, ita poscere impudens et improbus debet. Tempus usque occasionem statumque rerum intente versando, quatenus sibi oblata opportunitate non desit, presto sit ac vigilet ut letum mero, hilarem nuntiis, solutum venereis, festum iocis primus occupet, laudet, iactet, magnificet, postulet.

Grandopere item iuvabit cum donantur adesse, quoniam exhilarati[137] honore missorum, quo interdum ipsi quoque magnifici videantur, que[138] recepere dispergunt. Quo sepenumero evenit ne inverecundior quisque ad exposcendum abeat indonatus. Quippe, educata magnificentie prestantia, munifica negareque verecunda natura dominorum est, quoniam testimonium maioritatis est dare. Idcirco quanto quisque animo excelsiore nascitur, tanto ad erogandum presentior invenitur. Quare leti festique maxime liberales existunt. Alia in iactantiam, alia in pretium laudis fundunt. At ministri[139] voluptatum consciive facinorum haud modo nequiquam poscunt, sed ultro quoque donantur. Bombosolum Marchio, Montursium Carriger, Guido, Ravenne dominator, Gerundinum ditavit[140] et sublimavit. Bernabos quoque, Mediolani princeps,

---

131. regnantem PV.
132. precator V.
133. affactu V.
134. impiguabitur P.
135. pescatoris V.
136. prelaudavit PV.
137. exhilerati V.
138. quo V.
139. ministris PV.
140. dictavit V.

to approve the character he imitates. So the result is that the whole city catches the infection of the ruler's disease, as, for example, it will aid in his wars, his pursuit and cultivation of arms. At once the flatterers share his wishes and behavior, and the sinner is lauded for the desires of his soul; they will approve of war, brandish arms, take the garb of camp soldiers, and show the way straight to the sword. In short, whatever emotion moves their hearts will be anointed with the oil of the sinner, which is nothing other than the agreement of subverting and subverted minds. In this way the confessor of that Carrara who praised debauching a youth rather than a maiden, indeed took care that what he thought would sound better was spread abroad in spite of the truth, though it was public knowledge.

In addition, just as the courtier ought to be ready to fawn and flatter, so must he be shameless and forward in making demands. By carefully taking advantage of time, situation, and circumstances, in order that he may not miss any opportunity, let him be ready and vigilant to be the first to engage, praise, extol, magnify, and make requests of the ruler when he is happy with wine, joyful over news, relaxed in love, sportive with jests.

It will also be useful to be present when gifts are given, since, when men are rejoicing in the honor of their awards, they share what they have received so that they themselves may also seem generous. As a result, it often happens that a man who is not ashamed to ask does not go away without a gift. To be sure, the nature of lords, who are educated to excel in munificence, is generous and reluctant to refuse, since giving is a sign of nobility. Therefore the loftier the mind a man is born with, the more ready to pay out he is found to be. Happy and joyous men are especially liberal. They pour out some things for ostentation, some as a reward for honor. But the ministers of their pleasures or those who share their crimes not only ask with impunity, but also are spontaneously presented with gifts. The Marquis enriched and elevated Bombossolo; Carrara did the same for Montorso; Guido da Polenta, Lord of Ravenna, the same for Gerundino.[28] Bernabò,

fuit indulgentissimus medicine; aliique multa obsequio turpi largiter prebuerunt, quamquam[141] eiuscemodi exuberatio, velut qui largiuntur et quas ob res merentur qui suscipiunt, pudenda est. Ita nequaquam in ratione liberalitatis et munificentie ac per hoc[142] nec glorie quidem ascribenda; quicquid autem virtutis studio bonorumve suffragiis erogatur iustum decus ac laudem comparat.[143]

V-21. Dare largius[144] esse prestantis. Sed dudum comicus lamentatur inique fore comparatum ut qui minus haberent semper aliquid divitioribus adderent. Ita nunc quoque experimur; quin etiam, sapiens ille Hebreus quodam loco docet pauperes esse divitum pascua.

P-21. Dixit et legitur. Non quod fieri debet sed quod fieret admonuit. Esse autem excelsioris tribuere negari nequit, quoniam est actus principii[145] et celestis ordo fatetur. Nam hoc est proprium divine maiestatis ac maximum, ut quemadmodum a nullo extat, ita quicquam recipiat a nullo, tribuat autem cunctis. Sedem quippe propiorem[146] sortitis primo sue bonitatis munus inspirat, qui lege caritatis proximos orbes moderantibus accepte largitatis beneficium impartiuntur. Atque sic deinceps moderatrix queque natura, prestantior participatione[147] sue felicitatis, dempta refluoris[148] expectatione, ultro influit. Itaque amor divinus per moderatores celicos, velut irrefluos[149] fontes, indefessa largitate partiliter iuxta rerum modulum ad nos usque demanat. Huiusmodi sempiterno benignitatis[150] ordine Deus omnia diligit, dirigit, conservatque omnia,[151] quoniam omnium summus omnibus presidet.

Ita qui bene presunt, utilitati subiectorum indulgentes, accepte potestatis munus liberali erogatione diffundunt. Ex hoc nimirum fonte liberos educamus, protegimus, consulimus; atque ista dignitatis lex ad omnino inanimata quoque protenditur. Nam

---

141. quam V.
142. hec P.
143. comperat PV.
144. astrius PV.
145. quoniam . . . principii *om.* V. *Vide* note 150.
146. priorem V.
147. participationem PV.
148. refluoris: apparently coined.
149. irreflous: apparently coined.
150. sempiterno quoniam est actus principii benignitatis V. *Vide* note 145.
151. omnium V.

Prince of Milan, also was most generous to medicine;[29] and others granted many things liberally for base service, although generosity of this sort, like those who bestow it and like the activities by which the recipients earn it, is shameful. Thus this kind of giving is not to be reckoned as liberality or generosity nor consequently even as glory; but whatever is given through a zeal for virtue or the approval of good men acquires just honor and praise.

V-21. To give generously is the mark of an excellent man. But long ago the comic writer lamented that it was ordained unjustly that those who have less always add something to the riches of the more wealthy.[30] So we, too, are experiencing now; and even more, that wise Hebrew, in a certain passage, teaches that the poor are pastures for the rich.[31]

P-21. So he said, and so we read. He has reminded us not of what ought to happen, but of what does happen. Moreover, that giving is the province of a higher being cannot be denied, since it is a function of high rank, and the celestial order confirms it. For this is the characteristic of divine majesty, and the greatest one, that, just as divinity derives its existence from no one, thus it does not receive anything from anyone, but gives to all. First, in those who have been allotted the closest position, it instills the gift of its own goodness; and these bestow, through the law of charity, the benefit of the generosity they have received upon those governing the worlds below. And so in turn each ruling nature, more excellent because of the sharing of its felicity, flows on of its own accord without expectation of a return. Thus the divine love, through heavenly governors, like springs that do not flow back, with unwearied abundance flows down to us, share by share, according to our status. In the eternal regular progression of this loving-kindness, God loves all things, and directs and preserves all things, since He, as highest of all, presides over all.

Thus those who are good rulers, serving the welfare of their subjects, pour forth in liberal payment the gift of the power they have received. It is for this reason, in fact, that we educate our children, protect, and counsel them; and that same law of authority is also extended to things entirely

arborum rami frondes, fructus a radice tamquam a parente accipiunt, nec retribuunt. Belue rursus, suis queque pignoribus afficiuntur, fovent, et componunt. Quodque a maioribus dedicere, caritatem, studium, ac indulgentiam, minoribus conferunt. Datum nempe utilitatis in se et honoris continet rationem; idcirco testatur Aristoteles avaros et ambitiosos gratari muneribus quod utilitatem et honorationem referre viderentur.

At vero que superioris emanant largitate opis et beneficii potius vocabulum sortiuntur, eademque nonnumquam[152] adornamentis accedunt. Perexiguum namque regis obsonium[153] grandi largitioni[154] comparis antecellat. Namque familiaritas presidentiumque dilectio, ex virtutum meritis prodire iudicata, gradum efficit, quia non indignus laude censetur qui honore dignissimis[155] placet. Proinde, que regnantes impendunt, instruunt et exornant; eis autem oblata honoris ac fidei professionem gerunt, et exenia sunt nuncupanda quam dona, altera namque parte utilitate manca deficiunt. Quid[156] enim[157] afferant ad[158] abundantiam inexhaustam? Nichil preter honorem et amorem[159] Domino Deo possumus reddere pro omnibus que tribuit nobis. Quid est? Regi amplissimo urbanus quispiam vel agricola, cum tali collatione crescere nequeat, augmentum certe prestare non potest, quod fidem studiumque testetur potest.

V–22. Si dominatores acceptis minus adiuvantur, quid exactiones, tum private tum publice, quid tributa populos aggravant?

P–22. Sicut una quevis domus vel agrariis vel mercenariis proventibus vel mercatura consistit et regitur, ita urbes et regna vectigalibus tributisque, cum[160] etiam populis censuariis, amplitudinem et statum servant. Quod ergo est negotiatori lucrum, mercenario diaria solutio, et redditus civi fundanus, hoc imperiis vectigalia, tributa, indictiones,[161] et quicquid ex mulcta criminali fisco leges ascribunt, quicquid item victis hostibus eripitur[162] aut

152. nonquam V.
153. ob sompnium V.
154. largitione PV.
155. dignis V.
156. quam PV.
157. ei V.
158. ad *om.* V.
159. amore V.
160. tum V.
161. indiciones V.
162. arripitur V.

inanimate. For the branches of trees receive leaves and fruit from the root as it were from a parent, and do not make recompense. Animals, in turn, are all full of affection for their offspring, and they cherish and comfort them; and what they have learned from their forebears—love, care, and tenderness—they confer upon their descendants. Indeed, a gift contains in itself the grounds of profit and honor. Concerning this, Aristotle attests that the greedy and ambitious are pleased by gifts because these seem to confer profit and marks of honor.[32]

However, gifts that come from the generosity of a superior are in the form of power and favor, and also often confer distinction. For a very small present from a king exceeds great largess from one's peer. This distinction is made because it is assumed that the friendship and love of rulers are bestowed as a reward of virtue; thus the man who pleases those most worthy of honor is deemed not unworthy of praise. Now, gifts from rulers support and adorn, but presents offered to rulers are a profession of honor and loyalty, and should be called trifles rather than gifts, since they are deficient in some part because of an imperfect usefulness. What indeed could they add to an inexhaustible abundance? We can return to the Lord God nothing except honor and love for all that He gives to us. Why is this so? Since the status of a mighty king cannot be enhanced by such contributions, the gifts of a city dweller or a farmer surely can be seen only as a proof of fidelity and zeal.

V-22. If rulers are not supported by what they receive, why do taxes, private as well as public, and tributes burden the people?

P-22. Just as every kind of home depends on either agriculture, industry, or trade for its income and is regulated by them, so cities and kingdoms preserve their prosperity and status by means of imposts and tributes, as well as by taxing the population. Therefore, what profit is to the business man, what daily payment is to the worker, and farm income to the citizen, taxes are to empires, also tributes, levies, and whatever the law allows to the state treasury from fines imposed on criminals,

imperatur.[163] His iusti principis magnificentia instruitur, his gaudet, et a subiectorum coentionibus, rapinis, ceterisque tirannice cupiditatis artibus abstinet. Ac velut pace facultatibus civium parcit, sic insurgente bello cives ultro arma suscipiunt et quasi apes, "incolumi[164] rege mens omnibus una est." Quoniam ergo publice tanta supplentur, quod privata cuiusquam veneratione redundat, minime incrementum sed grati affectus testimonium est, quemadmodum quicquid offerimus superis[165] pie summisseque devotionis officium convenientius appellatur. Quo enim donare modo[166] ferar cui nichil sum donando profuturus? Quamobrem pleraque a feudatariis vasalisque annua redhibitione collata principibus habenda sunt honoris insignia. Iam vero clientes multa patronis, coloni quoque tribuunt multa. Verum que nequaquam spontali affectu demanant favoris aut opere pretia sunt, non autem dona. Est autem donum rei possesse datio ex affectu prodiens, virtutis eius respectu qui accipit. In predictis vero ceterisque similibus largitionibus quas minime dantis affectus emittit sed necessitas extorquet, iniquam versari consuetudinem comicus ipse causatur, ubi superiorum favor magis emitur[167] quam donatur. Sed evenit divini ordinis providentia ut quam locupletis gratiam pauper redimit, tam, quo potentis firmitas consistat, pauperis cultus ematur a divite. Quo fit ut, ultro citroque necessitate cohibente, ita egeat minorum presidio magnitudo sicut magnitudinis adminiculo ipsa minoritas.

Sed iam cepta redeat oratio. Quoniam hasce artes Ravennas servare non didicit, aruit quemadmodum nec iniusta probare nec obsequium celicole, quod aulicantibus potissimum evenit. Posthabere quotiens in dies et horas insidias divitibus strui, quotiens

163. imparatur P.
164. incolium V.
165. supis P.
166. meo P.
167. emittitur V.

together with whatever is seized or demanded from conquered enemies. By these means, the magnificence of a just prince is provided for, and in these he rejoices; and he abstains from forcing his subjects, from thefts, and from the other methods of greedy tyrants. And as in peacetime he is sparing of the resources of the citizens, so when war arises, the citizens willingly take up arms. Like bees, "when their king is safe, they are all of one mind."[33]

Since, therefore, so many things are publicly supplied, what comes through the private veneration of each individual is not an enrichment but a testimonial of grateful affection, just as whatever we offer to Heaven is more suitably called the performance of a pious and humble devotion. For how shall I be said to give to one who profits in no way by my giving? Therefore, most things received in return annually from feudal tenants and vassals are a mark of honor for the princes. Now, in fact, clients give many things to patrons, and peasants, too, give much. But contributions not willingly made from affection are rewards for favor or work; they are not gifts. A gift, however, is the giving of a possession motivated by affection, out of a regard for the virtue of the man who receives it. In the case of the aforementioned types of largess and similar ones, which do not arise from the affection of the giver, but which necessity demands, the comic writer himself complains that an unjust custom is involved, where the favor of superiors is bought rather than bestowed.[34] But through the providence of the divine order it happens that just as the poor buy the favor of the rich, so do the rich purchase the devotion of the poor in order to preserve their own power. Consequently, since necessity compels both, great men need the protection of the lesser just as lesser men themselves need the help of the great.

But now let us return to the subject we began. Since the Ravennate did not learn to use these skills, he wasted away, for he did not approve of wrongdoing nor of obsequiousness to the "god," which most of all falls to the courtiers' lot. They must attach no importance to the number of times one has to lay the daily and hourly ambushes for the rich, to

violare pacem, absistere a fide, immeritaque cede emulum tolli!
Nosces et audies quod probare non solum verum insuper approbare,
et contra reclamante[168] propheta dicere pro audientium libidine
"bonum malum et malum bonum," nisi tamquam amens mavis
infidusque reici, compellere. Verum profecto qui scripsit protulit.
Exeat aula qui vult esse pius, etiam qui iustus, qui vericola, qui
innocens; quare conscientiam ponat et se ad fas nefasque omne
componat qui gliscit in curia provectum.

Necesse preterea, quatenus solicitus ac diligens opere curialis
ad manumque gerendis[169] primus negotiis habeare, haud modo
familiarem operam sed divini quoque cultus omitti. Siquidem,
piorum hominum studia memorias obire, sanctorum ad sacra
perstare misteria, assistere verbo Dei, aulico vix tota etate continget.
Cur ita? Quia, ut legitur, nemo potest duobus dominis servire.
Si provehi flagitas honoribus aulicis uni eius servitio, proscriptis
ceteris, intendito illique totus vive. Quod arguisse intelligi satis[170]
valet qui ait totam prorsus vitam aliud agentibus elabi. Quamobrem
hisce rebus que memorate sunt illa quoque haud mediocris iactura
additur,[171] amissio temporis. Quantula vite portione sibi fruitur
curialis! Ab ortu lucis ad primam facem aut iugis assistes aut
atria cenaculaque obambulabis,[172] multis multigenisque confusus,
audiendo[173] vana vel fabulando vel etiam componendo. Atque ita
inerti statione, gressu vago, invia dictione,[174] tempus teritur. De
quibus prophete vaticinium impletur: "Transierunt in vanitate
dies eorum et anni eorum cum festinatione." Ad sexagesimum
usque annum, Montursius aulicam egit indignitatem et odium
retulit. Huic dierum nedum ac noctium sed ne horarum quidem
ius erat. Memini, quo biduana vacatione[175] frueretur, semel et

---

168. reclamantem V.
169. grandis V.
170. satis inteligi V.
171. adit V.
172. obarbulabis V.
173. aridiendo V.
174. dicione V.
175. vocacione V.

violate the peace, to betray a trust, or to remove a rival by unwarranted murder. The courtier will be compelled not only to approve these actions, but even to hold them in high esteem; and though the prophet decries it, he will have to say that "good is evil and evil good"[35] in accordance with the pleasure of the hearers, unless he prefers to be rejected as a disloyal madman! But certainly the one who wrote this made it well known. That man should depart the court who wishes to be pious and just, a cherisher of the truth, an innocent. The man who desires advancement in court must put aside his conscience and ready himself for either right or wrong.

It is necessary, furthermore, in order that you may be considered painstaking and diligent in curial work and foremost in carrying on the business at hand, that not only your personal work be neglected, but also divine worship. In fact, to apply himself to the works and histories of pious men, to persist in studying the sacred mysteries of the saints, to help the word of God, will scarcely be possible to a courtier in his entire life. Why so? Because, as we read, no one can serve two masters.[36] If you demand to be advanced in court offices, then be attentive in serving only this activity and live entirely for it; everything else is forbidden. This has been sufficiently proved by the saying that the whole of life slips away while men are doing something else. Therefore, to these things that have been mentioned, you must add something of no little cost, namely loss of time.

How small a portion of life does the courtier enjoy for himself! From dawn to dark you will either stand continually near at hand or make the rounds of the halls and dining rooms, confused by many things of many sorts, hearing, speaking, or even inventing trifles. And in this fashion, with idle standing, vague wandering, and devious talking, time is frittered away. Concerning such matters, this prophecy of the prophet is fulfilled: "Their days have passed in vanity and their years with swiftness."[37] Up to his sixtieth year Montorso performed unworthy deeds at court and incurred enmity. He in no way had control of his days and nights or even of his hours. I remember that, in order to enjoy a two-day vacation, time

iterum finxisse langorem. Tanti est curie ambitio ut te prorsus ipsum non habeas. Quid enim, dum opes exaggeres, inferioribus imperes, a vicaneis timearis? Erat homo probe sagax ad fingenda, ad aliena vigil perscrutanda, ad referenda non segnis vitia, que[176] quemque facile tirannis insinuant.

Horum iste de quo agimus usquequaque fuit imprudens; cumque nil conducibilius quam residuum tempus litterarum utilitati impendere arbitraretur, osus expertia virtutis otia, que ab servitiis fragmenta temporis superessent sibi colligebat in usumque vertebat. Qua quidem virtute cum debuit laudem, apud aularchas detractionem[177] meruit. Quid ita? Quia nimirum despicit aula aspernaturque simplices vita, mites, ius equumque preferentes. E regione autem simulator, fictor, varius relator, delatorque ilico fortunatur.

Magnopere item conducit haberi munificum et dapacem quatenus comparium favorem emat, superiorum redimat formam, preterea, si adest, cultu servare, si minus, utcumque fingere et citra invidiam cultum ornatumque producere. Nam mundus corporis et ornamenta gratiam cumulant et pretium nanciscuntur; quippe quorum magis exteriora pensantur, crebrius inde vocantur, addicuntur negotiis, legata mandataque ferunt. Eo maxime, si venustas in moribus, lepos in ore, in convictu iocunditas eluceat, facile ista in sublime aulicum tollunt.

V-23. Pape, mores ut aulicos numerose recenses! Nec ambigo quin esse ita opere pretium[178] sit. Culmen namque regnantium bonorum malorumque obsequio fulcitur. Quo fit ut si quem videas, uti est plurima portio, abiectum genere, excordem, sine doctrina, sine virtute, prestare, dubitari nequeat sceleribus gradum emeruisse. Nam ut locus ille virtutis officio probos, sic vitiorum

---

176. que vitia V que vita P.
177. detractiones P.
178. precipuum V.

and again he feigned illness. Ambition at court is of such importance that henceforth you do not own yourself. But what does this matter, when you are piling up wealth, ordering inferiors about, being an object of fear to the peasants? Montorso was a man exceedingly clever in contriving, watchful in investigating others' affairs, and not slow to report faults, traits that easily recommend one to tyrants.[38]

That man whom we are discussing, the Ravennate, was in all respects improvident of these things. And since he thought nothing was more profitable than to spend his free time on the enjoyment of literature, scorning idleness as devoid of virtue, he collected the fragments of time that were left over from his services and turned them into use. Although he should have been praised for this virtuous practice, he received only slander from the court officials. And why? Because indeed the court despises and scorns men who are honest and gentle in their lives, and who prefer the right and the just. But on the contrary the pretender, the feigner, the devious tale-bearer and informer straightway becomes prosperous.

It is also highly useful for the courtier to be thought bountiful and rich in order to buy the favor of his peers and to acquire the fine appearance of his superiors, particularly, if possible, to reproduce their style of dress, or if not, to fashion somehow and exhibit splendid and magnificent attire without regard for envy. For elegance and ornamentation of the body accumulate favor and find value; indeed, those people whose external appearance is esteemed are as a result frequently summoned, assigned to business, and made receivers of legacies and commissions. A courtier will easily rise on high especially if he displays attractiveness in his manners, charm on his lips, and affability in his social contacts.

V-23. The number of characteristics of courtiers that you list is remarkable! And I have no doubt that it is worthwhile, for the high position of rulers both good and bad is supported by service. Hence if you see in an eminent position a man who, like the majority, is of low birth, stupid, without learning, and without virtue, it cannot be doubted that he has attained his rank through his wickedness. For just as at court the good

opera quosdam provehit. Quare minus iam admiror si liber animus et evi memor seque frui gnarus ultro ab aulicis abstitit. Sunt tamen qui parum sani capitis existimant,[179] quia splendidis apud aulicos titulis fulgebat, ad pedagogii nebulas descendisse. Quippe inter primos locus ei fuisse vicissitudoque ac nomen fertur. Etiam domini se adiectione et scribi et appellari audiebat. Nunc, quod[180] cerdonibus tonsoribusque evenit, magister vocatur.

P–23. Qua potui memoria patefeci quibus moribus quove ingenio curialis fructus ubertas metitur. Sed quantula portione? Neque nossem,[181] neque possem quibus instruitur aula monstris hac potissimum etate contexere.[182] Ceterum quod hunc nescio quo inter primos loco et honore functum audis, cave ne id ei quasi ab aule assumpto munere sentias provenisse. Nam si quid claritudinis gratieve tum apud aulicos tum apud cives tulit, extimationi docti rectique hominis, que passim de ipso predicabatur, et nulli aulico favori collatum est. Itaque minus piguit linquere cuius absentia nichil esset amissurus. Unum, fateor, aula contulit : virtutes eius usu dabat agnosci. Et o superi donassent ut tam credita a dominatoribus sententia eius quam merita laudata fuisset! Numquam profecto in has calamitates Paduani incidissemus.

At vero pro speciosis illis maximeque domini, quod impresentiarum magistri vocabulum subeat, opinari videris eius adornamentis fore sublatum discretione rerum. Opido falleris. Duo quidem nomina sunt tota regione distantia, dominus et magister, quorum alterum quidem casus dare, alterum numquam valet. Quot a rastris, a strigili, dominatum asciverunt? Sepenumero exercitus ipsi, ceso imperatore, e vestigio alium surrogarunt. Notius est quam explicari velit exemplis quam repente tirannus tiranno

179. extimant V.
180. que V.
181. noscem V.
182. compescere V.

advance through virtuous performance, so do some advance through the workings of evil. I therefore do not wonder now if a free spirit, mindful of the times and knowing how to enjoy himself, of his own volition keeps away from courtiers. Still, there are those who think him of unsound mind to have descended to the obscurity of schoolteaching from the splendor of the illustrious titles he held among the men at court. Indeed, it is said that his place was among the highest, as well as his duties and name. He even used to hear himself described and addressed by the epithet *lord*. Now he is called by the name applied to craftsmen and barbers, *master*.

P–23. To the best of my memory, I have explained by what manners and wit generous curial reward is harvested. But by how small a number of persons? I could neither know nor relate with what monsters the court is peopled, particularly in this age. But because you hear that this man enjoyed some place and honor among the first rank, do not think this came to him as a result of gifts received from the court. For if he bore any fame or favor not only among courtiers but also among the citizens, it was conferred upon the worth of a learned and upright man, a worth that was proclaimed far and wide and was not based upon court favoritism. Hence it was not a matter of regret to him to leave, since his absence would cost him nothing. I admit the court gave him one thing: it made his fine qualities known through their practice. If only Heaven had permitted his opinion to be as much relied upon by the rulers as it was deservedly praised! Surely we Paduans would never have fallen into these calamities.

But indeed, as regards those handsome titles and especially that of lord, you seem to think that since they have been replaced by that of master, his splendor has been diminished by the change of circumstances. Certainly you are mistaken. In fact, the two names, lord and master, are entirely different; one of them can be given by chance, the other never. How many men have taken over leadership just after having put aside their hoes and currycombs? Often armies themselves, at the death of their general, have at once supplied another in his place. It is too well known to need examples how suddenly

succedat. Nox una, imo hora, ut evadat quispiam dominus efficit. Magister ut fiat vix plena vita contingat. Paulo ante, Verona capta, quot mox ipse introitus dici dominos effecit? Negari nequit magno discrimine subitus honor partus. Quid autem? An non principum nuptie celebritates, natalia, aliave solennia sine discrimine, sine metu, sine labore, quodque detestabilius est, sine merito, milites ac per hoc dominos creant?

V-24. Haud tempero michi quo minus tue narrationis cursum intercipiam. Quid quod iuniores ac scioli, imo pene pueri, cum e grammatice cunabulis ad dialetice rudimenta conscendunt,[183] magistri dicuntur et salutantur?

P-24. Ita iuris auditores mox domini appellatione venerari superbiunt. Primum honos iste sapientie cuius studium adiverunt,[184] demum persone que non est sed quam formare suscepta eruditio despondet tribuitur. Igitur illi magistri quoniam eo luminis intellectualis pervenire sperantur ut alios docere, isti vero domini, ut alios regere queant, intempestiva veneratione feruntur. Atque sic laudabilibus calcar initiis et testimonium future probitatis prodit utrimque vocabulum. Iuniores vero ac sciolos[185] error aut etiam[186] consuetudo vulgaris tam inconsulte magistros appellat quam ludibriose milites ac domini fiunt multi. Sed accipe in huiusmodi questione quid Galeotto Malateste dudum Johannes de Lignano Bononie respondit. Cum enim, astante legato, per otium dictio[187] vagaretur, mirari se Galeottus[188] inquit cur, iuris minus animadversa dignitate, iuniores ad doctoratus apicem proveherentur et scioli, quod minime evenire absque doctissimorum fame detractione valeret, Johannes "Amabo," ait, "exemplo vestro, qui militie indignos temere ascribitis, contagium traximus." Mordaciter nimium, sed vere profecto. Nam et pueri et militaris

---

183. consendunt V.
184. advertunt V.
185. sociolos P.
186. eciam aut V.
187. dicio V.
188. Galleotas P.

tyrant can succeed tyrant. One night, in fact one hour, suffices for some lord or other to emerge. To become a master, a whole lifetime is scarcely sufficient. Just recently, when Verona was captured, how many men did that entry soon cause to be called lords?[39] It cannot be denied that a sudden honor is born from a great crisis. And what else? Do not the marriage celebrations of princes, birthdays, or other solemn rites that contain no danger, fear, difficulty, or, what is more detestable, no merit, create soldiers and consequently lords?

V-24. I cannot keep from interrupting the course of your narrative. What of the fact that when young men and dilettantes, practically children, graduate from the cradles of grammar to the rudiments of dialectic, they are spoken of and greeted as masters?

P-24. In the same way law students are proud to be venerated by the name of lord. First that honor is paid to the discipline upon the study of which they have entered, then to the person who does not yet exist, but whom the education that has been undertaken promises to form. Therefore the young scholars are called masters, by premature veneration, since they are expected to reach that degree of intellectual light which will enable them to teach others; but the law students are called lords, also prematurely, because they are expected to rule others. And so, by laudable beginnings, the title provides each group a stimulus and promise of future excellence. But youths and dilettantes are as inadvisedly called masters by error or even common custom as many men ridiculously become soldiers and lords. Now, concerning a question of this sort, listen to what Giovanni da Legnano of Bologna recently replied to Galeotto Malatesta. For when in the presence of the ambassador a leisurely conversation was in progress, Galeotto said that he wondered why, in disregard for the dignity of the law, young men and dilettantes were being advanced to the height of the doctorate, something that could not occur without detracting from the reputation of highly learned men. Giovanni replied, "If you please, we have contracted the disease from you who foolishly enroll unworthy men in the military."[40] A somewhat sarcastic statement, but a true one! For both

glorie ludibrium histriones militiam assecuntur, et domini fiunt, ceu nescio quis Aldobrandinus, lixa et manipularis[189] timpanista, apud nos domini vocatione a cunctis, vel ab ipsis quoque principiis, clamatur, usque adeo glorie defensione contempta ut cum ipso non pudeat quem rident ac ludibriant appellationem habere communem.

Ex quo liquet quam vaga sit denominatio que ridiculis quoque contingat hominibus. Adde quod sive quisque natura sive casu sive merito prestat dominum rite se audit. Sic avus a[190] nepote, pater a liberis, vir ab uxore, a cliente patronus, iudex a reo, religiosus a layco, a discente preceptor, nauarchus a nautis, multique multifariam a multis audire se dominos queunt; magistros non queunt. Quippe id nomen ingenio rationisque prestantia comparatur,[191] unde valet qui magisterio fungatur dominus, licet non continuo qui dominus habeatur dici magister possit. Dominus siquidem, cum imperiosa coercendi potestate eminentiam in supposita designat, ideo timoris est potius quam amoris. Quod[192] per Malachiam Deus expressit: "Si ego," inquit, "dominus, ubi est timor meus? Si ego pater, ubi est honor meus?" Ex quo tam magister domino quam pregravare amor timori videtur, quam rursus amari prestat quam timeri. Nimirum domini appellatio Deo vero unice, sicut verus honor et gloria, congruit, ut cui extat in cuncta potestatis irrefragabilis plenitudo, et omnia ineffabili obedientia famulantur. Ideo canit ecclesia: "Tu solus sanctus, tu solus Dominus," quoniam solus potest quod vult, et nulla creatura potest quod ille[193] non vult.

Ex quo liquet vocabulum quo tumemus et superbimus tam falso quam indecenter assumi. Cur, forsan poscis? Quia nemo in quemquam[194] et[195] ne in quicquam quidem[196] ius plenum habet. Nichilominus superbia tirannica iam nomen acceptum a fonte fastidit, iam, se hominem ministrumque divine iustitie esse minime advertens, dominus vocari mavult, et qui audit et profert uterque fruitur falsitate. Neque enim cuiquam vere contingit, qui non valet omnia que iubet, ut impleantur, et

189. manipulatis V.
190. a *om.* V.
191. comperatur V.
192. quod. V.
193. ille *om.* V.
194. quamquam V.
195. sed PV.
196. quid V.

boys and actors make military service a mockery of glory and become lords, just as one Aldobrandino, a sutler and drummer of a maniple in our army, is acclaimed by the name of lord, even by the staff officers themselves. The defense of glory is so scorned that it is not a matter of shame to them to share a common title with a man whom they mock and make sport of.[41]

From this it is clear how meaningless is a name that is applied also to fools. In addition, whether a man is outstanding by nature or chance or merit, he is duly spoken of as lord. Thus the grandfather can be called lord by his grandson, the father by his children, the husband by his wife, the patron by his client, the judge by the defendant, the priest by the layman, the teacher by the pupil, the captain by the sailors, and many others in like manner; but they cannot be called masters. Indeed, this latter name is acquired by ability and excellence of reason; hence a man who fills an office can be called lord, though not necessarily can one considered a lord be called master. Since a lord, to be sure, marks his eminence over his subjects by his great power to compel, he is for this reason an object of fear rather than love. This was expressed by God through Malachi: "If I," he said, "am Lord, where is the fear of me? If I am father, where is the honor to me?"[42] From this, the master seems to outweigh the lord as much as love outweighs fear, as much, again, as it is better to be loved than to be feared.[43] In fact, the name of lord truly fits God in particular just as does true honor and glory, because for Him unbreakable fullness of power exists over all things, and all things serve Him with inexpressible obedience. Therefore the church sings: "You only are holy, You only are the Lord,"[44] since He alone can do what He wills, and no created thing can do what He does not will."

From this it is clear that this title that makes us swell with pride is assumed as falsely as it is unsuitably. Why, perhaps you ask? Because no one has full right over anyone else and not even over any thing; nevertheless the proud tyrant now scorns the origin of the name he has received; now ignoring that he is a human being and the servant of divine justice,

cui plura contradicant. Eia, perge, ubi talem contatus ostendas? Mensurno pactus stipendio famulus te dominum appellabit, loquetur, nominabit; sed quantulam in eum exerceas potestatem, quotiens omitti, quotiens perverti coirrasceris imperia? Non est speciosus adeo titulus iste tantaque dignus admiratione nisi apud improbum quemque sue conditionis oblitum, aliene potestatis ignarum. "Si violandum est ius, ob imperii causam violandum est." Ex Euripide[197] Iulius Cesar suam vocem fecit, ab scelestibus deinceps ac simili estuantibus libidine collaudatam. Verum qualem meruit exitum nacta haud minus continere periculi quam decoris ostendit. Non est, ut perversi quidam ferunt, redimendum vite[198] vocabulum precipue librantibus instituta esse imperia nequaquam ut populi serviliter pareant et privatorum facultates expleant imperantium voluptates, aut alieni pudicitiam thori secura libido defloret.[199] Sed ut publica potestate privatis sceleribus obvietur, pax custodiatur, violentia propulsetur, componat unius providentia cunctos ac dirigat quo merito primatus ac reverentia prestetur a singulis.

V–25. Tuus iste sermo de gubernatoris officio in hanc me coniecturam[200] divertit, uniusne principis an plurium dominatu ceu nostra ceu Tusca felicius urbs regatur. Ede, queso, quid censes.

P–25. Unius non modo optimi, tunc velut numen esset in terris, sed vel[201] mediocriter boni eligibilius esse regimen arbitror.

---

197. Euripede P.
198. vita PV.
199. defloret *ex* floret *corr.* V.
200. coniacturam V.
201. vel *om.* V.

he prefers to be called lord. And both the one who hears and the one who utters it enjoy the falsehood. For the name of lord does not truly belong to anyone who cannot have fulfilled all that he commands, and whom many things controvert. Come now, where may you seek and find such a person? A servant, hired for a monthly salary, will call, address, name you lord; but how little power can you exercise over him, how often do you grow angry that your orders are neglected or subverted! That title is not plausible and worthy of much respect except in the case of an evil man who is forgetful of his status and unmindful of the rights of others. "If law is to be violated, it should be violated for the sake of sole power." From Euripides, Julius Caesar made this his own maxim, one praised subsequently by the wicked and by men burning with like passions.[45] But by finding the kind of outcome it deserved, this saying showed that it contained as much danger as glory. The title should not, as certain perverse people say, be applied chiefly to those who consider that power has been established in order that people may obey like slaves and the resources of private citizens may satiate the appetites of the rulers, or that carefree lust may deflower the chastity of another's marriage bed. It should be bestowed upon one who believes that the purpose of public power is to prevent private crimes, guard peace, and avert violence; a man whose prudence would unite and guide all men, so that he would deservedly be accorded preeminence and reverence by all.

4. Relative Merits of a Monarchy and a Republic

V-25. Your discussion of the duty of a ruler has brought to mind another question, whether a city is ruled better by the authority of a single prince or that of many, like our own Venice or Florence. Please tell me what you think.

P-25. I think the rule of one is preferable, even when in the hands of only a moderately good man; when it is held by an

Quam in sententiam allicior quod omnis creature status, quo similior conditori, hoc pulchrior, ordinatior, et perfectior existit. Quare, cum rerum autor et rector unus sit, unius gubernamen, quoniam universi conformius, melius esse iudico. Cui rei illud quoque attestatur, quod in urbibus que multitudine temperantur,[202] quo serius consultiusque res geri queant,[203] ad paucorum numerum potestas contrahitur; uno enim nichil est[204] paucius.

V–26. Hoc[205] responderim: nonne decem prudentium uberior sententia quam solius? Et si uberior, cur non melior?

P–26. Quia numquam valens est quam[206] una. Quamquam enim plurium intelligentia plura concernat, haudquaquam[207] tamen consentienter[208] adeo ferventerque agenda disponit. Mirabile sit quinque nedum inveniri decem ad unum, omni dempta varietate, concordes. Velut enim duas facies sine differentia, ita duas voluntates sine discretione sententie difficile poteris invenire. Quin unum vix offeras cui nulla pulsetur varietate iudicium. Et licet una cunctorum ad unum ratio obiectum feratur, sensum nichilominus emulatio et arrogantia detorquebit humana. Quia dum quisque vel notitia rerum vel autoritate prestantior haberi tendit, minime que verior[209] sed que sua extet sententiam teneri certaverit.

Taceo studia partium, tecta odia, invisos civium honores quo estu distrahunt voluntates. Quanto item veneno aspergat avaritia senatum Iugurta decedens Roma testatus est: "O urbem," inquit, "venalem et facile perituram, si emptorem invenerit!" Quod[210] de vestra Carriger senex crebro[211] exprimebat, expertus pene cunctorum favores esse venales, qui cum ad privatum aliquid detorquentur, mox rei publice utilitas claudeat. Quod in uno

---

202. teperantur P.
203. queat V.
204. esse V.
205. hic V.
206. numquam . . . quam] non que valet esse tam PV.
207. haud quamquam V.
208. consentienter: apparently coined.
209. vereor V.
210. quid V.
211. crebro *om.* V.

excellent man, then it is as if a god had come down to earth. I am drawn to this belief because the more the condition of every created thing is like that of its creator, the more beautiful, well-ordered, and perfect it is. Therefore, since there is one creator of all things and one heavenly ruler, I consider the rule of one man on earth to be better in that it conforms to the scheme of the universe. In respect to this, proof is to be found also in cities that are ruled by the people; in order for matters to be accomplished with seriousness and sound deliberation, the power is restricted to a few persons. And there is no number smaller than one!

V–26. I could reply as follows: is not the judgment of ten prudent men fuller than that of a single man? And if fuller, why not better?

P–26. Because it does not have so much authority as that of one man. For although the intelligence of more people perceives more, it does not settle so unanimously and quickly matters needing to be done. It would be remarkable to find five men, not to say ten, agreeing on one thing without any differences! For just as you can hardly find two faces without dissimilarities, so it will be hard to find two persons of one mind and will. Even more, you can scarcely show one man who can arrive at a decision without wavering. And though a single reasoned judgment, by everyone's consensus, may be applied to one objective, still human jealousy and arrogance will distort the meaning. For as long as each man is eager to be considered superior either in his knowledge of affairs or in his authority, he will strive to hold not to that opinion which is truer, but to that which is his own.

I shall not mention the partisan zeal, the concealed hatreds, the envied honors of citizens, by the passion of which their wills are distracted. Moreover, with how much poison avarice bespatters the senate Jugurtha testified as he departed from Rome: "O city," he said, "for sale and easily to be destroyed, if it should find a purchaser!"[46] This is a saying that the old Carrara often applied to your city, after discovering that the favors of almost everyone were for sale.[47] When these are used for private interests, the public interest is neglected. This is

principe valet nullo modo contingere, quoniam adversum se contaminari ipse nequeat et omnem regni utilitatem omni attentione custodiet. At vos, posco, tantisper ignoscas si vestram rem publicam exempli gratia nominaverim per quam omnes sumo.
V–27. Age, ut iuvat, nomina. Nichil succenseo! Scio enim neque[212] odio neque livore sed veri studio tua verba prodire.
P–27. At vos, inquam, coacto senatu, cuncti num[213] de re publica indistracta cogitatione pensatis? Et nullis privato curis angimini? Alius piperis, cotoni alius, ille argenti, hic lane, ille uxoris zelo. Quis ere alieno, quis suo distrahitur? Et quota ordinis tanti portio incomminuta attentione in ordinem coit? Quia nimirum plus[214] utilitas presens quam sperata sentitus, urget quemque quod proprium novit ac diligit. Dominatori vero quia proprium sunt[215] universa, et emolumentum iacturamque singulorum propius[216] sentit. Quicquid imperii autoritatem pondusque respicit, ad id totus iacendo, vescendo, deambulando refertur et impendet. Adde quod ad gratiam, liberalitatem, clementiam verti facilis, facile suadetur. Exoratur facile quandoquidem amari optet et coli; que nisi munificentia et placabilitate non assequetur.

Multitudo autem surda et pene inflexibilis ad[217] beneficium, ad veniam. Nam nisi consonent universi, frustra postulabis. Quod ferre desideras, inhibebit alius, quatenus publice utilitatis asseratur diligens asservator, officium liberalitatis impleri; alius, ut cultor iusti rigidus metuatur, veniam negabit erranti. Amplo alter animo dona et largitiones magnificas suadebit; contra, qui angusto singula digerit, publicis facultatibus censebit esse parcendum. Quid multa? Dum sua quisque passione raptatur, difficile est plures habere

---

212. neque *om.* V.
213. non V.
214. populus V.
215. sunt proprium P.
216. proprius V.
217. *ex* ab *corr.* V.

something that cannot possibly happen in the case of a single prince, since he cannot be contaminated against himself, and he safeguards all interests and the well-being of his kingdom with all his attention. But meanwhile I ask you to pardon me if I name your commonwealth as an example to represent all republics.

V-27. Do as you like. Name it, I am not angry! For I know that your words do not come from malice or envy but from a love of truth.

P-27. Well, then, I say, when the senate is assembled, do you all deliberate concerning the commonwealth with undivided thought? And are you bothered by no private worries? One man is distracted by his zeal for pepper, another for cotton, one for silver, another for wool, another for his wife. Who is worried by his own debts, who by those of others? And how large a part of such a great body meets with undivided attention? Certainly a present advantage is noticed more than one that is hoped for, and what each man knows and cherishes as his personal concern presses upon him. But because all things are the ruler's concern, he feels as his own both the profit and loss of individuals. Whether resting, eating, or walking about, he is wholly given and dedicated to whatever concerns the authority and weight of his power. In addition, being easily inclined to favor, generosity, and clemency, he is easily pursuaded. He heeds entreaties readily since he desires to be loved and honored; he will not attain his desire except through liberality and placability.

But the multitude is deaf and almost inflexible with regard to favor and pardon. For unless they all agree, you will ask in vain. What you desire to obtain, one man, in order to be acclaimed as a diligent preserver of the public funds, will prevent being granted by the liberals; another, so that he may be considered a rigorous observer of justice, will deny a pardon to an erring person. One with generous mind will recommend gifts and magnificent largess; on the other hand, a man stingy in his own business will think he should be sparing with the public resources. What more do you need? When each one is in the grip of his own passions, it is difficult to make several

concordes ac per hoc et impetrari quod cupitur.

V–28. Quid quod periculosissima sors est, ubi unius furori impune quod libet licet? Velut premium ita ad penam facile unus impellitur.

P–28. Nichil est adeo nature adversum hominis quam sevitia, quam feritas. Solvit enim sociam caritatem que mutuis simul opitulationibus affectus contrahit. Iustus autem princeps de iustis enim sermo est. Sicut imperio, ita quibus ornatur imperium, multitudine gloriabitur. Ideo tamquam sedulus pastor oves morbidas sanare medicine remedio, insanabiles et contagiosas subtrahi cede curabit. Ac per hoc pronus ad gratiam, ad penam lentus agetur. Ex animi prestantia indiscusse donabit, ex gravitate discusse damnabit. Ac ceu optimus paterfamilias singula circumspectans fiet de singulorum incolumitate solicitus. In ducatu autem politico, quia nullus est cunctorum pastor, nullus ovibus[218] studet, sed suo quisque negotio propius insudat, cum, senatu dimisso, sua quisque negotia repetit. Quotusquisque illo aciem refert quod in commune digessit! Adde quod virtutes principis magnanimitas, munificentia, benignitas, iustitia, moderatio, clementia raro in privatis, in uno, rarius in pluribus inveniuntur. In dominantibus aut[219] vere sunt aut verarum simulacrum iactant. Quippe, amplissima orti fortuna magnificeque educati, magnis etiam assueti, proni redduntur ad magna. Item maiorum imagines nec non proprie estus glorie tum ad magnifica, tum ad liberalia factaque clementer calcar additur. Hinc rursus facilius donant, remittunt facilius, quia nec in acquirendo laborant, nec patiuntur iacturam largiendo. Ideo etiam presentiores ad veniam quoniam emereri quibus ignoscunt et offendi non posse cognoscunt. Privato

---

218. oves PV.
219. autem V.

men agree and consequently to get what is desired.

V-28. What of the fact that it is a very dangerous situation when the madness of one man is permitted to do with impunity whatever it pleases? A single individual is driven as easily to punishment as to reward.

P-28. Nothing is so contrary to the nature of man as savagery or ferocity, for it destroys the social amity that creates affections through mutual assistance. Moreover, the just prince is truly a sermon on just men. As he glories in his power, so will he glory in those by whom his rule is honored, the people. Therefore, like a careful shepherd, he will take pains to heal the sick sheep by the remedy of medicine and to destroy the incurable and contagious. For this reason he will be influenced readily to favor, reluctantly to punishment. Upon excellence of mind he will bestow countless gifts, but cruelty he will carefully punish. And like a good father of a family overseeing all details, he will become concerned with the lack of individual welfare. However, under the people's leadership, because no one is shepherd for all, no one is concerned for the sheep; but each man labors diligently at his own business when, at the dismissal of the senate, each returns to his own affairs. How few bring sharp attention there, because generally they have other concerns.

In addition, the virtues of a prince—magnanimity, generosity, benevolence, justice, moderation, clemency—are rarely found among private citizens even in the case of one man, but even more rarely in the case of a group. Among rulers they are either true virtues or give the appearance of true ones. To be sure, the fact that princes are born to the most ample fortunes and are magnificently educated and accustomed to greatness instills in them a desire for greatness. Similarly, the memory of their ancestors and ardor for personal glory are an additional spur not only to magnificent deeds but to generosities and acts of clemency. They also give gifts and make payments more easily, because they perform no labor in acquiring these and suffer no loss in bestowing them. They are even more ready to pardon because they know they lay under obligation the persons whom they pardon and cannot be hurt by them.

autem natura, tametsi regias virtutes impresserit, raro tamen usus facultatem exhibuit. Quemadmodum insuper labor in acquirendo sentitur, sic manus in dispergendo contrahitur. Quo fit ut parcius utantur qui divitias peperere. Idcirco, ut predixi, princeps, quia comminui non sentit, liberali effusione letatur, et glorie detrimentum arbitratur non impartiri quod donando nitet amplius quam servando.

Porro quam, uno principe, rerum protendatur felicitas, hinc latissime claret quod ingenia philosophorum, poetarum, oratorum, historias describentium[220] alumnata, fota provectaque a principibus animumve principis gerentibus reperies. Augusto orbis domino, Maro, Flaccus, Naso, ad nostra usque tempora celebres, aliique[221] incelebres non pauci, indulgentia liberali vacationem et facultates otiis habuerunt. Deinde orbem Iustiniano moderante, formam et ordinem iuris civilis utilitas cepit. Nostram prope etatem rex Robertus physicos, theologos, poetas, oratores, accumulatissimo honore effusaque largitione confovit. Quisquis in orbe terrarum litteris fructum expetisset, ad eius regiam minime frustra confluebat, erat enim tamquam sacrum studiosorum domicilium patens. Bernardinus, Ravenne dominator, Bocacii studia magnifice instruxit. Cuius ante avus Guido sic Dantis presentia gloriabatur, ut non modo ad nutum cuncta suppeditaret, verum etiam tamquam privatus eius conversatione familiariter uteretur. Sic deinceps Iacobus de Carraria Petrarcham a Mediolani tiranno Paduam blanda elicuit instantia, cui et liberalem magnifice et amicum familiariter se prestitit. Quem mox dominator filius haud minus asserta dilectionis[222] munificentieque attestatione percoluit. Nicolaus insuper, Marchio Estensis, litteris plusquam militariter indulgens, qui poeticam[223] et historias nossent,[224] munifice admisit, eorumque presentia velut deliciis fruebatur. Novissime omnium in hac virtutis laude[225] Iohannes Galeaz liberalitatem supergressus est, non dico poetas et oratores, qui rarissimi comparent, sed medicos

---

220. describendo V.
221. *ex* aliisque *corr.* V.
222. dilecionis V.
223. poetas PV.
224. noscent V.
225. laudibus V.

Monarchy versus Republic

But although nature may have put upon a private person the stamp of royal virtues, rarely has she given him the opportunity of their use. Moreover, because he is conscious of his labor in acquiring possessions, he is loath to give them away. Hence those who have produced riches use them sparingly. Therefore, as I said before, the prince, because he does not feel himself diminished, rejoices in generous giving and thinks it a detriment to his glory not to share what is more splendid to give than to keep.

Furthermore, when there is a single prince, how the benefits of his good fortune are extended to others is exceedingly clear from the fact that you will find that the talents of philosophers, poets, orators, and the writers of history have been nourished, fostered, and furthered by princes or those with the spirit of princes. When Augustus was master of the world, Vergil, Horace, and Ovid, still famous in our times, and many others unknown, had free time and means for leisure activities because of his liberal generosity.[48] Later when Justinian was ruling the world, the beneficial civil law received form and order.[49] Near our own time King Robert encouraged doctors, theologians, poets, and orators with prolific honors and abundant largess. All in the world who sought the rewards of the study of letters poured into his kingdom, and not in vain, for it lay open as a sacred domicile of scholars.[50] Bernardino da Polenta, Lord of Ravenna, provided generously for the studies of Boccaccio. Before him his grandfather Guido so gloried in the presence of Dante that he not only furnished him everything at his whim, but even like a private citizen intimately enjoyed his company.[51] Similarly, Giacomo da Carrara enticed Petrarch to Padua away from the Milanese tyrant with flattering insistence, and showed himself grandly liberal and an intimate friend to him. Afterwards his son as ruler cherished Petrarch with no less firm evidence of love and generosity.[52] Furthermore, Niccolò, Marquis of Este, fonder of the literary than of the military, received generously those who knew poetry and history and enjoyed their presence as if it were a delight.[53] Most recent of all in this honoring of virtue, Giangaleazzo went beyond liberality—I do not speak of poets and orators, who very

etiam et[226] iurisconsultos qui predicarentur ad eliciendum fruendumque indiscussa erogatione[227] munificum.[228]

Quid? Producta nimis series si tum priscos tum nostros evolvere pergam, qui incredibili voluptate studiosos ascivere. Et ascitos benignissimis suffragiis sunt prosecuti, quod, ubi imperet multitudo, raro leges, factum rarius cernes. Profecto poetica numquam,[229] oratoria, philosophia, cronographia, ceteraque[230] sublimis opere studia, dempta principantium liberalitate et cura, eo decoris incrementique pervenissent. Quot item viri militares, rei familiaris angustia contracti, quot nobilitate singularique aliqua dote[231] laudabiles, principum gratia, recepti sublevatique sunt? At dominans multitudo nullius virtutem gratis respicit, mercenarias recipit, otiosas aspernatur. Dum enim quisque vel stringit nummum vel extra limen gloriam[232] non licetur, poetas ut non sapit ita contemnit, et mavult canes alere quam philosophum aut lectorem. Quod quam officiat glorie silentio coercere non possum! Vestra res publica, florens et magnifica, quam nulla Europe felicitate rerumque amplitudine equiperat, uno dumtaxat urbis nomine pervagatur. Cum autem clarissimis viris speciosissimisque exemplis fulserit[233] per tot secula, domi ac militie illustria facinora quis novit? Quis legit? Quis meminit? Suis nota temporibus, obducta nunc oblivionis nube, laudibus vacant.

V–29. Infitiari nequit et absque nota ruboris audiri. Que res publica terra marique totum orbem gestarum rerum gloria eo usque maximis editis operibus percensuit, memoratuque digniora tum pace tum bello gessit? Quorum quidem si florerent historie, vix Peno Romanoque cederemus, verum insudamus[234] suam quisque domum auro locupletare quem fama; quamquam minime desunt,

---

226. et *om* V.
227. erragacione V.
228. munificus PV.
229. nonquam poetica V.
230. ceteteraque V.
231. docte V.
232. gloria V
233. fulxerit V.
234. instudemus PV.

infrequently appeared, but doctors and lawyers, who were well known for getting and enjoying the bounty of uncounted salaries.[54]

Why say more? My discourse would be too long if I should proceed to describe not only former rulers but those of our time who have with unbelievable pleasure admitted scholars. And they have honored with very generous applause those they have taken in, something you will seldom read of when the people are ruling, and more rarely see done. Certainly never would poetry, oratory, philosophy, history, and other studies of high attainment have reached this degree of honor and wealth without the love and generosity of princes. Likewise, how many military men constrained by the difficulties of their personal life, how many men praiseworthy for nobility and some singular talent, have, thanks to princes, been received and elevated? But a ruling multitude does not without recompense have a regard for anyone's virtue; it accepts accomplishments that produce money, it scorns those of leisure time. For since each man either piles up money or considers valueless any glory beyond his doorstep, since he is ignorant of poets, he scorns them, and prefers to support dogs rather than a philosopher or a teacher. I cannot keep silent about the injury to glory! Your commonwealth, flourishing and magnificent, which is equaled by none in Europe in felicity and abundance of goods, is well known only by the name of the city. Although it has shone brightly with splendid men and excellent examples through so many centuries, who knows their illustrious deeds in war and peace? Who reads of them? Who remembers them? Well-known in their own times, but now shrouded by a cloud of oblivion, they have no praises.

V-29. This cannot be denied, nor heard without the blush of shame. What other commonwealth has covered the whole world by land and sea to such an extent with the glory of its deeds, producing the greatest of accomplishments, and has done things more worthy of commemoration, both in peace and in war? Truly, if there were histories of these deeds, we should scarcely yield to Phoenician or Roman! But each one of us is more eager to enrich his home with gold than with fame.

arbitror, qui gesta annalibus cogant.

P–29. Caduca profecto conviviorumque simillima predicatio; nam maternis aut nudis vocibus alligantur. Quo fit ut, quemadmodum rudes picture, spectentur ac ilicet pretereantur. At vero scita ac dives oratio splendorem indit rebus et imprimit maiestatem, efficitque ut ex lectione voluptas, ex voluptate laus, ex laude fama prodeat. Illud preterea meritis laudibus officit, quod eam si qui lucubrationem capessunt vestrigene[235] sunt et abrogatur[236] rerum fides. Nam sicut propria laus indecenter exprimitur, sic proprie gentis honor sine mendacii suspicione aut culpa iactantie non extollitur. Unde Roma ab externis scriptoribus gestarum rerum gloriam plurimum mutuata est, quorum otia principes[237] fortuna vel animo, plenis favoribus aluerunt. Quippe, rarum ac celeste munus, eloquentia, non est negotii et indigentie, sed quietis et opulentie. "Oportet," inquit Aristotiles, "preexistere victum et vestitum et reliquum famulatum." Quatenus ergo scriptoris partus prodeat absolutus, voluptate necesse est et libertate fruatur,[238] quod monarcha dominante sepe, politia[239] raro, contigisse memoratur.

V–30. Nequaquam falleris, quia tacitis raro studiis erogatur e publico. Quemadmodum enim plus sentit, ita plus utili[240] quam glorie annuit multitudo. Hinc mercatura nobis quam poesis aut philosophia pondus habet, licetque amplius qui vias maris quam celi aut virtutis, et navis flexus quam planetarum novit. Idcirco omnium qui operas prostituunt eoque vehementius quo instantius callidiusque apud nos fortuna provehitur; his autem qui sequestres seducta virtutis opera seque frui nituntur, laus forte contingere fructus vero vix posset.

P–30. Nec minus apud nos. Simulac optimorum spreta cura

---

235. vestrigene : coined.
236. abrogam V.
237. princeps V.
238. feratur PV.
239. politica PV.
240. *ex* utilis *corr.* V.

However, I think we do not lack writers to collect these deeds in annals.

P-29. A perishable sort of publication, certainly, and very similar to table conversation; for such writings are confined to their mother tongue and unadorned speech.[55] So the result is that, like crude pictures, they are looked at and immediately passed over. But learned and rich speech adds splendor to facts and impresses majesty upon them, so that pleasure comes from reading, praise from pleasure, and fame from praise. Besides, it is damaging to merited praises when those who undertake this night labor are native born, and the facts are thus deprived of credibility. For as it is unseemly to express praise of oneself, so the honor of one's own people is not extolled without suspicion of falsehood or the charge of boastfulness. Hence, Rome obtained glory for her deeds for the most part from foreign writers, whose leisure time was supported by princes, through fortune or judgment, with full benefits. Indeed, the rare and heavenly gift of eloquence is not born from hard labor and want but from quiet and plenty. "It is necessary," says Aristotle, "for food to preexist, and clothing, and other forms of services."[56] Therefore, in order that the offspring of a writer may come forth complete, it is necessary for him to enjoy pleasure and freedom, a condition that is said to have existed often under the rule of a monarch, but seldom under that of the people.

V-30. You are not wrong, because seldom is money paid out from the public purse for quiet studies. For as the people understand utility better, so they are more favorable to that than to glory. Hence trade has weight with us rather than poetry or philosophy; and a man is esteemed more for knowing the paths of the sea than those of the sky or of virtue, and the movements of a ship rather than those of the planets. Therefore, all men who eagerly display their accomplishments in public advance their fortunes among us the more quickly and skillfully; but those who in solitude attempt to enjoy themselves and their secluded work of virtue can seldom chance upon the honor of rewards.

P-30. This is not less true among us. As soon as interest in

studiorum castrensibus mercenariis impensus est favor et pretium et a sapientie studiosis tamquam ignavis[241] belloque malis aversus. Sed eorum, quamvis suum otium a rei publice negotiis procul agunt, haud est, ut arbitrantur, inutilis et repudianda vocatio,[242] nec iacture deputandum quicquid eis impenditur. Cum enim nichil agere videntur, plus sepenumero quam turbulenti plerique et qui curiosissimi[243] in re populari iudicantur ad communem utilitatem conferunt. Magna namque et salutaria, bona diutiusque constitura,[244] pertractant; et sine invidia, sine ambitione, sine querela degentes presentibus recte vivendo et utilia scribendo posteris consulunt. Tam mehercule, opinor, ad bene vivendum virtutis exemplum quam ad bene pinguendum iusta valet imago. Quod si noster hic dominator poetas et philosophos uti siccarios predonesve coluisset, has numquam angustias deflessemus.

Intueris tamen quanta vi licet vestris inferior viribus obstet et prodeat. Quid hoc? Certe quia unus omnia circumspicit, unus deliberat,[245] unus iubet. Simulac autem res provisa est, actutum impletur. Vos vero, cogendo senatum,[246] rogando sententias, disserendo, disceptando negotia, tempus teritis; ac repetentes agenda, prorogatis ipsaque prorogatione rimis produntur. Nam sicut vina[247] diligens licet attentio per dolia plura vix potest absque effusione distribuere, sic difficile est ut nulla parte fatiscat in plures deliberatio circumducta. At cogitatio dominantis non ante sentitur quam in opus imperium[248] traducatur. Quamobrem senatus consulta, quoniam sepe fissuris extillant, vel dilata impediuntur vel obstructis artibus evertuntur. Quid, preterea, quod unus dominus ferventius amatur, timetur instantius, ceu qui in dextra contineat et probis meritum et penam inferre[249] ignavis. Idcirco

241. ignavibus PV.
242. vacacio V.
243. curosissimi V.
244. constituta V.
245. unus deliberat om. V.
246. senatu PV.
247. una V.
248. impium V.
249. refere V.

the fine arts was scorned, favor and reward were dealt out to mercenary camp soldiers and were withdrawn from men desirous of learning, as from the cowardly and useless in war. But their vocation, although they spend their leisure time apart from the affairs of the commonwealth, is not, as men think, useless and worthy of repudiation; nor should anything paid out to them be counted as a loss. For when they seem to be doing nothing, very often they are contributing more to the common good than most bustling people and those who are considered busiest in public affairs. For the scholars deal with great matters that are good, wholesome, and destined to be longlasting; and living without envy, without ambition, without complaint, they give useful counsel to those now alive by living rightly, and to those to come by their writings. By heaven, in my opinion an example of virtue is as important for a good life as a true image is for a good painting. If this lord of ours had cherished poets and philosophers as he has cutthroats and robbers, we would never have been bewailing such hard times!

Nevertheless, you see with how much strength this inferior man can withstand your forces and gain ground. How can this be? Assuredly because one man oversees everything, makes the decisions, gives the orders. As soon as a thing is foreseen, it is instantly accomplished. But as for you Venetians, by calling together the senate, asking for their opinions, discussing, debating matters of business, you waste time; and by repeating the things to be done you prolong them, and by the very prolongation they become fissured by cracks. For just as the most painstaking care can scarcely distribute wine into several jars without spilling it, so it is difficult for a deliberation conducted by a number of people not to fall apart in some way. The planning of a ruler is not known before his order is translated into an action. But the decrees of the senate, since they often seep out through the cracks, are either, when spread abroad, hindered, or overturned by skillful obstructions. Furthermore, consider that a single lord is more ardently loved and more intensely feared, as one who holds in his right hand the power to bestow reward on the good and punishment on the wicked.

presens armatis addit audaciam, segnitiem demit. Ductores autem multitudinisque propositi non amantur, quia benefici non sperantur nec venerantur. Non enim licent, dum perfunctoria[250] et non solida dignitas extimatur. Quo fit ut plus virium exercitui adhortatiuncula[251] principis addat quam quevis munera privatorum. Nature siquidem opus est ut quem fortuna sublimet admirationem[252] quoque superadiciat ex ipso que venerandi usu gignitur in animis populorum, quedam reputatio maiestatis, quod nequit privato contingere. Cui si ulla ad tempus dignitas agenda mandatur, non illi honos aut reverentia, sed ei vicaria[253] cuius gerit imaginem redditur. Plerumque etiam vitia que tegebantur exerit et, qua potuit licere, despicitur.

Esto animum principis conferas: utique magnitudinis et munificentie referre vim quam non didicit nesciet. Sicut enim ceterarum artium, ita dominandi melius dexteriusque negotium ducitur, si annis teneris usus impresserit. Audaciter dixerim artium nullam difficiliorem, et tamen nulla magis cupitur aut[254] minore scientia tractatur. Pretura vero popularis nec mera[255] nec diuturna vix concedet in habitum; cum enim incipit disci, traditur successori. Unde si quid magni regendo concepisset, privatus obliterat. Principi continuatione ipsa dominandi virtus scientiaque imprimitur, ex quo pondus quoque dignitatis assequitur.[256] Cumque non est nisi homo et[257] nonnumquam animi feditate minus quam homo, tamen absque adoratione et reverentia non aditur. Quare hisce rationibus unius sceptro quam plurium felicius agi urbium gubernacula reor.

V–31. Etsi quod fers de regnante singulari tua suadere nititur oratio et iuvat rationes audire, nulla tamen felicitate et opibus est nostre civitas adequanda; et nichilominus multitudine guber-

---

250. profunctoria PV.
251. adhotaciuncula V.
252. admiracione V.
253. vicariam PV.
254. nec PV.
255. nec mera *om.* V.
256. exequitur V.
257. et *om.* V.

Therefore, by his presence he adds courage to his army and removes laziness. But the leaders and officials of the people are not loved because they are not expected to be generous, nor are they venerated. They are not held in high esteem since their office is considered perfunctory and unstable. Therefore, the exhortation of a prince adds more strength to an army than any manner of gifts from private citizens. In fact, it is an accomplishment of nature that the man whom fortune raises on high consequently acquires admiration, too, which is born in the minds of people from their habit of venerating a certain imputation of majesty—none of which can befall a private citizen. If at some time an office is entrusted to a citizen to be performed, he receives neither honor nor reverence, but only a vicarious reverence whose image he bears. Generally he also reveals flaws that were concealed, and he is despised insofar as it is permitted.

Suppose you compare his to the mind of a prince; undoubtedly he will not know how to represent a vigorous greatness and generosity that he has not learned. For, like the other arts, that of ruling is conducted better and more skillfully if practice has impressed it upon us from our early years. I would be bold to say none of the arts is more difficult, and yet none is more desired or handled with less knowledge. Indeed, leadership by the people, being neither genuine nor long lasting, will scarcely become a matter of habit; for as soon as it begins to be learned, it is passed on to a successor. If, then, one has begun something of importance in his term of office, a private citizen obliterates it. Through the very continuity of a prince's reign, virtue and knowledge are marked upon him. From this also comes the authority of his office. And although he is only a man and sometimes, through baseness of mind, less than a man, still he is not approached except with adoration and reverence. Therefore, for these reasons, I think that cities are more felicitously governed by the rule of one man than of many.[57]

V-31. Although your discussion attempts to make convincing what you say about a single ruler, and it is interesting to hear your reasons, nevertheless no city is the equal of ours

natur. Quod sententiam tuam videtur subruere![258]
P–31. Ubi similem prodes? Nam quemadmodum situ, totius vite ratione a ceteris variat. Oligarchicus[259] principatus est diligenti pene tirannidi[260] compar, propter quod Franciscus prior tirannorum urbem nominare solebat. Que si unius ductoris clavo gavisa fuisset, iam maria omnia terrasque susciperet.[261] Vicine profecto urbes que pluribus subesse fastidiunt regi Venetiarum ultro paruissent. Itaque minime quod tenor ille principandi solius regimini pregravet,[262] sed deteriorum collatione precellitis.[263] Nam vetus dictum est: cui caput languet, cetera membra dolent. Circumsitarum urbium cui non doluit, imo cum non dolet, caput? Ex quo tabe et macie cernuntur exhauste. Nam quemadmodum in capite vires resident animales indeque cerebri virtute sensus corpori ministrantur, sic ex virtute presidentis ordo ac modus fingitur civitatis, divina attestante scriptura qualis est rector civitatis, tales habitantes in ea. Quare ne[264] vero contranitamur. Regibus primum genus hominum coiisse et ortas urbes excretasque licet affirmemus. Per reges Romanum fundatum est et vires cepit imperium. Deinde, ubi regi superbo superbi cives parere contempserunt, populariter res acta est, Deus bone, quanto fluctu et turbine civitatis, primo tribunis[265] plebis, deinde militaribus, mox insolentia decemvirali populum urbemque vexantibus! Infitiari non possumus Romanum populum sub consulibus magna gessisse, licet despectum sepe atque derisum. Sed quantulum est ad eam collatum[266] magnitudinem imperii et dignitatis ad quam sub Cesaribus exauctam sublimatamque[267] legimus.

An tamen forsan Romanorum et non aliarum gentium regibus regna floruerunt? Imo etiam reginis imperantibus ad incrementum et gloriam pervenerunt. Semiramis, Thamaris, Marpesia regna duxerunt, protexerunt, auxerunt. Atqui Atheniensium et Lacede-

---

258. subivere P.
259. olingarchius V.
260. tirannide P.
261. suspiceret PV.
262. pergravet V.
263. percellitis V.
264. ni PV.
265. tribunus V.
266. collata PV.
267. sublimatam exauctamque V.

in fortune and wealth; and yet it is governed by many. This fact seems to disprove your belief!

P-31. Where can you show a city like it? For Venice differs from others not only in its location but in the manner of its whole life. It has an oligarchical government, almost the equal of a diligent tyranny; and on account of this Francesco il Vecchio was accustomed to call it the City of Tyrants. If it had enjoyed the direction of a single helmsman, now it would be mistress of all the seas and lands. Certainly neighboring cities that disdain to submit to the rule of the people would of their own accord have obeyed a king of Venice. There, you excel not because that method of ruling is superior to the regime of a single man, but only through comparison with lesser peoples. For there is an old saying: when the head is sick the rest of the body suffers.[58] Of the surrounding cities, whose head has not suffered, in fact, does not still suffer? As a result, they are perceived to be exhausted by sickness and disease. For just as the life force resides in the head, and from there by virtue of the brain the senses serve the body, thus by virtue of the ruler the order and direction of the state are fashioned. As divine Scripture testifies, whatever sort of ruler a city has, such are its inhabitants.[59] Therefore let us not rebel against this. We can confirm that the first race of men and the rising and expanding cities united under kings. Through kings the Roman rule was founded and grew strong. Then when proud citizens scorned to obey a proud king, a government of the people was formed—oh, good God, with what disturbance and commotion of the state, when first the tribunes of the people, then the soldiers, and then the insolent decemvirs harassed the people and the city! We cannot deny that the Roman people, though often despised and derided, performed great deeds under their consuls. But how little a thing it is when compared to that magnitude of empire and dignity to which we read the city was raised and exalted under the Caesars.

Or, however, perhaps kingdoms flourished under kings for the Romans and not for other peoples? Not so; for even under the reign of queens others attained growth and glory. Semiramis, Thamaris, Marpesia headed kingdoms, protected them, and

moniorum predicata res publica opesque et bellis externis et civili seditione semper turbulentissime fatigate sunt, sub regibus respirarunt.

Quid longius peregrinor? Quid externa vexo? Quid maius, quid imperiosius nostra urbe civiliter gubernata? Sed, velut ceterarum multitudo, continuo se non ferens, odio atque ambitu nequissimo vicissim impetere et morsare sese ac cedibus et rapinis devorare cepit, quousque perniciosi cives factionibus tirannos exteros induxerunt. Tandem plebe dissipata, cesa funditus nobilitate, suorum tirannidem erexerunt. Quibus dominantibus, pax viguit, et civitas, calcatis potentiorum[268] motibus, tirannica potestate respiravit. Si ergo multitudinis imperium ad iusti unius domini conferas editumque utrimque provectum metiare, tute fatebere unius etate regentis quam seculo populi urbi felicitatem magis adolevisse.

Vestram utique[269] urbem loci[270] commoditas et securitas opulentam[271] frequentemque reddit. Cui tamen si detraxeris excrementa adiacentium regionum et urbium eversarum, quid civium supererit? Atque ad hanc ipsam amplitudinem et decorem lustris seculorum vix pervasit, at satis est unius principis etas urbem ac populum in decus opesque provehere. Urbem Romam Cesar Augustus (taceo signa ab hostibus recepta, victas gentes, ultroque deditos reges, directos legibus populos, ab incendiis restauratas urbes, stratas silicibus vias) principio[272] et facultatibus exauxit illustravitque ornamentis, ut obiens gloriaretur invenisse latericiam, marmoream reliquere. Plus glorie maiestati Romane, Augusto moderante, quam multis ante seculis accrevisse memoratur.

Nostra denique etate Ludovicus, rex Hunnorum, regnum illud discissum inhumanum, sine lege, sine more cultuque divino, erexit,

---

268. potencium V.
269. uti V.
270. lo V.
271. opulenta V.
272. principibus PV.

enlarged them.⁶⁰ And the famed republic and wealth of the Athenians and the Lacedemonians were always violently exhausted by both foreign wars and civil sedition; under kings they drew a fresh breath.

Why go further? Why keep mentioning foreign situations? What was greater, what more powerful than our city when kindly ruled? But like many other cities, unable to live at peace with itself, it began to attack and snap at itself by turns with hatred and wicked ambition, and to devour itself with murder and rapine, until the destructive citizens by their factions brought in tyrants from outside. At last when the common people were scattered and the nobility utterly destroyed, they raised up a tyranny from their own people. With these men ruling, peace flourished; and the city, after the rebellions of the powerful were crushed, breathed freely again under the power of its tyrants. If then you compare the power of the people to that of one just ruler and measure the advantages offered by each, you will admit that in the lifetime of a single ruler greater happiness has come to the city than in a century of popular rule.

Assuredly the convenience and security of your city's location makes it rich and populous. Yet if you take away from it the outgrowths of adjacent regions and conquered cities, what will be left of your citizenry? And it barely arrived at this very greatness and beauty through the passing of centuries; but the lifetime of one prince is sufficient to advance a city and people to honor and wealth. Under Caesar Augustus—I shall not mention the standards taken from enemies, the conquered population, the voluntary surrender of kings, the peoples who were given laws, the restoration of cities after fires, the paving of streets—Rome was exalted by his princely rule and wealth and was made illustrious with adornments, so that when he was dying he boasted he had found it a city of brick and was leaving it a city of marble.⁶¹ More glory is said to have accrued to Roman majesty under the rule of Augustus than in many centuries before.

Finally, in our times, Louis, King of the Huns, raised up that divided and savage kingdom, lawless, without divine

composuit, ampliavit. Et cum prius brutorum appareret, hominum fecit, subque disciplina ac lege vite rationalis reformavit, et venerandum regibus formidandumque reddidit. Quo[273] olim, suam virtutem subiectis[274] emetiens gentibus, indigne[275] eiusmodi se populorum imperium sortitum esse comploravit; brevique ante obitum, compositis ab se exauctisque rebus, stragem et eversionem divino sui spiritus vaticinio[276] imminere predixit.

Haud verebor post duo, alterum orbis, regnorum alterum, lumina, senioris Francisci urbanas laudes supponere, qui, suscepto Padue sceptro, menia urbis supplevit, vacua spatia domibus constructis ornavit, artes auxit, lanificinam induxit, civium facultates promovit, studia litterarum unice excoluit. Quid loquar pontes, aquarum ductus,[277] amnes circumactos, valles exhaustas in arvaque versas, doctos montes uvis florere[278] peregrinis, turres oppidaque constructa, alia fossis murisque munita? Tot denique et tanta fecit, ut minime etatis unius hominis sed multorum opera nescius iudicaret. Brevique, nondum senex, eo decoris et amplitudinis rem provexit Euganeam, ut populus toto seculo non implesset. Num ambigis? Ad vos parumper oculum retrahe et intueberis turrim Cluse a magnificentia Venetica, omni cessante obice, lustro non exactam, claustraque pelagi, lustris pluribus coerceri cepta, adhuc[279] infecta spectari. Adeo lenta sunt populorum negotia, solicita dominorum! Communitates presentibus estuant malis, torpenter assurgunt[280] ad futura.

Haud me tempero quin alium, vestris affinem aquis, principem Estensem, Nicholaum, non hunc ephebum sed penultimum ex

---

273. quod PV.
274. subiectis *om.* V.
275. indigne *om.* V.
276. *ex* faticinio *corr.* P.
277. devotus V.
278. fluere PV.
279. ad hec V.
280. asurgant V.

teaching or worship, put it in order, and ennobled it. And though previously it appeared a kingdom of brutes, he made it a kingdom of men. He reformed it under the discipline and the law of rational life and caused it to be respected and feared by kings. As a result, imparting his own virtue to subject nations, he once complained that he had unworthily acquired power over people; and a short time before his death, when everything had been put in order by him and improved, he predicted through the divine prophecy of his spirit that destruction and overthrow were imminent.[62]

I do not hesitate to add after these two luminaries, the one of the world, the other of kingdoms, the urban accomplishments of Francesco il Vecchio, who after taking over the rule of Padua repaired the walls of the city, adorned empty spaces with the construction of homes, encouraged the arts, introduced wool-working, increased the prosperity of the citizens, and fostered humanistic studies to an extraordinary degree. Need I mention the bridges, aqueducts, rechanneled rivers, exhausted valleys turned into arable fields, mountains taught to flourish with imported grapevines, the construction of towers and towns, and other places fortified by trenches and walls? He did, in short, so many great things that anyone who did not know would judge them the work not of one man's lifetime but of many men's. And in a short time, when not yet an old man, he brought Padua's circumstances to such a degree of beauty and richness as a popular rule could not have reached in a whole century.[63] Surely you do not dispute this. Turn your eyes upon yourselves for a little while, and you will see that the tower of Chioggia has not been completed in five years by magnificent Venice, though no hindrance stands in the way, and that even though efforts have been made for several decades to close up your dams, they are unfinished till now.[64] So slow are the accomplishments of the people, so distracted their leaders! Communities are highly concerned for their present troubles but are aroused only sluggishly by those in the future.

I shall not resist adding one other, a neighbor to your waters, Niccolò, Prince of Este (not this youth but the next

germanis, subiciam. Nam ceno immeabilem et gravem odore Ferariam illimem ac salubrem reddidit, vicos lateribus ac saxo stravit, domos asseritias[281] pro[282] lapideis[283] dimisit, castra et turres erexit, oppida munivit. Sic denique prudentia et circumspectione augmento urbis ornamentoque indulsit, ut pro mensura nulla vicinarum opulentior neque frequentior speciosiorque visatur.

Age, si potes, que civitas eo dignitatis populi estate concrevit?[284] Considera vicinam in fronte Bononiam, quanta opum, quanta studiorum ac sapientie, quanta civium et advenarum rerumque omnium gloria preeminebat, principe Mediolanensi pastore. Sedis Romane deinde ex auro versa mox in scoriam simulac populus usurpavit[285] imperium, ambitione atque avaritia deflagravit. Demum seditione, odio civili, suorum exiliis cedibusque lacerata, nomen ac decus amisit, donec ad unius redacta moderamen respiravit et in flores fructumque reviruit.

Ex quo liquet quod humana fragilitas, in facinus prona, nisi regis aut legis coerceatur habenis, ruat in preceps. Quare, ambiguitate decisa, conducibilius ac divinius urbes ac regna mecum fateare oportet unius quam multitudinis ducatu componi. Quod hinc quoque animadvertas licet. Creator nempe Deus hominem continuo sub obedientie lege constituit. Quid ita? Quia nimirum intelligi voluit ut posteritas nisi sub eadem lege felix esse non posset. Id prope omnia confitentur. A nobis primum exempla captemus.

Si rationi sensus non obtemperent, indecora hominis vita perversaque ac damnabilis fuerit. Que domus, ampla licet et opulens, patrifamilias detractante[286] familia, constiterit? Unum gubernatorem, cui pareatur ad nutum, navigantium salus efflagitat. In officina vulgarium unus ministeria sortitur, obtemperant singuli. Ecclesia militans reverentiam uni et obedientiam profitetur. Claustrales unius discipline, quatenus fructuosior existat tran-

---

281. asseritias: perhaps a coined adjective. *Cf.* assericium, "board-work, flooring."
282. pro *addidi.*
283. lapideas **PV**.
284. concreverit **P**.
285. usurpat **P** exurpat **V**.
286. detractione **V**.

to last of the brothers). For he made Ferrara, which was impassable with filth and thick with odors, clean and healthful; he paved the streets with brick and rock, he replaced wooden houses with stone ones, he erected forts and towers, he fortified the towns. Finally, by his foresight and circumspection, he so furthered the growth and beautification of the city that not any of the neighboring cities were seen to be proportionately more wealthy or more populous and beautiful.[65]

Tell me now, if you can, what city has grown to such heights in a period of popular rule? Consider Bologna, the neighbor in front of you. When the prince of Milan was her shepherd, she excelled for the glory of wealth, studies, and learning, the glory of citizens and strangers and all things. Then, losing her splendor as the jewel of the Roman See as soon as the people usurped the power, she burned with ambition and avarice. At last, wounded by sedition, civil hatred, and the exile and slaughter of her people, she lost her name and glory, until, being returned to the guidance of one man, she drew breath again and blossomed once more into flower and fruit.[66]

From this it is clear that human frailty, being prone to wickedness, unless checked by the reins of kings or law will fall headlong into ruin. Therefore, shedding all doubt, you will have to agree with me that cities and kingdoms are directed more fitly and more in accordance with divine will under the leadership of one man than under that of many. You can realize it also from this fact: God, our Creator, at once set man under the law of obedience. Why so? Because surely He wished it to be understood that future ages could not be happy except under the same law. Almost all things demonstrate this principle. Let us take examples first from ourselves.

If the senses did not yield to reason, the life of man would be dishonorable, perverse, and deserving of condemnation. What home, however prosperous and rich, would stand firm if the family rejected the head of the household? The safety of sailors requires a single captain, whose slightest wish is to be obeyed. In a workshop of ordinary men, one assigns duties and the others obey him. The Church Militant professes reverence and obedience to one. Cloistered monks are subjected

quilliorque spiritualis religio, subduntur. Quam damnabiliter superbiret impenderetque ruine, si, moderamen superioris pars discissa[287] contemnens, propria usurparet vivere libertate! Omnis prope Teutonis plaga, velut Italia[288] Romanum Imperatorem dominum[289] veneratur et dicit. Ast Argentina, Rheno supersita, orbis principi subesse et parere dedignatur, et tamquam pars abrupta caput superba contemnit. Quemadmodum autem illa, sic ex Latiis, reiecto unius principis solio, superbam sibi arrogant libertatem.

V–32.   Ista moliri videtur assertio anteferre tirannidem libertati. Apud veteres autem nullum infestius quam nomen tiranni susceptum est. Legibus quoque non modo impunitas verum etiam premia tirannicidis constituta sunt. Quid ergo? An non laudabilius tirannus occiditur quam salvatur?

P–32.   Libertatem utique probo et tecum pariter. Et quisquis idem sapit, tirannidem funditus odit,[290] sed eam libertatem prefert[291] quam unius, non multorum, iustitia dispenset, quoniam solidior quidem et tranquillior. Nam ubi unus dominatur, suo quisque negotio prorsus publici securus vacat. In multitudinis autem imperio dominus quisque haberi vult, habere non vult. Quod, quam ab ordinis sinceritate absistat, dubitari nequit. Atqui fateor priscorum institutis tirannicidia laudibus celebrata; sed nec nunc quemquam ita coniecto desipere ut malit[292] tirannum tolli quam vivere. Sane cum unius regimen probo, eius intelligo qui subiectos regat, non premat, quia ratio eligendi principis est ut eligatur non qui opibus seu potentia imaginumque vetustate, sed sapientia, iustitia, animive magnitudine prestet, quemque ratio magis agat quam cupido, quantum loco ceteros tantum moribus antecedens. Ceterum lex tirannicidis[293] illa favens humane sapientie

---

287. discusa V.
288. Italie PV.
289. dominum *om.* V.
290. odio PV.
291. prefert *addidi.*
292. non malit PV.
293. tirampnicis V.

to the discipline of one so that their religious spiritual life may be more fruitful and tranquil. How reprehensibly would they show arrogance and be headed for destruction if some, segregating themselves and scorning the leadership of their superior, should unlawfully assume the privilege of living in personal independence. Almost all the region of the Germans, like Italy, calls the Roman Emperor lord and venerates him. But Strasbourg, located beyond the Rhine, scorns to be subject to the ruler of the world and obey him, and, like a part broken off, haughtily disdains its head.[67] Moreover, like that city, some cities of Italy, also rejecting the rule of one prince, take arrogant liberty upon themselves.

V–32. That assertion of yours seems to be trying to make tyranny preferable to freedom! But among the ancients no name was more detested than that of tyrant. Under the laws not only were tyrannicides granted impunity but rewards were even decreed for them. What about this? Is it not more praiseworthy to kill a tyrant than to save him?

P–32. Naturally I approve of liberty as much as you do. And whoever is wise regards tyranny wholly with hatred; but he prefers that liberty which the justice of one man, not of many, dispenses, since it is surely more reliable and tranquil. For when one man rules, everyone then has time for his own affairs, being free from public business. But under the command of the people, each person wishes to be considered a ruler and not to have one. How contrary this situation is to the soundness of order cannot be doubted. I admit that under the institutions of the ancients, tyrannicide was celebrated with praises;[68] but I do not think anyone now is so foolish as to prefer that a tyrant be destroyed rather than live. To be sure, when I aprove of the rule of one man, I mean of one who guides his subjects, not oppresses them;[69] since the wise method of choosing a prince selects a man not because he excels in wealth or power or the antiquity of his ancestral images, but because he excels in wisdom, justice, and greatness of mind, and because reason leads him rather than greed—a man exceeding others as much in character as in position.[70] For the rest, that law favoring tyrannicides was a product of human wisdom

terreneque superbie et non divine iustitie fuit. Omnem siquidem potestatem a Domino Deo esse et ratio convincit et sacrarum litterarum sanctio perhibet. Quamobrem, siquando superior deseviat,[294] sanctius toleratur[295] quam cede subruitur. Id gener ille sanctus regis exemplo ostendit, cum enim socerum, hostem et persequentem seque etiam obsidentem, perimere potuisset,[296] studuit placare quam perdere. Cur ita? Quoniam Dei esse[297] opus regem novit, et regis iniquitatem Dei iudicium extimavit. Recte quidem, quia ut ait apostolus: "Ministri Dei sunt in hoc ipsum servientes eisque ob hoc tributa prestantur." Quid igitur agendum infensis prepositorum iniuria? Nequaquam mox in exitium coniurare, non struere insidias, non ferro insurgere, sed vel cedere, fieri si queat, vel equanimiter divinum iudicium tolerare debent, pieque precari ut dominanti iustitiam colere et gravatis patientie arma[298] largiri dignetur. Impleant interim apostolicum dogma: "Reddite,"[299] inquit, "omnibus debita, cui honorem honorem, cui vectigal vectigal, cui tributum tributum, cui timorem timorem." Ex huiusmodi humili patientia et humilitate patienti, passo meritum cumulatur. Omnis profecto et tirannica et quevis undequaque vita molestia virtutem erudit, vitium efficit,[300] ac per hoc in penam aut meritum cedit. Da, queso, si habes, meram illam dominationem in qua inferior non reperiat unde queratur, nisi fortasse florentem[301] vestram pretereo, que tametsi ceteris libertate degentibus prestet, tamen a minime paucis, nedum exteris, sed ab his ipsis quidem quos alumnatis medio sinu qua nescio fortuna, nec amatur nec laudatur.

Age porro, quid plus offensant dominantes? Rapiunt tua, vim inferunt, famulari cogunt, iniuriant[302] hoc pacto. Quis tiranno sub non est? Hic enim fastum contumeliamque uxoris, hic liberorum contumaciam et rapinam; dolos iste ac tedia

---

294. sceviat V.
295. tollatur V.
296. perime pocius set V.
297. esse om. V.
298. arma paciencie V.
299. redire V
300. afficit PV.
301. florentinam PV.
302. iniuriantur V.

and earthly pride and not of divine justice, since indeed reason convinces, and the sanctity of sacred literature proclaims, that all power is from the Lord God.

Therefore, whenever a superior is mad, it is more holy that he be tolerated than killed. That pious son-in-law of the king shows this by his example, for although he had the power to kill his father-in-law, who as an enemy pursued and even surrounded him, he was eager to placate rather than destroy him. Why so? Because he knew the king was the handiwork of God and thought the injustice of the king was the judgment of God.[71] Rightly indeed, since as the apostle says: "They are servants of God attending to this very thing and therefore tributes should be paid to them."[72] What therefore ought to be done by those who are harmed by the wrongdoing of their rulers? They ought not to conspire for their deaths, nor lay ambushes, nor rise up with the sword, but either leave, if possible, or endure the divine judgment with equanimity and piously pray that God may deign to cultivate justice in the ruler and to bestow the armor of patience on the oppressed. Meanwhile let them follow the apostle's doctrine: "Give," he says, "to all what is due: to whom honor is due, honor; to whom taxes, taxes; to whom tribute, tribute; to whom fear, fear."[73] From this sort of humble patience and patient humility, merit is earned by the one who has suffered. Indeed, every trouble caused by a tyrant or any kind of trouble in life either teaches virtue or brings about misdoing, and therefore results in either punishment or reward. Give me an example, if you have one, of that pure rule in which an inferior does not find something to complain of, unless perhaps I omit your prosperous government! And it, although better than others living under liberty, nevertheless is neither loved nor praised by many, I do not say by foreigners, but those very men whom you nurture in the depths of your embrace with all kinds of fortune.

Come now, what other harm do rulers do? They seize your belongings, use force, compel you to serve them; they do injury in this way. Who is not subject to a tyrant? One man is forced to endure the arrogance and insults of his wife, another the disobedience and rapacity of his children, this man the decep-

famulantium, ille vicini superbiam, sociorum alius fraudem et tolerare compellitur et vitare non potest nec ulcisci.[303] Imo, quod adversius est, quos sentit infestos alere et curare necesse est! Dominos autem sorte communi supportat, qui siquidem pluribus molesti, festi etiam pluribus sunt. Ut obsunt plerumque, sic prosunt.

In communi vero dominatu singulis quisque cum defert, crimen auditur, creditur, in questionemque trahitur. At nisi consonet multitudo, nequiquam[304] probitas, quamvis predicata, invatur. Animadverte igitur quenam sit speranda fortuna : ubi per se officere singuli, prodesse nemo valet. Quare ut nec in domesticis malis mox ad arma, sed potius ad patientiam virtus animi retorquenda, ita ubi superior potestas improbe dominatur. Prestat enim iniuriam tolerare quam plurium exitio, quod in nece tiranni ferme semper eveniat, vindicare quod turbet. Sed fare, quid est unius solium dedignari quam fugere quod iubemur, obedire dominis carnalibus et subici omni creature propter Deum? Quod quidem non videtur aliud quam nature ordini, imo vero divino repugnare. At cense quam se divina lex prodat. Illi ipsi qui superioris illius ordinis regule obtemperare intolerabili superbia renuunt, ultro constitutis legibus substernunter et acerbius serviunt dominantes, quam si[305] regio famulatu subditi paruissent. Quid tandem? Erigunt qui onus curamque omnium gestet, et, extans imperii ac potestatis expers, non vim dignitatis sed imaginem referat. Sed in contrarium sepe cedit, nam quanto[306] fuerit autoritas comminuta gerendi muneris tanto minuitur effectus.[307]

Natos parens iussa detractantes eliminat. Comitus remiges non tantum abnuentes sed lente quoque obeuntes imperia dimittit. Nullus artifex nequiter obtemperantem[308] operarium retinet. Atqui

---

303. nec ulcisci *om.* V.
304. nequaquam V.
305. si *addidi.*
306. quantum PV.
307. affectus PV.
308. operantem V.

Monarchy versus Republic

tions and nuisances of his servants, that man the haughtiness of his neighbor, still another the cheating of his companions—and these things can be neither avoided nor avenged. Even more, what is worse, it is necessary both to support and take care of those who are bothersome! But man puts up with his rulers in his common fate; and those rulers, if troublesome to many, are also a source of pleasure to many. As they are a hindrance frequently, so too are they useful.

Now, under the rule of the people, since each man reports to individuals, when a charge against him is heard, it is believed and he is dragged into court. Yet, unless all reach an agreement, his honesty, although well-known, is of no avail. See, therefore, what sort of fortune is to be expected; where individuals can do harm per se, no one can benefit. Thus, as in domestic troubles strength of mind should be turned not to arms but rather to patience, so it should be when a superior power governs wrongly. For it is better to endure injury than to avenge the trouble by the death of many men, which nearly always is the result of the murder of a tyrant. But tell me: what is disdain for the rule of one man except avoiding what we are commanded, that is, to obey our earthly masters and be subject to all creation because of God? This indeed seems nothing else than to fight against the order of nature, and, even more, the divine order. Now consider how the divine law reveals itself. Those very men who with intolerable pride refuse to obey the regulations of that superior order voluntarily subject themselves to constitutional laws and do harsher service in ruling than they would have done if they had subjected themselves in servitude to a king and obeyed him. What finally happens? They raise up one to bear the burdens and cares of all and, since he is without power and dominion, to have no strength of dignity but only its image. But it often has negative results, for the more the authority of an office is lessened, the more its effects are lessened.

A parent turns his children out of doors when they ignore his orders. A ship's captain dismisses oarsmen not only if they disobey his commands, but also if they are slow in carrying them out. No craftsman retains a workman who obeys

si unus in civitate quispiam, si duo, si decem, si denique vicus, ab ordine et obedientia rei publice sese abiungentes, suo sibi iure ac libertate vivere moliantur, ilicet quam exquisitis ceteros suppliciis adversum se ruituros inveniant! Et quod in paucis irrevocabili animadversione corripitur, in plena urbe toleratur[309] minime, tamquam fas equumve sit verum quia, dempto vindice orbis, in consuetudinem abiit. Et si qui principantur[310] luxuria quam virtute, cogniti merito contemnuntur. Haud est idcirco, quarundam licet urbium multitudinis dicione[311] felicitas predicetur, quod illud simulacrum libertatis pertinax arrogantia non pariat et unius equi presidentis custodia non excellat. Nempe, dempto dominante, civitas[312] quid putari valet nisi velut exercitus sine duce, navis sine rectore, sine anima corpus? Optimus enim princeps pro omnibus excubat. Ceteris securis, unus ordinem, tranquillitatem, uber opportunarum rerum providentia vigili procurat.

Imperante vero multitudine, plures necesse est fieri curiosos,[313] et fit, quoniam utrumque officiose nequit impleri, aut rei communis aut proprie utilitatis negotium minatur. In quo evidens paulo ante Bononia dedit exemplum. Nam dominante ecclesie pontificatu, singulis propia curantibus, pace letabantur, redundabant opibus. Postea vero quam imperium usurparunt, ambitu deflagravere; et dum magistratu quisque urbano grandescere nititur, familiare sivit[314] studium, et, fervens ad publica, tepuit ad propria. Qua quidem re liquet summam[315] rerum sedulo magis[316] curari populumque sedatius agere, uno presidente, qui nullo alio munere distrahatur. Eo plane studio qui preerant nequaquam apud veteres domini sed patris patrie, ducis, et rectoris

---

309. tollatur V.
310. principiantur V.
311. dictione V.
312. civitas dominante PV.
313. curosos PV.
314. sinit V.
315. summa V.
316. magis sedulo V.

poorly. And if any one person in a city, if two, or ten, or even a whole neighborhood should separate themselves from the orderliness and obedience of the commonwealth and attempt to live for themselves under their own law and liberty, they would immediately find the other citizens ready to fall upon them with choice punishments! And what is censured with uncontrollable aversion in the case of a few is not at all tolerable in the case of a whole city—as if a fact is right or just because, ignoring the protector of the world, it has become customary! And if any persons rule with extravagance instead of with righteousness, as soon as they are recognized they are deservedly scorned. Therefore, though the felicity of certain cities under the sway of the people is proclaimed, it does not exist, for the reason that the obstinate arrogance of liberty does not produce that image and is not distinguished by the guardianship of one just man. In fact, without a ruler, what can a city resemble except an army without a general, a ship without a helmsman, a body without a soul? An excellent prince keeps watch over all. While others are free from cares, one man by his careful providence procures order, tranquillity, and an abundance of useful goods.

But when the people are governing, it is necessary that many become full of responsibilities; and, since two pursuits cannot be performed dutifully, either the common interest or private advantage is neglected. Concerning this, not long ago Bologna gave a clear example. For when the episcopate of the church was ruling and individuals were looking after their own affairs, the people enjoyed peace and abundant wealth. But after they usurped power they were inflamed by ambition; and when every man was striving to become great by means of an urban magistracy, he let go his private pursuits and, fervent with regard to public affairs, grew indifferent toward his own.[74] Therefore it is clear that the sum total of things is cared for more sedulously and the people live more quietly under one ruler, who is distracted by no other duty. To be sure, those men who were preeminent in this occupation among the ancients delighted in the full and true honor of being addressed and regarded not by the name of lord, but by the

appellatione acclamari et haberi plenis verisque[317] laudibus exultabant. Nam Augustus, felicissimus idem et principum maximus, non ab exteris modo appellari dominus sed ne ab ipsa quidem[318] familia voluit, et eum sibi titulum prorsus interdixit. Eant nunc et extorqueant sibi tirannuli quod[319] orbis regnator sibi arrogandum non putavit. Magnificus sane atque mirabilis qui suum et caprarum possessoribus congruat! Dicitur enim gregis et armenti dominus qui[320] numquam magistri nomen asciscat, quippe ad mentis lumen attinens quo prorsus carent rationis expertes.[321]

V–33. Exaggeratis[322] operose rationibus monarchatum preferre conaris, quas tametsi dicendi serie delectavit audivisse, nostram tamen politeam malo. Nec adduci possem quin regio cuivis[323] solio anteponam. Sed procede, ac cepta contexe.

P–33. Rogasti, et moriger ego tibi in medium posui quid de unius pluriumve gubernatione sentirem. Sed ut ait apostolus: "Suo quisque sensu abundat." Et comicus :[324] "Quot capita, tot sententie." Nec in eo quidem dumtaxat, qua distet a politico monarchus utilitate, sed fere[325] cunctis in rebus sententie pro capabilitate hominum variant. Audis ipse quam his in duabus voculis, dominus et magister, opinionum ratio dissideat.[326] Nam dominos alii, magistros alii appellari gloriantur, parum satis advertentes nominum dignitatem, cum alterum casus et fortuna, ceu premisimus, officiosa ratio comparet. Preter hec erudire ad pietatem, ad iustitiam, ad vite cultum rerumque notitiam, ad artes item famulares magistri, non domini munus est. Quare stultus et

---

317. ac veris V.
318. quoque PV.
319. quam P que V.
320. quod PV.
321. expertia PV.
322. ex agregatis V.
323. cuius V.
324. comitus V.
325. *ex* ifere *corr.* P.
326. desideat V.

name of father of their country, leader, and guide. For Augustus, at once the most fortunate and the greatest of princes, was unwilling to be called lord not only by foreigners but even by his own household, and in fact forbade this title to himself.[75] Let petty tyrants go now and turn to their own use what the ruler of the world did not think should be applied to himself. A magnificent and marvelous man, to be sure, is one who corresponds to the keepers of pigs and goats! Indeed, the man called lord of the flock and herd would never claim the name of master, thus displaying a mental clarity completely lacking in those without reason!

V-33. You are trying to show monarchy in a favorable light by painstakingly piling up arguments; and even though it has been a pleasure to hear your exposition, I still prefer our commonwealth. Nor could I be influenced not to place it before any sort of royal rule! But proceed, continue what you have begun.

5. Relative Merits of a Master and a Lord

P-33. You asked, and in compliance with your request I have set forth plainly my opinion concerning the rule of one or of many. But as the apostle says, "Let each man be abundant in his own understanding."[76] And the comic poet: "There are as many opinions as there are men."[77] And not in this only, through what advantages the monarch differs from the poular representative, but in almost all things opinions of men vary in accordance with their understanding. You yourself have heard how in the case of these two names, lord and master, reasoning is at variance. For some glory in being called lords, others masters, paying insufficient attention to the value of the names, since chance and fortune produce a lord, as we have shown, and careful planning a master. In addition, it is the function of a master, not a lord, to educate for dutifulness, justice, refinement of life, and knowledge of facts,

indoctus sepe³²⁷ dominus fertur, non autem magister, qui omnino extat doctus.³²⁸ Ex quo rursum magistralis dignitas liquet, quod fortuna reflante nequit amitti, facilis autem vertex³²⁹ domini evertit insigne. Vidimus reges, vidimus tirannos, exules, captos serviliter, defunctos, quos ne noti quidem pro dominis putavere. Narrabo in hac vanitate superbie quemadmodum argentarius vestras, Bartholomeus, quempiam ex patriciorum ordine monuit. Secundo namque bello Euganiensi, cum Veneta multifarie oppressa res publica laboraret, "Vigila," infit, "patricie, vestrum ne imperium subsidat. Vestra plurimum refert. Nam si exulare cogaris, nusquam gentium dominus, Andreas, eris." (Id erat patricio nomen.) "At quoquo transferar gentium, magister habebor. Adverte, ni obaudis huiusmodi commonitioni,³³⁰ quam dominus magistro subsit."³³¹

Idque ipsum per hoc quoque manifestum est, quod illud plures sepe domini quo vocarentur ultro deposuere, sepe rursus inviti detinuere. Nemo unde magister existeret dediscere voluit. Quam multis insuper dominos esse tam sibi quam suis quoque exitiosum sepenumero extitit; quam raro magisterii locus offuit. Cum igitur nequaquam omni tempore dominari conducat, esse vero docendi peritus³³² semper velle quisque debeat. Alterius tituli manifestatur humilitas, quam ei substet merito quod nulla vicissitudine mereatur omitti. Quid quod artes ipsas quibus bene agitur, imo sine quibus bene vita non agitur, litterarum item ac scientie habitum magistris sortimur autoribus; a dominis autem precipue nostris³³³ quid preter desidiam vitiaque condiscimus?

V-34.   Negari nequit quin ubique magister honorem et pondus, dominus autem sepe invidiam, sepe etiam odium nanciscitur. Nostra res publica qui esse ac dici dominus gliscat horret ac premit, magistros honorat et fovet moti velut arbitror quod publice

---

327. sepe *om.* V.
328. indoctus PV.
329. vertebra PV.
330. commonitione PV.
331. subsistat PV.
332. paratus V.
333. nostre vis PV.

and also for the skills of serving. Hence a lord is often said to be stupid and unlearned, but not a master, who is highly learned. Consequently, the worth of a master is obvious, because it cannot be lost if fortune blows the wrong way; but a light breeze can overturn a lord's symbols of power. We have seen kings and tyrants exiled, enslaved, destroyed, whom not even their friends considered lords. I will relate as an example of this vain pride how a silversmith of your nation, Bartolomeo, warned a certain man of patrician rank. For in the second Paduan war, when the Venetian commonwealth was laboring under all sorts of difficulties, he said, "Be on your guard, patrician, lest your power decrease. This is of the greatest importance to you. For if you are compelled to go into exile, nowhere in the world will you be a lord, Andreas." (That was the patrician's name.) "But wherever in the world I may be transferred, I shall be considered a master. You will see, unless you heed this warning, how inferior a lord is to a master."[78]

And this fact is clear, also, in that many lords have willingly put aside that name by which they were called, and again often unwillingly kept it. No one has wished to unlearn the things that have made him a master. Furthermore, to how many men has it been deadly to be lords, not only to themselves but to their possessions as well; and how rarely has the position of master done any harm! Although it is not agreeable at all times to be a lord, surely every one ought always to wish to be skilled in teaching. The insignificance of the title of lord is obvious from its inferiority to that merit which deservedly is not neglected under any circumstances. Consider that we acquire the very arts by which life is lived well, in fact without which life is not lived well, and also the accomplishments of literature and knowledge, with masters as our mentors. But from our lords what especially do we learn except slothfulness and vice?

V-34.   It is undeniable that everywhere a master finds honor and influence, but a lord often envy or even hatred. Our commonwealth dreads the man who ardently desires to be and to be called a lord, and it suppresses him. It honors and

libertati honos ille plerumque abroget, urbes evertat, magistri vero eruditionis utilitate provehant.

P-34. Recte quidem censent, quia nulla truculentior pestis civibus quam ubi summum locum nequitia sortitur. Sed animadverte rursum quod dominorum collatione servi, magistrorum autem discipuli nuncupantur. Ex quo liquet quam[334] subest discipulo servus, a magistro tam dominum anteiri. Amplius, ad magistri presentiam quatenus adipiscantur unde redeant meliores propria utilitate conveniunt; ad dominos autem ut assistatur et parcatur ipsorum dominorum voluptate coitur. Insuper ille auditoribus, tamquam ratio superior sensibus, regaliter, hic despotice velut anima corpori suppositis imperat. Ad hec magistralis cura qui subiciantur efficere meliores annititur, et ceu faber erarius lima doctrine caliginem mentis deruginat splendidamque reddit; ac penitus enutritam famulatu vocis discenti formam insigillat. Indulgentia vero dominantis quo secunda, hoc elatos insolentesque remittit. Etiam quicquid erogatur a dominis forinsecus instruit et deperire eripique valet. At magistri munus introrsus ornat et confert quod externe violentie non formidet incursum.

Quid sibi vult sapiens imperator, institutionum suarum limine, dum imperatoriam maiestatem armat legibus, decorat armis, nisi quod sapientia legis vim condit armatam? Ante namque precipitium[335] se inconsulta ferocitas, velut ad victoriam erudita virtus, extollit. Ideo rei publice fortitudo armatur sapientibus, fortibus ornatur, quoniam ea demum speciosa sunt bella que armantur cohortante iustitia. Quo datur intelligi preposito gentibus strenuitatem et sapientiam convenire, idcirco lex armat[336] principem, quia vires sine prudentia freneticant. E regione splendet armatus quia

---

334. quod V.
335. precipuum V.
336. amat V.

encourages masters, in my opinion, because while a lord generally takes away from the public liberty and disrupts cities, masters advance them through the benefits of learning.

P-34. Their judgment is right, because no plague is harder on the citizens than when wickedness holds chief place. But notice, again, that in relationship to lords men are called servants, but to masters, pupils. From this it is clear that as a servant is inferior to a pupil, so the lord is surpassed by the master. Besides, people gather in the presence of a master to acquire the means of going away improved to their own advantage; but they go to lords in order to be helped and pardoned according to the pleasure of the lords themselves. Furthermore, the master gives instructions to his students in the manner in which superior reason does to the senses, like a king; but the lord commands his subordinates despotically, as the soul does the body. In addition, the concern of the master strives to make better those who are subject to him, and, like a craftsman in bronze, he strips off the rusty covering of the mind with the file of his teaching and makes it gleam; and he imprints deeply upon the learner a design created by the working of his words. But the more favorable the indulgence of the lord is, the more it makes men haughty and insolent. Also, whatever is expended by lords equips externally and can perish and be taken away. But the gifts of the master adorn internally and confer something that does not fear the inroads of external violence.

What does a wise emperor mean when at the beginning of his administration he arms his imperial majesty with laws and embellishes it with arms, except that the wisdom of the law tempers armed power? For untutored ferocity rises up on the edge of a precipice, whereas trained might leads to victory. Therefore the strength of the commonwealth is armed by the wise and adorned by the strong, since, in short, those wars are splendid which are armed by the urgings of justice. From the foregoing, one realizes that activity and wisdom go hand in hand for nations, and therefore the law arms the prince because strength without prudence runs amuck. When armed he is illustrious because his propensity for good-

probitatis inanis est pronitas, si viribus deseratur. Lex item efficit ut[337] princeps ametur armatus, arma vero ut timeatur inermis. Quanto itaque dilectio metu fecundior, magistri appellatio tanto splendidior quam domini. Quippe legibus erudimur quomodo principatus feliciter armatur. Ferri terrore scelestorum coercetur audacia. Adde quod innocens quisque nascitur ac per hoc minime indigens tribunalis. Nobis autem error et inscitia connati cathedram mox exposcunt.

Sed a puerilibus studiis ad hominum assurgamus, complectamur in quapiam orbis plaga aureum, Saturno rege, seculum degentibus sine avaritia, sine ambitione, sine dolo vitam mortalibus. Si quod ob unum, Deo providente, superior potestas maxime instituta creditur innoxie pacificeque iuvatur, domini titulus frustra sit, magisterii directorisve utilitas non sit. Unde qui populos ad civile fedus formamve[338] componerent, nequaquam domini, ut diximus, sed reges ac gubernatores ac[339] patres dicti sunt.

V–35. Haud testate satis consequi videtur quod asseveras, quia rerum ordo videtur obtestare. Nam si summa ab imis collatio demigret, una domus, una civitas, unum regnum, ipse orbis, demum celum celitesque unum aliquem imperantem moderantemque cetera, quo sit[340] felicior vita, recognoscunt; et tamen huic antelata videtur refragari sententia.

P–35. Forte patula minus luce spectantibus; interdum enim vel plano calle plante cecutientium offenduntur. Ita qui rerum qualitates, umbrata veritate,[341] recipiunt plerumque admiratione pulsantur. At si qua dominus ratione fundatur capessas, paulo ante diserta minime videbuntur adversari. Nisi enim quod[342] prioritatis dignitate preiret constitueretur, nec ordo quidem prorsus in rebus existeret. Quemadmodum namque sine causa, ita sine superiore nichil preter unum extat omnino; ac rursum veluti cause effectus quod est, sic dignitatis quoque prestantiam debet

---

337. ut ut V.
338. formave V.
339. et V.
340. fit V.
341. virtute V.
342. que V.

ness is vain if it lacks strength. The law likewise makes the prince loved when armed, but the arms make him feared by the unarmed. Therefore, just as love is more productive than fear, so the name of master is more splendid than that of lord. Indeed, we are educated by the laws in the same way the principate is felicitously armed. The boldness of wicked men is restrained by fear of the sword. Every man furthermore is born innocent and consequently not in need of a judgment seat, but the error and ignorance born along with us soon demand that chair.

But let us proceed from childish pursuits to those of men. Let us suppose a Golden Age in some region of the world, with Saturn as king, where mortals pass their life without avarice, without ambition, without guile.[79] If the title of lord is needless because the superior power is believed to have been set up for one by God's wisdom and is given support peacefully and harmlessly, there is also no use for instruction or direction. Hence those who settled the people under a civil treaty or orders were not called lords, as we have said, but kings and governors and fathers.

V-35. What you claim does not seem to follow clearly enough, because the arrangement of things appears to testify against it. For, moving from the lowest comparison to the highest, one home, one city, one kingdom, the world itself, and finally the heavens and the heaven-dwellers recognize someone ruling and governing others in order that life may be happier; and yet your aforementioned opinion seems to oppose this.

P-35. Perhaps it seems so for those looking in a dim light; for sometimes even on a smooth path the blind stub their toes. Thus those who perceive the characteristics of things when the truth is in shadow generally are struck with bewilderment. But if you understand by what reasoning a lord is established, the words spoken a little while ago will not seem to be contrary. For unless there were established a precedence in the honor of rank, then order would not exist in creation. Just as without a cause so without a superior nothing except One exists at all; and again, as the effect must attribute its

ascribere. Ceterum si quicquid excelsius est, Iustino teste, iustam habet venerationem. Infitiari indignum est quod iure prestet fore etiam veneratione dignissimum. Hoc ex fonte nature liberi parentes, liberorum nati avos, maritum uxor, soceros generi, patronum cliens, magistrum discipulus, servus dominum, grandevum iunior, domini appellatione condecorat. Tam, mehercule, quisquis etate vel cultu fortunave precellere videtur, ea nominatione obvii nuncupamus. Quare speciosum nequaquam titulum hunc de fastigiose solummodo potestatis sed dignitatis quoque ac meriti attestatione prodire intime speculanti patebit.[343] Unde eruditoribus congruenter preponitur, quandoquidem[344] ipsa docendi prestantia suam dignitatis gerat imaginem, sed eo a domini ratione seiunctam quod peritiam qua sine intelligi dominus valet designare constat.

Quamobrem mundi redemptor "Vos," ait, "vocatis me Magister et Domine; et benedicitis: sum etenim." Quippe viam indicando salutis magisterii vicem implebat; et omnipotenter miracula faciendo cui omnia ad nutum parerent, dominum ostendebat. At rursus, "Si ego," inquit, "lavi pedes vestros, Dominus et Magister, vos debetis alter alterius lavare pedes." Hic autem quod dominus antefertur, divine misterium preceptionis aperitur. Nam prelate[345] humilitatis actionem voluit adverti ut[346] cuius arbitrio cuncti[347] famularentur, usque ad lavandum pedes, servis conspicati substerni fastigium, pietatis exemplum discerent emulari. Ideo sane magister ab apostolis dicebatur quia eos doctrina potius quam imperio dirigebat. Ab his autem quos imperio non medicina sanabat, dominus vocabatur. Ideo utrumque sibi dignissime attribuit qui verissime utriusque merito potens fuit. Nec idcirco in hac sibi quisquam vanitate complaceat, quod in[348] quibus splendor ullus dignitatis emicat, nequaquam magistros sed dominos salutamus. Id enim evenit non ut laudatio magistri prematur, sed quod de

---

343. patebit *om*. P.
344. quando quid V.
345. plante V.
346. et V.
347. cuncta PV.
348. in *om*. V.

existence to its cause, so too it must attribute to it superiority of rank. If something is higher, according to Justinus, it possesses a just reverence.[80] It is unworthy to deny that what rightly is superior is also most worthy of reverence. From this natural source children honor their parents with the name of lord, the sons of the children their grandfathers, the wife her husband, the sons-in-law their fathers-in-law, the client his patron, the pupil his teacher, the servant his master, and the young man the old man. By heavens, whoever seems to be preeminent in age or culture or fortune we call by this name when we meet him. Therefore, it will be clear to one looking deeply that this fine title appears as evidence not only of extreme power but also of rank and merit. Hence it is fitly applied to teachers, since the very excellence of teaching bears its own image of high rank; but the rank differs from the principle of a lord in that it is understood to designate a skill not necessary to the meaning of lord.

Therefore the Redeemer of the world says, "You call me Master and Lord, and you are right; for so I am."[81] Indeed, by showing the way of salvation He performed the office of a master; and by omnipotently performing miracles He showed Himself a lord whose nod was obeyed by all things. And again He said, "If I have washed your feet, being Lord and Master, you ought to wash each other's feet."[82] But here, because the name Lord is spoken first, the mystery of His divine teaching is revealed. For He wished the act of humility that He displayed to be observed so that by its authority all men might serve, even to the washing of feet, perceiving that the One of highest rank was beneath the servants, and so that they might learn to emulate the example of piety. For this reason He was called Master by the apostles, because He guided them by teaching rather than by command. However, by those whom He healed by command, not by medication, He was called Lord. Therefore He added each name most worthily to Himself, as He most truly was possessed of the merit of each. And therefore no one should be complacent with foolish notions because of the fact that we greet as lords, not masters, those in whom some splendor of high rank gleams. For this happens, not to

magisterio ambigi de superioritate que ore vel cultu referatur non potest, vel quod latius domini vocabulum protenditur;[349] quandoquidem temere fortunatus quilibet dominus vocatur, magister continuo dici nequit. Servire preterea omnes feliciori possumus, erudiri autem apti non sumus. Nam calones, lanii, ceptarii, cunctaque forensis turba prestantem quemque habere dominum quod inferior existat, et non magistrum quod erudiri possit valet.

Iam vero quanta magistri honos excelleat dignitate etiam inde liquet quod omne sapientie studium prasim aut theoricam respicit, quorum alterum in[350] cognitione, alterum in veritatis operatione perficitur. Ex quibus duplex quoque vite munus active contemplativeque nascitur. De contemplantis[351] precellentia, Christo Mariam perlaudante,[352] ambigi non oportet. Idem[353] insuper vir doctissimus in Philosophie Consolatione libellos dextre, sceptrum leve collocando monstravit. Per quod intelligi datur sinistra politicam, dextra studiosam vocationem[354] designari; sed politica dominum, studiosa nominari magistrum efficit. Quo satis magisterii primatus claret. Amplius in celestium gloria premiorum qui alios docuere, non qui imperavere,[355] aureole qua preter virgines martiresque in beatorum nemo regia letatur, radiant claritate, quos Danielis quoque vaticinium comparat[356] stellis eternitatis. Quid quod satis est ad cumulandam taxandamque magisterii prestantiam,[357] quod dominatio tertia sede a cherubin subsidet? Nosti autem cherubin scientie plenitudinem importare, qua gratia[358] magisterii corona suscipitur. Nunc et postpone[359] dominationis vocabulum ei per quod scientie lumen accipitur, cum a Deo preexistere[360] dominationi cherubin audias in celo.

Ceterum quia in[361] terra sumus terrenaque mole opacamur et

349. pretenditur V.
350. in *inser. supra* V.
351. contemplatis V.
352. prelaudante P. prelaudantem V.
353. inde V.
354. vacacionem V.
355. imparavere P.
356. comperat V.
357. prestantia P.
358. gratiam V.
359. prepone PV.
360. presistere PV.
361. in *addidi*.

A Master versus a Lord

suppress honor to a master, but because there can be no doubt concerning the master's superiority, which is revealed by his speech or culture, or because the name of lord is used more extensively, since indeed every fortunate man is carelessly called lord; but he cannot necessarily be said to be a master. Furthermore, we are all able to serve a more fortunate man, but we are not all suitable to be taught. For soldiers' servants, butchers, onion dealers, and the whole marketplace mob can have some superior as their lord because they are his inferiors; and yet they cannot have a master because they cannot be educated.

How much the office of a master excels in greatness is evident also in that every pursuit of learning has reference to either practice or theory, one of which is perfected in knowledge of the truth, the other in its operation. From these also comes the twofold function of life, the active and the contemplative. Concerning the superiority of the life of contemplation, there ought not to be any doubt, because of Christ's praise of Mary.[83] Furthermore, a very learned man demonstrated the same thing in his *Consolation of Philosophy* by placing books in the right hand and a scepter in the left.[84] This means that the vocation of government is designated on the left, and that of study on the right. Since government gives the name of lord, and study the name of master, the primacy of the position of master is clear. Those who have taught others, not those who have commanded, shine more brightly in the glory of celestial rewards, with the brilliance of the aureole that no one in the palace of the blessed enjoys except virgins and martyrs, whom the prophecy of Daniel also compares with the stars of eternity.[85] Does not the fact that dominion sits in the third seat from the cherubim sufficiently complete the evaluation of the preeminence of a master's office? Morever, you know the cherubim bring in an abundance of knowledge, and by this grace the crown of the master is received. Now, too, set the name of dominion below that through which the light of knowledge is received, since you hear that the cherubim exist from God in Heaven before dominion.

But because we are on earth and are darkened and oppressed

premimur a spiritaliumque intellectione deficimus, relabamur[362] ad sensibilia, de quibus est mortalibus promptius iudicare. Respondeas hoc velim : in ludo Schachorum quis regi propior,[363] miles an alphilus?

V-36. Hoccine rogas? Nemo dubitaverit dempto medio alphilum[364] assidere. Quid inde?

P-36. Quid? Certe quod alphilus sapientis personam gerit. Miles ad arma, iste ad consultum ascitur. Quo nimirum ordine sapientie subdi imperium innuitur, nam sapiens consulit quod fortis exequatur. Quantum itaque intelligentie fortitudo, tantum magistro dominus cedit. Actio enim intelligentis est, non autem intellectus agentis. Nam ab intellectu actio, ab actione potius experientia, et inde ars gignitur. Hinc convenientissime iungitur domino[365] magister. At magister dominus non auditur, quoniam qui magister existat esse dominus queat, qui vero dominus ilico non magister.

V-37. Iam cerno magistri voce qui erudire alios possit, vel erudiat signari. Cur autem qui iura docent vel discunt domini quam magistri, sicut qui liberales artes philosophiamque non domini sed magistri dicantur? Nosse[366] desidero.

P-37. Si ad exarata superius cordis oculum reflexeris, quod nunc deposcis facile, arbitror, illucescet. Ex antelatis bipartito sapientie studium omne procedere, in cognitione et actione veritatis, totamque hisce philosophiam inservire audivisse te puto. Nam sicut duplici natura, sublimi una, luculenta, ac celesti, que anima dicitur, altera vero ima, opaca, terrena, que corpus appellatur, consistimus,[367] ita mortales, partim sapientie negotium ad anime, partim ad temporalis vite felicitatem referentes, active contemplativeque vite fructum exequuntur. Atqui dictum est activam dominis veluti contemplativam magistris magis attribui. Cum ergo liqueat[368] rationales scientias, queque de sensibilis

---

362. relabimur V.
363. proprior V.
364. alphilum medio PV.
365. domine PV.
366. nosce V.
367. constituimus V.
368. liqueat *addidi.*

by the earthly mass and are lacking in knowledge of spiritual things, let us pass over to matters of the senses, concerning which it is easier for mortals to judge. I should like you to answer this: in the game of chess which is nearer the king, the knight or the bishop?

V-36. What a question! No one could doubt that the bishop sits by the king, without an intervening place. What of this?

P-36. What? Why, because the bishop takes the role of a wise man. The knight is used for warfare, the other for consultation. In fact, by this arrangement power is meant to be subjected to wisdom, for the wise man makes the plans that the strong man is to carry out. Therefore the lord yields to the master as much as strength yields to intelligence. Action is a characteristic of an intelligent man, but intellect is not characteristic of an active man, since action is born from the intellect, experience from action, and from that, art. Hence a master is united quite suitably with a lord. But the lord is not spoken of as a master: the one who is a master is able to be a lord, but the lord necessarily cannot be a master.

V-37. Now I understand by the word master a man who can educate others or be designed to educate. But why are those who teach or learn the law called lords rather than masters, when those who study the liberal arts and philosophy are called not lords but masters? I should like to know.

P-37. If you turn your mind's eye to the facts noted previously, what you now ask will, I think, easily be cleared up. From what was said before I think you understood that the whole study of knowledge proceeds in two directions, to either the perceiving or the performing of truth, and that all of philosophy serves these two. For as we consist of a twofold nature, one sublime, bright, and celestial, which is called the soul, but the other lowly, dark and terrestrial, which is called the body, so mortals, referring the business of knowledge in part to the happiness of the soul and in part to that of temporal life, pursue the rewards of both an active and a contemplative life. Now it has been said that the active life is more appropriate to lords as the contemplative is more appropriate to masters. Since it is clear that the rational sciences, which deal

altiorisve nature causis negotiantur, ad anime pertinere dignitatem; que[369] vero rerum humanarum normam distributionemque, ut sunt contractus conventionesque urbane, iudiciarie cause ac testamentarie dispositiones, profiterentur, ad communionem magis hominum vitamque civilem referri, et has quidem leges, illas vero usitata nuncupatione scientias potius dici liqueat. Qui leges discunt et docent, tamquam civilis vite moderatores et correctores,[370] domini appellantur.

V–38. Vehementer assertionis tue ordo iuvat compellitque affirmare que probas. Verum superest quod adversari videatur et scrupulum gignat : qui bene dominetur, quam qui bene docet, anteponi, idque multitudinis assensum iri sententiam.

P–38. Haud miror. Ut enim sentiunt, ita iudicant. Scrupulum efficit quia dominantis officium docentisque minime prospicaci satis luce contuimini. Haud enim una est utriusque ratio nec tota rursum provincia sequestrantur. Nam quid est bene imperare nisi subiectos in equitatem vite dirigere? Quid docere nisi lumen veritatis infundere? At nemo quemquam[371] valet in veritate vite continere nisi didicerit veritatem. Adeo vicino federe connectuntur ut ipsa quoque dignitatis gravitas magistratus nomen non aspernetur. "Dominus," inquit sapiens, "sedet in solio ut omne malum in circuitu dissipet"; magister vero in cathedra ut omne bonum instruat circumstantes. Iubet ille ut subditi faciant intellecta; docet iste ut intelligant facienda. Hic rursus instruit imperanda;[372] ille imperat que didicit facienda. Dominus inutiliter preest nisi obediatur cum dicit, ceu frustra[373] magister nisi intelligatur cum docet. Porro tamen inesse magisterio prestantic rei dignitas astruitur,[374] ut aule regiarumve prefecti consuetudine prope trita magistri ferantur. Sic apud veteres quoque urbana officia magistratus appellabantur.

369. quo P.
370. correptores V.
371. quamquam V.
372. imparanda P.
373. frustra *om.* V.
374. astruit PV.

A Master versus a Lord 155

with causes of a sensitive or higher nature, pertain to the dignity of the soul, but the skills dealing with the pattern and arrangements of human affairs, such as urban contracts and agreements, judiciary cases, and testamentary dispositions, are concerned rather with the community of men and civil life, it is obvious that the latter are called laws, but the former are better called by the usual name of sciences. Men who learn and teach the laws, like guides and governors of civil life, are called lords.

V-38. Your logical presentation is helpful and makes me agree with your proof. But there remains something that is an apparent contradiction and poses a problem: that is, the one who rules well is preferred to the one who teaches well, and this will be found to be the opinion of the majority of people.

P-38. I do not wonder. For as they feel, so do they judge. The difficulty exists because we do not consider the function of the ruler and that of the teacher in a sufficiently clear light. For there is not one single principle for each, nor, on the other hand, are they separate in their entire scope. What is ruling well except to guide one's subjects into stability of life? What is teaching except to pour in the light of truth? But no one is able to hold anyone in the truth of life unless he has learned the truth. They are bound together by so close a tie that even the authority of high office does not scorn the name of magistrate. "The lord," says the wise man, "sits on a throne so that he may dispel all evil around him";[86] but the master sits in a chair so that he may teach all good to those standing about. The one orders his subjects to do what they have learned; the other teaches them to learn what they have to do. One explains what is to be ordered; the other orders what he has learned. The lord has his high rank to no avail if he is not obeyed when he speaks, and so does the master if he is not understood when he teaches. Nevertheless, a high degree of superiority is inherent in the office of the master, with the result that the officials of the court or palaces according to an almost timeworn custom are called masters. So, too, among the ancients, whose city offices were called magistracies.

Audio nunc item frequenter "magnus ille magister est in regia Francie." Quamobrem? Quia talis habetur cui autoritas imperandi[375] ordinandique intelligentia lege plena sub rege consistat. Quod utique apud barbaros facile perpendas, in quibus cui rerum aulicarum a principibus dispensatio sit et collata prelatio, "lophmaster" agnoscitur. Sic item Ordo Templarium eum qui universis presidet Rodi nequaquam dominum sed magistrum dicat. Preterea apud nonnullos inoluit qui militantibus famulantur, quos impresentiarum pagios, olim ragacios, audiebamus, dominos suos appellare magistros. Quoniam tamen a pluribus bene dominari sentitur, a pluribus perlaudatur.[376]

Attende[377] rerum affinitatem: litterarum studium prestat bene dominari; bene autem dominari gratiam fecundat studiorum. Quam rem utinam ductor Euganeus[378] animadvertisset, et tam decertasset sapiens esse[379] quam potens! Sed dum scientiarum studia negligit, colit armorum. Se suosque ruina miserabili involvit, atque admonuit dominia felicius sapientia servari quam armis. Nec ab re Minervam Iunonemque a Troianis defecisse vates intexuere carminibus. Nam cum sapientia et opes, quibus regna potissimum confoventur, urbes deserunt, exiguo labore ab hostibus evertuntur. Quamquam autem Iuno, cui divitiarum potestas ascribitur, legatur favisse Troianis, Minerva tamen ad Grecos transeunte, non potuit quin caperetur Troia defendi. Adeo plus sapientia quam[380] opes regna tuetur. Habes quid de vi utriusque nominis teneam; de utroque ferre tute pro arbitrio sententiam potes.

V-39. Adornatis adeo armatisque rationibus magistro autoritatem attribuis ut deinceps amplius arbitrer veneratione dignissimum. Quamquam, more depravato ac superbissima vanitate, si opiduli imbellisve turricule cuivis possessio contingat, nisi dominus appelletur impatienter ferat et furat. Quin etiam, sacrosancti dudum presules,[381] licet nunc sacrosancta tantummodo presulum nomina superent,[382] patres ac pastores haberi et amari gaudebant.

---

375. imparandi P.
376. prelaudatur PV.
377. attente V.
378. et Euganeus V.
379. esse sapiens V.
380. sapiencia plusquam V.
381. presules dudum V.
382. supent P.

A Master versus a Lord

Now I also hear frequently "that master is great in the court of France."[87] Why? Because such is considered the man whose power of command and knowledge of regulations exist with full legal rights under the king. You can see this readily in the barbarians, among whom the man who is entrusted by the princes with the management of court affairs is known as "lophmaster." So, too, the Order of Templars proclaims the man who presides over all at Rhodes not lord but master.[88] Besides, among some who serve military men, whom we hear of now as pages and formerly as servants, the custom has grown to address their lords as masters. Since, however, being ruled well is experienced by many, it is highly praised by many.

Notice the relationships: the study of letters maintains good government, and good government gives abundant encouragement to studies. If only the Paduan leader had had regard for this fact and had striven as hard to be wise as he did to be powerful! But while he neglects the study of the sciences, he encourages that of arms. He has involved himself and his people in miserable ruin and reminded us that dominions are kept happier by wisdom than by arms. On this subject, the poets told in song that Minerva and Juno had deserted the Trojans. For when wisdom and wealth, by which kingdoms chiefly are nourished, forsake cities, they are overthrown with little trouble by the enemy. But although Juno, to whom the power of riches is ascribed, is said to have favored the Trojans, nevertheless when Minerva crossed over to the Greeks, nothing could prevent Troy from being taken. Thus wisdom more than wealth protects kingdoms.[89]

You see what I think about the meaning of each name; you can form an opinion about each according to your judgment.
V-39. You attribute importance to a master by means of such logical and powerful reasoning that finally I believe him to be the most worthy of reverence! Even so, because of depraved custom and empty pride, if someone becomes owner of a small town or a peaceful little tower, unless he is called lord he displays impatience and anger. Even more, bishops, formerly most holy men (though now only the names of the bishops are holy), used to rejoice in being thought of and

Quid dico "gaudebant?" Imo, tamquam elatum nimis preconium vocis vera humilitate vitantes, servos se appellari mallebant, quam nimirum humilem pietatis expressionem pontificum pontifex servum se Dei servorum scribendo fatetur. At vero nec patres nec pastores, quia non sunt, merito dici volunt, sed velut abiectissima ludibriosaque vocabula odiunt et domini amant, efflagitant ac letis[383] auribus captant. Unde calcatur titulus spiritualis et temporalis ac terrenus arrogatur, ut quivis episcopellus in sue diocesis atrio, querat dominus appellari secularique metui potestate. Illud insuper improbe voluntatis sigillat affectum,[384] quod gentilicia cognomina, abusi lege dicendi, dignitatibus anteferunt, quasi vero minime satis fulgore dignitatis innotescant et genus suscepto pontificio et non generi pontificium sit honori. Qui profecto dignitate ordinis se indignos produnt, hoc ipso quo aura terreni flatus ordini iniuriam faciunt. Neque enim ad pontificatum provehi certant pontem erecturi (unde pontifices nuncupantur) quo a simplicioribus migretur ad vitam, sed ut monstruose vivendo in mortem precipitium fiant, nec item ut pinguedine sacra alant pauperes Christi, sed genus ac penates extollant opibus Christi. Num[385] id mentior? Recense episcoporum abbatuum[386] claustra. Recense: nurus, matrone, pueri, puelle, servarum greges, crepundia, mamme frequentes occurrent. Quanto divinius sacer Augustinus, qui cohabitare sorori negavit, proferens memorabile rudimentum,[387] "Que cum sorore mea sunt," inquit, "sorores mee non sunt." Fit igitur, quemadmodum adeptis[388] prelaturis abutuntur, nullum apud populos pretium mereantur et dignitates fedando cum dignitatibus contemnantur.

Dicam et nequiquam forte dicam. Nichilominus, nos mare, procellas, cautes, estum, gelu, terre salique monstra, piratas ac

---

383. lectis V.
384. effectum V.
385. non V.
386. abbacium V.
387. erudimentum V.
388. adeptis *om.* V.

loved as fathers and pastors. Why do I say they rejoiced? In fact, as if avoiding with real humility too lofty a commendation in a title, they preferred to be called servants, truly a humble expression of piety, which the priest of priests evinces in writing that he is the servant of servants of God.[90] But indeed now they rightly wish to be called neither fathers nor pastors, for these they are not; in fact, as they hate these names as being lowly and ridiculous, they love the name of lord, they demand it, and snatch it up with joyful ears. Hence the spiritual title is trodden underfoot, and the temporal, earthly one is assumed; so that every bishop in the court of his diocese seeks to be called lord and to be feared for his secular power. In addition, the objectives of their wicked desires are crowned by the fact that, abusing the law of speaking, they prefer gentile surnames to titles; as if indeed they do not become adequately famous through the brilliance of their office, and as if their family is an honor to the bishopric instead of the bishopric's being an honor to their family. Those who show themselves unworthy of the high rank of their order do injury to that order as by a blast of terrestrial wind. For they do not strive to be advanced to the pontificate in order to erect a bridge (from which the pontifices derive their names) by which simpler men may pass over to life; but so that by living unnaturally they may become a jumping-off place to death.[91] Nor do they nourish with holy abundance the poor of Christ, but exalt their own family and homes with the wealth of Christ. Surely I do not lie about this! Count up the cloisters of the episcopal abbeys: count the daughters-in-law, matrons, boys, girls, flocks of women servants, babies' playthings, nurses running about in throngs. How much more admirably did the holy Augustine, who refused to live with his sister, say in setting forth his memorable first principle, "Those who are with my sister are not my sisters."[92] The result is, since they abuse the bishoprics that they have acquired, that they have no honor among the people and by debasing their high office are despised along with it.

Let me say this, and perhaps I may say it to no purpose. Nevertheless, we dare the sea, the storms and craggy shoals,

barbaros, alioque sub celo nationes, lucri studio, multa cura, periculo magnoque labore experimur insani prorsus ac dementes. Que sane mercatura facilior[389] minusque discriminis continens et emolumenti plus redundans quam sacrorum? Magnum ducitur seculari commercio si certis periculis certisve laboribus centenarius trigenarium pepererit, esto etiam quinquagenarium. At in lege[390] Levitica semel emitur unde annuis circulis millenario millenarius redeat aut geminet. Haud luso![391] Gozadinus, ut pomposie pater evaderet, quatuor millibus emit emendi licentiam totidemque ei qui venderet sacra erogatione porrexit. Provida[392] nimirum impense iactura octo millibus mercari ducatis, ut annali vicissitudine millia quatuor emetantur. Proxime diocesis pastor quinque milibus constitit, minutis vix totidem licet. Felix utique emptio que anniversaria prope id revehat;[393] sed haud[394] minore tributo emit alius abbatiam unde abraderet non minora. Omitto feraces prebendas et pinguia sacerdotia, que[395] pari vindemia proveniunt. Sed que usura, que navigatio tam secunda, que tam provida ratio mercandi iugi adeo infallibilique ferar augmento? Ingens, crede, sapere est paupertinam avitamque substantiam in aurum liquare et emptione adipisci unde annus tibi vel summam vel auctam remittat de portatis. Itaque nichil mirum si obesi genas, si anulatis manibus, si purpuratis cucullis incedunt, denique si luxuria in moribus, si in animo superbia repullulat.

Verum sinamus vaccas pingues in monte Samarie et redeamus unde est decisa narratio, a qua, tamquam nondum omne soluisses,[396] ita[397] ratiocinationem abruperas.

P-39. Et quis, inquam, superest?

V-40. Cunctorum, meo iudicio, difficillimus nec de pari extricabilis : cur Deus ipse, cum dicatur et laudetur omnium ore prophetarum Pater et Dominus, nusquam Magister Deus auditur?

389. falacior V.
390. lege *om.* V.
391. luso: apparently a coined verb. *Cf.* lusantes, note 448.
392. pro invidia V.
393. redeat V.
394. aut V.
395. qua V.
396. *ex* soluisset *corr.* V.
397. ita *om.* V.

heat, cold, monsters of land and water, pirates and barbarians, and nations under another sky, all from our desire for profit, with much trouble, danger, and great labor. We must be insane and out of our minds! After all, what commercial venture is easier, less dangerous, and more profitable than that of the sacred ministry? In world trade it is considered a great success if, despite the certain dangers and work, one receives a profit of thirty, perhaps even fifty, percent. But in the law of the Levite priesthood an investment of a thousand gives a return of a thousand, or twice that, annually.[93] I am not joking! Gozzadino, so that his father might go about in pomp, bought him the buying license for four thousand and presented in payment just as much to the one who sold the sacred rites.[94] So his foresighted outlay of eight thousand ducats earns four thousand annually. The bishopric of the nearest diocese costs five thousand, and it brings in nearly as much in small lots. Lucky indeed is the purchase that annually brings almost its price as a return! But another, for no less money, buys an abbey from which he will derive no less. I pass over the fruitful state allowances and rich priesthoods, which produce an equal harvest. But what usury, what navigation is so favorable, what method of trade so careful, that I am borne along with a constant and unfailing profit? Believe me, it is a great thing to know how to melt one's poor ancestral possessions into gold and to purchase a means of producing annually either that sum or a larger one from the revenues! And so it is not at all remarkable if they strut about fat in the cheeks, with ringed hands and purple hoods, in short, if extravagance flourishes in their customs and pride in their hearts![95]

But let us leave the "fat cows on the mount of Samaria"[96] and return to the point where the narrative was cut off, where, as if you had not yet made everything clear, you interrupted your explanation.

P-39. And who, I say, is left?

V-40. In my opinion the most difficult of all, and not readily explainable: since God Himself is spoken of and praised by the tongue of all the prophets as Father and Lord, why is He never called God the Master?

P–40. Eia, difficiliora abs te[398] manebam! Attentionem exaggerasti meis sensibus dum nodum[399] ipsum ancipiti adeo dubietate incipiens suspenderas. Sed, reor, vel[400] e vestigio perspicaci ratiocinatione absolvam, vel ceu nexum Alexander Gordianum, difficultate explicandi reiecta, precidam.

Meministi superioribus esse prolatum hoc ipsum quod dominus diceretur imperiose[401] cuiusdam summeque vim potestatis designare, ut, qui vere dominus extet, liceat ei ulla sine parentium refragatione efficere cuncta que cupiat. Divine autem potestati, quemadmodum condidit omnia, sic dempta prorsus omni repugnantia, famulantur universa. Nos vero quibus imperamus, quatenus fieri valeat quod iubetur, necesse est voluntatis nostre speciem, modum, et ordinem eos ipsos qui debeant parere moneamus. At Deitas ipsa, simplici invariabilique sue maiestatis nutu, simul docendo iubet docetque iubendo quod a creato natura perfici destinat; ut quod nos per temporales motus iubemus et docemus pura dumtaxat divina voluntate compleatur. Nam docere et iubere, diverse mortalibus actiones, idem sunt Deo quod simpliciter velle. Cum igitur, obtemperante illi universa[402] natura, nequaquam oporteat docere quod velit, sed tantummodo velle quod fiat, Dominus legitur, non magister. Pater autem, quia creavit cuncta et creata componit et servat, pietate iustissima nuncupatur.

V–41. Delectasti me vehementr tum eleganti serie narrationis, tum ipsa multo magis veritate summe, quam alias exagitatam nusquam audivi; et dubitavisse opere[403] pretium fuit, quoniam indiscusse rei materiam lumine rationum meis, et si qui forte

---

398. abs te dificiliora V.
399. nondum V.
400. velut V.
401. impiose P.
402. diversa V.
403. opere opere P.

P–40. Well, I was expecting something more difficult from you! By beginning with so wavering an uncertainty and holding back the knotty point itself, you made me give you all my attention. But I think either I will solve it at once with clear reasoning or I will cut it off as Alexander did the Gordian knot, thus dispensing with the difficulty of explanation![97]

You remember we brought out by what was said earlier that calling a man lord indicates the might of a certain very high power of command, so that the man who truly is a lord can accomplish all that he desires without any opposition from his subjects. Moreover, the divine power, as it has made all things, therefore is served by the whole universe without any refusal. But it is necessary for us, so that our orders may be carried out when we give them, to teach the appearance, manner, and arrangement of our wishes to those who are to obey. But Deity itself, by the simple and unvarying will of its majesty, simultaneously commands by teaching and teaches by commanding what nature intends to be accomplished by its creatures; so that what we through our temporal activities both command and teach is fulfilled by the pure divine will alone. For teaching and commanding, two different activities for mortals, are to God the same as simply willing. Since therefore, because all nature obeys Him and it is not necessary for Him to teach what He wills but only for Him to will what is to be done, He is called Lord, not Master; and because He created all things and directs and preserves His creations, He is addressed as Father with the truest piety.

6. The Good Life

V–41. I have enjoyed very much your fine exposition, and even more the true facts of your summation, which I have nowhere else heard related; and it was worth my while to have had doubts, since by the clarity of your reasoning you

lecturi sunt, oculis illustrasti.[404] Ceterum, quia usque huc propitia veritate meis questionibus satisfactum est, quatenus reliquie antelate ambiguitatis nulle resideant, cupio exolvas quod nisi admirabundus pensare nequeo, quid amicus ille tuus ab eo vite statu, quo satis clarus, satis etiam carus, tum civibus, tum exteris ducebatur, ad imitatem huiuscemodi[405] scholasticam maioribus functus sese contraxerit.

P–41. Haud tu quidem unus, verum et alii cause nescii, hoc ipsum stupent, et hoc est quod sepenumero sermones vulgi fatigat, quod eorum quibus admirantur rationes prorsus ignorant quam sibi in aula successerit. Diserte adeo copioseque libris intexuit ut me assertore non egeat. Pariet fortasse hactenus voluptatem otiosis utilitatemque descriptio. Nempe bene vivendi paucis notitia, paucissimis facultas, patet; neque enim que probantur[406] ab ineruditis continuo eligenda sunt,[407] nec sanus omnino quem medicine iudicant[408] imperiti. Dixerim quod vel tute admireris vel risent minus advertentes, prorsus uti cupias ita vivere bonam vitam semper dici non oportere.

V–42. Quenam, amabo, alia bona[409] est, si qua fruaris optato non est?

P–42. Uti minime constat quicumque letatur[410] bene letari (alias poeta nequaquam mala mentis gaudia protulisset), ita cuicumque temporalibus ad nutum frui contigit, haud continuo feliciter vivit. Hac namque ratione qui adulteriis, qui rapinis, qui sero luxu exultarent, et stulti et insensati voluptatibus emarcentes bene vivere dicerentur, quorum licet voti compotem statum sapiens nemo probaverit. Atqui primum omnium ea una vita bona est, qua hic bene merendo pervenitur ad vitam celestem.[411] Sed presens intentio non de his qui, defecatis usquequaque desideriis, e ceno

---

404. illustrati V.
405. huhuiscemodi V.
406. probatur PV.
407. vult PV.
408. indicare V.
409. bonam V.
410. letetatur V.
411. celestem *addidi*.

The Good Life

have illuminated the substance of an undiscussed subject for my eyes and for the eyes of any who will by chance read this. But because my questions have so far been satisfied with pleasant truth, I wish in order to leave no remnants of doubt that you would explain a matter that I cannot ponder without amazement: why that friend of yours retired from a condition of life in which he was deemed quite famous, even beloved, not only by citizens, but by foreigners, to the low rank of schoolmaster after performing more important tasks.[98]

P-41. Not only you but also others, being ignorant of the reason, are puzzled by this fact, and this very often occupies the conversations of ordinary people, because the thinking on which their wonder is based does not comprehend what his circumstances were in the court. He has so learnedly and copiously explained it in his books that he does not need me as an advocate.[99] Perhaps an outline to this extent will give pleasure and profit to those with leisure time. To be sure, the knowledge of how to live well is available only to a few, and the ability to a very few; in fact, things that are approved of by the uneducated are not consequently preferable, nor is that man necessarily healthy who is pronounced so by those unskilled in medicine. I would say, because you regard him with astonishment and less observant men laugh at him, that as a result the way you desire to live ought not always to be called the good life.

V-42. What other life is good, tell me, if it is not one where you can enjoy what you wish for?

P-42. As it is not agreed that whoever rejoices rejoices in a good way (otherwise the poet would not have written about the sinful joys of the mind[100]), thus whoever happens to enjoy temporal things as he pleases does not as a result live happily. For by this reasoning those who revel in adulteries, rapes, and midnight debaucheries, stupidly and senselessly wasting away from their excesses, would be said to live well, although no intelligent person could approve an existence that gratified such desires. But first of all, that life alone is good wherein by meriting well here one arrives at eternal life. However, my present intent does not concern those who, being completely

temporali in superna rapiuntur et dicere cum apostolo queunt:
"Nostra conversatio in celis est"; sed de his qui in vita civili
versantur transcurrit, in qua tenor vite corruptibilis minore
solicitudine minoreve crimine et honestiore voluptate ac libertate
uberiore peragitur. Reris, arbitror, aulicam me fortasse dicturum,
quoniam regnantibus familiares reverendi civibus ac pene imperare principali aura videantur.

V–43. Haud reor, nec parem abs te sententiam manebam. Et si
protulisses, lucem tue mentis, quam hactenus perspicuam sensi,
caligare censuissem! Imo, nulla alia miserior, incertior, discriminosior ac anceps, perditaque magis suique prorsus ignara.
Stipendia unius voluntate ac voluptate donantur, varia inconstantia, velut humani et precipue malignorum variant affectus.
Mane places, vesperi uno vel altero emulantis susurrulo eiceris.
Preterea datur vel quod[412] ab innoxiis eripitur, vel quod[413] tribuentis arbitrio rapiatur. Omne tempus, hora omnis, suspenditur.
Prandes, cenas, quiescis, iuberis ad aulam, ilico surgendum iter
imperatur.[414] Ire necesse est, quamquam mala valitudo, necessitas
familiaris, domesticarumque occupationum utilitas revocet. Vades,
inquam, per estum, per nives, per saxa, per hostes, per certa
discrimina. Tanti est mensurna provisio regiisque penetralibus
non excludi et dicier, verbi causa, famulus domini Padue. Bellus
nimirum titulus, tantisque periculis emendus! Tranquillius,
mehercule, mediocris fortune quivis e civibus nostris ac liberius
vitam degit, seque absolutius possidet.

P–43. Modo michi sapere videris, modo places! Verebar, uti
vulgus, ne aulari fulgore perstringereris. Nam si familiaritas
dilectioque regnantium, non, inquam, omnium sed eorum tantummodo qui sapientia et virtute principantur, inter optanda

---

412. quidem P.
413. quidem P.
414. imparatur P.

The Good Life

purged of their desires, are carried off on high from worldly uncleanliness and are able to say with the apostle, "Our abode is in Heaven."[101] But it does touch upon those who are engaged in civil life in which the course of life, though liable to corruption, is run with fewer worries or reproaches, and more decent pleasures and abundant freedom. You imagine, I suppose, that perhaps I am going to speak of court life, since the intimates of rulers seem to be revered by the citizens and seem almost to command with a princely aura.

V-43. I do not imagine it, nor was I expecting any such statement from you! And if you had made one, I would have thought the light of your mind, which until now I considered brilliant, had grown dark! On the contrary, no other life is more miserable, uncertain, full of peril and doubt, more corrupt and ignorant of its own self. Salaries are granted at the will and pleasure of one man, with varying irregularity as human feelings vary, and especially those of spiteful men. You are welcomed in the morning; in the evening, thanks to the whispers of one or another rival, you are tossed out. Furthermore, what is given to you is either seized from innocent people or can be taken away at the discretion of the giver. At all times, every hour, you are in suspense. You may be having breakfast, dining, or sleeping: you are summoned to court, your journey is ordered to be undertaken immediately. It is essential to go, even though bad health, family requirements, or pressing domestic interests call you back. You will go, I say, through heat, snow, and rocks, through the midst of enemies and certain dangers. So important is it to you to have the monthly provision and not be shut out from the royal inner chambers, and to be called, for example, a servant of the lord of Padua! Surely a beautiful title and one worthy of being bought by such great dangers! By heaven, any one of our citizens of modest fortune passes his life more tranquilly and freely and possesses himself more completely.

P-43. Now you seem to me to be wise, now you please me! I was afraid that, like the common crowd, you were enthralled by the splendor of the court. For if the friendship and love of rulers, not, I mean, of all, but only of those who rule with

numeratur, eis tamen ipsis famulatu[415] servitur, proprieque abnegatio voluntatis est. Miserrima tamen illorum et infelicissima quibus infidis ac levibus obtemperare contigerit.[416] Quod sapiens Hebreus non ignorans oravit: "Animo infronito, Domine, et irreverenti ne tradideris me." Sed quoniam ita sentis, consequitur ut, omissa curiali, de reliquis[417] quenam extet iocundior vita perquiramus.

Haudquaquam[418] inpresentiarum omnes per felicitatis numeros componere molior[419] hunc quem feliciter vivere hic statuo, neque[420] eam vitam quam plerique[421] audacius spondere presumpserunt quam monstrare potuerunt. Quis enim rimari ad exactum fragmenta quibus vite mortalis felicitas consummatur turbato otio tardoque speraverit ingenio? Sed que inveniri parique valeat molior. Neque hunc felicem ab hominum morbis ac moribus segregem fingo. Nonne extet iniurium ducere cum hominibus vitam consentire et malle cum hominibus mala non sentire? At secundior[422] si conditio tutior liberiorve contingat, hunc optabili vita frui libera satis voce confiteri possumus. Tribus hec[423] rebus, quantum ad presens attinet, loco, sufficientia, et opera comparatur.[424] Porro cum urbanis alii menibus, hi ruris libertate magis delectentur, quid habeat voluptatis et commoditatis villa tametsi prope cunctorum attestatione predicetur, minime tamen pigebit in illius paulisper iocunditate versari.[425]

V–44. Quin etiam magnopere suscipiam gratum; nam quo ab ruris abiuncti deliciis vivimus, hoc suavius audimus. Sed in multis plus valet avaritia quam natura. Quippe iste, celo aperto, virenti solo, et fontes visere et colles nemoraque gaudet. Ille[426]

---

415. famulari P.
416. contingerit V.
417. reliquarum PV.
418. haud quamquam V.
419. molior *addidi*.
420. namque V.
421. plerumque V.
422. securior V.
423. hoc V.
424. comperatur V.
425. servari V.
426. illa PV.

wisdom and virtue, are counted among desirable possessions, still even they must be given service, and one's own wishes must be foregone. However, the most wretched and unhappy life belongs to those whose lot it is to obey unreliable and fickle men. The wise Hebrew, not being ignorant of this, prayed, "Lord, do not hand me over to a rash and irreverent mind."[102] But since you perceive this, it follows that, omitting the court, we must inquire which of the other kinds of life is pleasing.

I do not at present attempt to describe through all categories of happiness this man whom I consider as living happily here, nor that life which most men have presumed to promise more rashly than they have been able to show. For who, when his leisure is disturbed and his mind slowed down, could expect to examine in detail the fragments of which the happiness of mortal life is made? But I am aiming for a life that can be found and created. I do not picture this happy man isolated from the disorders and habits of mankind. Would it not be wrong to agree to live with men and prefer not to feel the troubles of men? But if one happens to have a fairly safe and free existence, we can admit readily enough that he is enjoying a desirable life. This life, as far as it relates to the present, is attained by three things: location, adequate income, and occupation. Now, since some are satisfied by city walls but others more by the freedom of the country, even though the pleasures and conveniences of a country home are proclaimed by nearly everyone, still we shall not mind discussing its delights for a little while.

7. *Country versus City Life*

V–44. No, indeed, I shall be very glad to. For the farther we live from the joys of the country, the sweeter they are to hear about. But in many men greed is stronger than nature. To be sure, one man delights in seeing the springs and hills and forests under the open sky and on the green earth. But another

vero sese muris sepit, terminis angustat, et celum, sidera, ipsum quoque solem, cum latissime benignitate divina mortalibus offerantur, intercipit sibi, ut nec ortum intueri nec occasum, quin vix meridie sublimen, queat.

P-44. Ita est, et libet hinc Flacciano[427] inclamare preconio: "Beatus ille, qui procul negotiis, ut prisca gens mortalium, paterna bobus exercet rura suis, solutus omni fenore." Hanc certe beatitudinem semper amavi, sed potui sinistra sorte admirari magis quam imitari. Quod, si liceret componere michi fatum,[428] urbicarum vanitatum illecebris anteferrem. Preposuit olim Dioclitianus imperio, et Ludovicus, felicissimus regum, nemorali[429] quiete vite reliquias consecravit. Quidni iuvet ruris ameni sedes preter glareosum aque labentis rivum, colliculis austrum ab aquilone spectantibus? Hic equidem salubrior lene spirantis aure flatus, sedes urbana omni a fece remotior, a vanitate, a luxuria, a falsitate, ab invidia. Istic nec vitiorum exempla contaminant, improbe nec voluptates exurunt, emula nec solicitudo cogitationes dissipat. Vernant floribus colles, herbent prata, gemmascunt[430] pomeria, aviumque concentu[431] nemus omne susurrat. Quanta illa iocunditas messium, quanta vindemiarum! Nulla delectatio equiparat. Quis enumeret quas fruges, quos fructus autumni reddat ubertas? Quam iuvat[432] manu poma legere[433] que condas dum iuvenescentia succedant, incorrupta suavitate mansura! Quanto cum applausu exeniabis amicis racemos quoque, pariliter suspensos[434] liciis, non suo tempore leto miraculo hospitibus apponendos.

Numquam damnabile otium, numquam segnities iniqua, numquam meditatio surrepit, quia labor utilis semper succedit. Nullo namque[435] tempore quod ares, quod fodias, quod plantes, quod vellas, quod amputes, vel inseras serasve non restat. Pluvia vero ab agris arcente, aut lentis qualos brillis aut cistas gallinarias

---

427. flagiciano V.
428. factum V.
429. memorali V.
430. gemmescunt PV
431. contentu V.
432. vivat P.
433. legere poma V.
434. suspendere PV.
435. nonquam V.

surrounds himself with walls, hems himself in by boundaries, and cuts off from himself the sky, the stars, even the very sun, although these are offered to mortals far and wide through divine generosity, so that he is not able to see the sun either rise or set, and in fact barely sees it on high at midday.

P–44. That is true. We can here quote Horace: "Happy the man who, far from businesses, like the ancient race of mortals ploughs his ancestral land with his oxen, free of all usury."[103] This state of happiness I have certainly always loved, but because of unlucky fate I have had to admire it more than imitate it. If I were permitted to arrange my lot, I would prefer rural contentment to the enticements of the city's vanities. Once Diocletian preferred it to an empire; and Louis, most fortunate of kings, consecrated the remaining years of his life to peacefulness in the forest.[104].

Why would not an abode in the charming countryside be delightful, beside a pebbly brook of flowing water, with little hills facing south and turning their backs to the north? Here indeed is a healthful breeze of gently wafting air, a site far from all impurities of the city, from vanity, luxury, falsity, and envy. Here instances of vice do not contaminate nor sinful pleasures burn, nor does jealous care dispel one's thoughts. The hills bloom with flowers, the meadows are verdant, the apple trees bud forth, and all the woods rustle with the song of birds. How great is the joy of the harvest, of the vintage! There is no delight to equal it. Who can count the grain and fruit that the abundance of autumn brings? How pleasant it is to pluck apples to store up when they are ready and ripening, their sweetness destined to remain uncorrupted. To what great applause will you give as presents to your friends clusters of grapes as well, hanging evenly on trellises, set before your guests out of season by a happy miracle.

Never do reprehensible inactivity, or hurtful sloth, or periods of meditation creep upon you, because there is always useful work at hand. For at no time is there not something for you to plough, to dig, to plant, to pick, to prune, to graft, to sow. Then when the rain keeps you from the fields, you weave baskets or chicken coops from pliant willow and withes

intexis vel quibus arborum colligatur ubertas. Sunt et calopodia, sunt dalmate[436] a luto hiberno munimenta, que, imbre coercente vel longis noctibus, fabrices. Nunc[437] est item naxarum et gurgustiorum opera superabundans[438] ad pisces cancrosve inescandos; preterea, aut rastra stivasque instaurabis aut plaustra resarcies, nec furcarum opera accedet uncorumque frustra. At simul ista ad exactum maneant, iuvabit retia carcaresque[439] volucribus struere. Interim sine ambitione, sine odio, sine improba spe, fluit etas innoxie. Iam vero, quanta illa felicitas gregum et armentorum colentium et pascentium rura tua! Nam, prodente iam progne diluculum, sedulus ruricola surgit, vernaculos excitat, ministeria distinguit : hos arare, hos arva stercorare, ad serendum illos, alios ad plantandum feracia extirpandumve noxia destinat. Inter hec pater ipse ruris emissos operarios paula mora insequitur, falculamque gestans fundi oras ambit, modo coronatas plantariis fossas, arature modo ordines, ut trite glebe, ut rubis radicibusque emundatum equor appareat. Speculabundus operas singula recenset, deinde[440] luxuriantes ipse palmites[441] succidit, retorquet ordinibus oberrantes. Et peragrando ruris plagas corpus vegetat et pascit animum pleni agri culturam speculando. Plantaria deinceps fructiferarum arborum, nunc racemiferos ordines, nunc propagines pubescentes lustrat. Tum ut herbeant prata, ut pascant greges, ut iumenta contemplatur, arcere item sues a satis, capellas a pampinis commonet pueros. Visere postremo nemusculum migrat, quasque portiones[424] igni dedendas, quas domesticis asservandas usibus, quasque suillis animo premetitur. Denique, beata functus[443] circumspectione, ad atria redit, et ipsa exercitatione, vigorato calore, ac digestione peracta exuscitatur appetitus.[444] Ipse letus sine metu, sine solicitu-

---

436. dalmare PV.
437. non PV
438. superhabundas V.
439. *ex* carcere que *corr.* V, s *inser. supra.*
440. de hinc V.
441. palmittes ipse V.
442. portiones *addidi.*
443. fructus V.
444. exuscitatur appetitus *om.* V.

Country versus City Life

to bind the productive trees. There are also clogs and wooden shoes, protection from the winter mud, for you to make when rain keeps you in, or during the long nights. Now there is likewise plenty of work with weels and creels for catching fish or crabs; you will also repair hoes and plough handles or mend wagons; and work on the forks and hooks will not be useless. As soon as those things are in order, it will be good to construct nets and snares for birds.

Meanwhile, without ambition, without hatred, without improper expectations, time flows on innocently. Now indeed, how great is that bounteousness of flocks and herds that inhabit and feed on your land! For when the swallow is already proclaiming the break of day, the hard-working farmer arises, rouses his house-servants, and assigns the chores: he chooses some to plough, some to manure the fields, some to sow, and others to set out fertile plants or dig up weeds. In the midst of all this the father of the farm himself follows shortly after the workers who have been sent forth; and carrying a pruning hook he walks around the boundaries of his farm, visiting now the millraces crowned with new-planted orchards, now the regular rows of plowed land, where the clods of earth have been crushed so that a level surface appears, cleared of brambles and roots. Looking over the work he considers each thing individually; then he cuts down the over-luxuriant vine sprigs and twists back those wandering out of the rows. By roving through the countryside his body grows healthy, and his soul is fed by the sight of the cultivation of the whole farm. Next he inspects the orchards of fruit trees, then the rows of grapevines, then the flourishing shoots. Afterwards, so that the meadows may be green for the herds to graze in, looking at the beasts of burden he cautions the boys to keep the pigs away from the crops and the goats from the vine shoots. Finally he goes to look at the scrub and figures out in his mind what parts are to be burned, what saved for household uses, and what for the pigs. At last, having performed his cheerful inspection, he returns home, his appetite aroused by the exercise itself, by the generated warmth, and by his completed digestion. He himself, happy, without fear, without worry, eats the

dine, mandit oblata, luxu nullo, strepitu nullo infesta, sed nulla quoque arte saporata. Nam sapor et mense condimentum genita exercitio fames est; iuvant cuncta quia sapiunt cuncta. At luxuriam nil delectat urbanam quia nil sapit, et non sapit quia natura non cupit; que non cupit quia non capit. Iste vero avide ingerit quia bene digerit; bene autem digerit quoniam citra vim ignis intimi comedit viresque tempestiva exercitatione corroborat.

Idcirco in huiuscemodi vite genere iudices frustra sunt nec medici procurantur; quippe ad naturam vivitur. Labor membra durat noxiumque exudat humorem. Podagra, scabies, impetigo, ceteraque morborum agmina urbanas comitantia delicias raro contingunt, nec diurturnis tabent morbis verum senio potius; aut, vi laboris exiccato[445] humore, deserunt ipsi[446] potius vitam quam illis vita deficiat. Nempe interquiescendum campestribus operis refectionem mandat. Ipse de hinc bovilia oviliaque, tum etiam haras revisit, claustra refirmat, coaptat, premunitque[447] presepia. Vitulos hic iacentes, inde lusantes[448] edulos, illic exoptantium matres turmas agnorum computat. Crescit animus, dilatatur spes tanta sobole et iuventute domestica. Anserum vero gallinarumque studium, quod, uti ruralis commodi minime extrema portio, est nullatenus contemnendum,[449] matronarum cure cessit. Sunt enim mensis repentinis quotidianisque peropportunum[450] supplementum.[451] Pape, quanta delectatione, deciduo iam sole, ex dumetis gregum armentorumque coitio, remugiunt alumnis iuvence; capelle ovesque, tarda implorantibus ubera natis, balatu redire se nuntiant. Omne curtile hinc natorum, hinc parentum piis affectibus resonat, he quatenus expleant ieiunia filiorum, hi quo matribus subeant. Quanto sanctius tutiusque bucularum,

---

445. oxiccato P.
446. ipi V.
447. premiuntque P.
448. lusantes: *cf.* luso, note 391.
449. contemnendus P.
450. pre opportunum P.
451. sunt . . supplementum *om.* V.

proffered food, which has been impaired by no excesses, no disturbances, and is unseasoned by art. For the savor and seasoning of his meal is the hunger born from exercise; all things are pleasing because all things have savor. But nothing delights the extravagant tastes of the city-dweller because nothing has savor; and there is no savor for there is no natural desire. The desire does not exist because it is not possible. But the farmer eats heartily because he digests well, and his digestion is good since he does not eat more than he burns for energy, and he builds up his strength by regular exercise. Therefore, in a life of this sort judges are useless and doctors are not needed; truly one lives in accordance with nature. Labor hardens the body and sweats out harmful humors. Gout, itch, impetigo, and legions of the other disorders accompanying city indulgences rarely occur. Men do not waste away with chronic ailments but rather with old age; or, when the humors are dried out by dint of hard labor, men desert life rather than life's failing them.

The farmer orders rest to be taken now and then, to refresh the men for the work in the fields. He himself next revisits the ox stalls and sheepfolds, then the coops; he strengthens the bars and fits them and reinforces the stables. He counts the calves lying here, the frolicking kids, and there the flocks of lambs eager for their mothers. His heart swells, his hopes are enlarged by so many offspring and domestic young ones. And since the care of geese and chickens is far from being the least useful in the country, it is by no means to be scorned, but is entrusted to the diligence of the matrons. These fowls are certainly a very convenient supplement to both unexpected and regular meals. With what great joy, when the sun has already set, do the flocks and herds gather from the thickets! The young cows give answering lows to their young; the goats and sheep bleat their return to their offspring, who are crying for the slow-arriving udders. The whole yard resounds, on one side with the dutiful affectionate sounds of the young, on the other with those of the mothers, the latter in order to appease the hunger of their young, the former to get up to their dams. How much purer and safer it is to see the

ovium, capellarumque facies et voces audire malim quam tube hostilis timpanive crepitum ac mercenariorum acclamationes bellatorum! Illi sicut gignuntur affectus edunt, isti pro tristibus mentiuntur leta plerumque, et "iuvat"[452] sepenumero iterant, ubi in arcano mortem imprecantur. Armenta gregesque preterea numquam sine incremento stabula repetunt; hi vero iniquitatis operarii sine iactura numquam proficiscuntur.[453] Casa ergo, curtile, caula, septaque omni mugientium remugientiumque letitia redundant. Exuberantia interim nurus matroneque multralia referunt, suspenditur recens fumo caseus, exuccatus arcili reconditur. Serum mox infantibus puerisve custodibus recoquitur, unde recocta nominatur, opimatque cenam. Residuum satellites canes potant.[454] Huiuscemodi nempe studiis nec bella nec rapine fraudesve struuntur. Cum hilaritate cenatur, absque suspicione dormitur.

Habet etiam haud insuavis occupatio festos dies, nam pueri qua nidulentur aves inquirunt, aut prenotatos nidos exhauriunt. Retibus alii adultas laqueisve edaces inescant, fallunt sonoris hi[455] frondibus aut implicant visco, pars sepes araneis et aplude[456] cumulos inumbrant. Cura alia versat alios, quorum alii rivos fluentaque rimantur, et spicis inherentes immersis aut gurgustiis inclusos pisces educunt; pars[457] iaculis, pars sagenis insecuntur. Venandi vero alacritas, quam avide animos complectitur! Glandiferos enim lucos, feraces lacunas annotant, ubi tendiculis apros captent aut cane ac venabulis sternant. Captum exultatione triumphali in tecta reportant. Vescuntur festis epulis, vicinosque prede hostilis distributione dignantur. Nec scio cunctas nec explicare queo, toto licet itinere narrans, fortunati ruricole voluptates.

V-45. Quamquam illas ita edisseras ut esse fortunatissimum quemque ruris accolam affirmare descriptio premissa compellat,

---

452. vivat V.
453. reproficiscuntur P.
454. potat PV.
455. hi sonoris V.
456. ablunde P ablonde V.
457. par V.

faces and hear the voices of heifers, sheep, and goats than the blare of an enemy's trumpet or clash of his drum, and the shouts of mercenary warriors! As kindly feelings arise, farmers express them; but soldiers for the most part falsely say they are happy when they are sad and often repeat "We're having a good time" when secretly they are praying for death. Furthermore, flocks and herds never return to the stables without a profit; but these workers of iniquity never set forth without expense. Therefore the cottage, yard, sheepfold, and all the enclosures of animals lowing and lowing back in answer echo with happiness. Meanwhile the daughters-in-law and the matrons bring back the overflowing milk pails; cheese fresh from the smoke is hung up, and when it has been pressed, it is stored in a box. Then the whey is cooked again for the babies or their youthful caretakers (whence it is called *ricotta*), and it enriches the dinner. The attendant dogs drink the residue. Certainly, amid occupations like these, no one plans wars or plunderings or deceptions. Dinner is eaten with joyfulness, sleep is taken free from suspicion.

This not-unpleasant work also has its holidays, for the boys search for birds' nests or empty the nests they have previously noted. Some lure the greedy adult birds by means of baited nets or snares, others trick them with rustling leaves or entangle them in birdlime, and some cover hedges and piles of chaff with fowling nets. A different interest engages others, who explore rivers and flowing streams and pull out fish stuck on immersed hooks or caught in fish-traps; some try for them with spears, others with seines. And the liveliness of hunting, how eagerly it seizes their minds! For they take note of the acorn-bearing groves and the fertile ponds where they can catch wild boars with nooses or bring them down with dogs and hunting spears. When a boar is caught, they bring it home with triumphant exultation. They eat festive banquets and consider their neighbors worthy of a share of the fierce prey. I do not know nor can I describe, even if I use up our whole journey, all the pleasures of the fortunate country-dweller![105]

V-45.   Although you describe those pleasures in such a way that your words make me agree that every countryman is

nichilominus mirari non desino cur paucis ruranei[458] status urbanique[459] multis votum incesserit.

P–45. Quemadmodum delirantium et voluptates vanaque captantium,[460] nec non pompam laudis umbratilem illecebrasque fugaces, quam sapientium et eruditorum ac frugem vere virtutis amantium numerus maior impendet; ita sanctius et tranquillum vite genus paucioribus cessit. Namque alium ambitus involvit, alius avaritia raptatur, alter dum frui deliciis extuat turpiter servit. Nec sic me hos urbana impediri statione dicere presumas quasi sentirem hec vitia, ambitionem, cupiditatem, voluptates ad urbis cohabitationem mortales evocavisse. Laudabilia enim initia, ut ferme[461] solet, in pluribus improbi actus insecuti sunt. Sapientia, nempe, creatrix hominem condidit ut socio indigeret et delectaretur. Ideo commodissima ratio iocundissimaque ad communionem populos univit, quatenus sermonis quoque et obsequii mutua utilitate fruerentur. Verumque, ut vates ait: "Pauci quos equus amavit Jupiter et[462] ardens erexit ad ethera virtus." Ita perpauci quibus sese frui tumultuariisque a rebus vindicari[463] ac letari presentaneis contigisset.[464] Que sors quidem si cui indulta est, aut rus aut ruris par statio compensavit.

V–46. Libens haurio que doces; sed quid voto si cuncti ruris agerentur? Liberalium utique[465] artium philosophia, iuris ac medendi scientia, cultus denique morum prorsus absisteret. Attendis ipse quam villicolarum ab urbicolis[466] mores distent.

P–46. Magno ambitu fateor et civilem pariter urbanamque societatem opido humanam ad felicitatem attinere, quatenus omnifariarum artium et doctrinarum adminiculis[467] instantis vite imbecillitas instruatur. Verumtamen ita me agri amatorem suscipere noris ut in urbanis quoque moribus et virtute civili absolutum esse concipiam quem in summo nimirum felicitatis collocare ausim si cum[468] voluptate rusticationis asciverit dulcedinem[469] litterarum,

458. ruranei: apparently coined.
459. urbani quam PV.
460. septantium PV.
461. firme V.
462. aut V.
463. vendicare PV.
464. contingisset V.
465. utque V.
466. *ex* urbiculis *corr.* P.
467. aminiculis V.
468. cum *om.* V.
469. dulcedine V.

most fortunate, still I do not cease to wonder why a desire for country life comes to only a few, while city life attracts many.
P–45. Just as there is a greater number of people who foolishly pursue vain pleasures, the shadowy pomp of honor, and fleeting charms, than of men who are wise and learned and lovers of the rewards of true virtue, so a pure, calm sort of life is led by fewer people. For a desire for ostentation envelops one man, another is smitten by greed, still another is a base slave to the passions he burns to taste. Now, do not assume that I am hereby claiming that these people are ensnared by living in the city as if I believe that these vices —ambition, greed, passions—had necessarily enticed mortals to life in the city. In fact, for most people sinful activities have come, as a rule, after praiseworthy beginnings. Actually, the Creator's wisdom made man to need and enjoy companionship, and thus a very useful and pleasant plan has united people in communities in order that they may enjoy the mutual benefits of conversation and service. But, as the poet says: "There are few whom just Jupiter has loved and shining virtue has raised to the heavens."[106] So there have been very few whose lot it was to enjoy themselves, to be freed from tumultuous circumstances, and to be happy with the affairs of the moment. If indeed this fate has been granted to anyone, either the country or a place like the country has bestowed it.
V–46. It is a pleasure to hear what you say. But what if all were driven by a desire for the country? Surely the philosophy of the liberal arts, the sciences of law and medicine, in short, all civilized practices would henceforth cease. You yourself notice how different are the customs of farm people from those of city-dwellers.
P–46. I admit that in a broad sense civil and urban societies certainly tend toward human well-being, so that the frailty of our hard-pressed lives may be provided with the support of all sorts of skills and doctrines. You have learned to accept me as a great admirer of the country. Nevertheless, I would be so bold as to rank at the highest point of happiness the man whom I conceive to be free amid city ways and civil virtue, if only he could acquire the sweetness of literature

quatenus animi tranquillitate declinet potius urbis cupiditates quam virtutes. Atqui nosti[470] castitatem incontinentie prestare, plures tamen posthabent honorem castitatis. Sunt pariter qui ruris alacritatem norint et ament, preceps tamen error abducit. Civium sane collectio est uti multis cum multis, ruris vero secessio ut uni cum paucis sors iocunda contingat. Velut igitur indocti plures quam docti sunt, sic pauciores iter innoxium carpunt. In quo sane[471] Ravennatis sententia iuvat : "Etsi ceteri," inquit, "urbis rapiantur amore, mihi beatius est rure quam urbium[472] muris contineri, et prata florentia frondestresque umbras quam plateas porticusque lustrare, et item avium concentus[473] quam insane multitudinis fremitum[474] aure concipere. Quisquis denique urbicam sortem proferat, cedo, ruris ego antepono." Sic ille. Ast idem[475] sero non intellexit.

Unus pridem ex urbe nostra felicitatem rusticam auspicatus[476] seu solido iudicio seu vitiis infensus urbanis, Simeon a Statutis, locuplex quidem ac moderatus civis, etsi modice litteratus. Nam secessit in predium suburbanum; ibi stationem secus, adversa fronte, sacellum memoriam Virginis Matris construi et ornari curavit, ubi debitas laudum[477] vices Domino Deo reddebat. Reliquum temporis nunc equo, iam grandevus, interdum pedes sua rura circuibat, quorum glebas, Libio teste apud Aristotilem, nil adeo quam domini[478] vestigia fecundat. Colonos quoque modo attentiores presentia reddebat, modo remissos cohortationibus castigabat. Plerumque venatu piscatuque aut aucupiis indulgere una pergens exhortabatur. In his deliciis et animi tranquillitate, integer mentis senex diem obiit, fabricato humatus sacello.

Referam alterum in huiuscemodi genere felicitatis, Stenum, ortum educatumque rure suburbano, sed qui rura fortunasque

---

470. nosci P.
471. statim V.
472. urbi uni P.
473. conceptus V.
474. frenitum V.
475. indem V.
476. aspicatus V.
477. laudium V.
478. domini quam V.

with the pleasure of country living and in this way could avoid through tranquillity of mind the passions rather than the virtues of the city. And you know that chastity is preferable to incontinence, yet many ignore that honorable state. There are also those who know and love the joy of the country, yet rash error leads them away from it. To be sure, a gathering of citizens brings to many the pleasure of associating with many; but a retreat to the country offers to a person the pleasure of being with a few. Therefore, just as there are more unlearned people than learned, so fewer take the innocent way. In this regard a saying of the Ravennate is pertinent: "Even if others," he said, "are caught by love of the city, to me it is more blessed to be surrounded by the countryside than by city walls, to walk through flowering meadows and leafy shade instead of city squares and porticos, and to hear the singing of the birds instead of the uproar of the raving mob. In a word, let whoever wishes prefer his life in the city, but as for me, I'll take the country!"[107] Such was his feeling. And he did not learn too late.

Once a man from our city was pleased to move to the country, either from good judgment or in anger at the vices of the city. This was Simone degli Statuti,[108] a rich man and a temperate citizen, although of modest learning. He retired to a suburban estate, and there beside his house and facing it he had built and ornamented a chapel as a memorial to the Virgin Mother, where he rendered just praises to the Lord God. For the rest of his days, being now an old man, he went sometimes on horseback, sometimes on foot, around his farm, whose soil was fertilized by nothing so well as the footprints of the master, as Aristotle says, quoting the Libyan.[109] Also, by his presence he sometimes kept his tenants busier and sometimes chided them with admonitions when they were remiss. Often going with them, he encouraged them to engage in hunting, fishing, or bird-catching. In the midst of these pleasures and with a tranquil heart, the old man died sound of mind and was buried in the chapel he had built.

Let me tell you about another man with this sort of happiness, Steno,[110] born and reared in the suburban country-

exuperaret animum esset nactus. Sane dives agris, armentis, gregibus, multaque[479] familia: quatuor de quadraginta numerus erat, filii iam patres, nepotes ex fratribus predefunctis, et ipsi quoque parentes. Ampla domus frequens nuribus, pueris, adolescentibus, servis. Stenus autem ipse, vividus ac recens, iuvenili autoritate cuncta regebat. Equarum huic turme[480] dextrarios etiam alebat, electum genus equorum, quo honore in omni pene hesperia excellit Euganea. Huic iugalium boum, huic pascualium armenta septa complebant, capre insuper feteque haud facile numerabiles. Tantus preterea suine pecudis numerus quantus vix clauditur, etiam[481] ovium. Iam vero altilia quis enumeret, cum anseres ducenarium[482] prope transcenderent.

Quod ut minus ducatur[483] mirum, secus amnem Brentam domus iacebat, in quo et molendina habebat, non tantummodo familiarem ad usum, sed unde emolumenta quoque ampla referrentur. Quid dicam? Steni opes regias edes complectebatur, quibus ea magnitudine animi uteretur ut diversorium viatorum, et quo se conferret omnis nobilitas vaga, pateret. Lete liberaliterque susceptos magnifice habebat. Exuberantibus enim cunctarum rerum copiis, facile erat quovis eventu et adventu mensas instruere, gallina, capone, anaticulis, edo, agno,[484] suculis. Omitto columbulos quorum parentes geminis columbariis quasi apes effervebant. Ad fluminis adhuc[485] ripam lintres residebant. Repente[486] quispiam e familia iussus exigua mora emulis argento cum pisciculis aderat insperatus. Vecturas hospitum haud secus ac proprias ingenue[487] expleri iubebat; cubicula ei regia plume anserine dabat ubertas.

Quid moror? Nichil a felicitate[188] vite expetende[489] aberat preter notitiam litterarum, quarum usus,[490] si festos pluviosve[491] dies vel hibernarum spatia noctium temperare licuisset, foret; prorsus quantam habet presens vita summam[492] beatitudinis assecutus, sed quanta valet ignaris litterarum contingere, totam Stenus divitiarum, peculii, familie, loci sortitus est. Quis princeps,
    479. multusque PV.
    480. hinc fine P.
    481. aliis PV.
    482. ducentenarium PV.
    483. ducar PV.
    484. angno V.
    485. ad hec PV.
    486. repente om. V.
    487. ingene V.
    488. ad felicitatem PV.
    489. expectende V.
    490. usu PV
    491. pluviosque V.
    492. summa V.

side. He possessed a mind that surpassed his lands and fortune, though he was, to be sure, rich in fields, flocks, herds, and a large household. It was thirty-six in number, sons already fathers, nephews from dead brothers and also themselves parents. The spacious home was crowded with daughters-in-law, children, young people, servants. Steno himself, vigorous and fresh, ruled all with a lively authority. Herds of mares produced destriers, or war-horses, for him, a choice breed of horse, an achievement in which Padua surpasses almost all the west. Penned herds of plow-oxen and grazing animals made up a full complement for him and also breeding goats too numerous to be easily counted. There was besides so great a number of swine that they could scarcely be enclosed, and likewise of sheep. Who could count the fattened poultry, since the geese almost passed a total of two hundred! Lest you consider all this remarkable, his house was situated next to the Brenta River, where he also had mill-houses, not only for his personal use but also as a source of ample revenue. Need I say more? The dwelling place of Steno enclosed the riches of royalty, which he used in the generosity of his heart to provide a lodging for travelers and a gathering place for all the itinerant nobility. He kept in grand style those whom he had joyfully and freely taken in. For since the supply of all things was abundant, it was easy under any circumstances and for any arrivals to set a table with chicken, capons, ducklings, kids, lambs, and suckling pigs, not to mention the little doves whose parents swarmed like bees from twin columbaria. Skiffs lay beside the bank of the river; and when anyone of the household received a sudden order, with little delay he was ready quicker than expected with small silvery fish. Steno ordered conveyances to be supplied freely for the guests, as if their own. An abundance of goose down furnished royal beds for them.

Enough said. Nothing was missing from the happiness of his excellent life except the knowledge of literature, which would have enjoyably tempered the holidays or rainy days or long winter nights. Possessing the great amount of happiness that his life now holds, as much as can come to those ignorant of literature, Steno has acquired the blessings of riches, property,

quis urbanus paratius, letius, securiusve haberet cuncta que vita deposceret? Talis igitur vita meo in primis iudicio, si qua valet temporaliter esse leta vel fingi, eligenda videtur, quoniam innocens, tranquilla, secura, omnia sponte suppeditans.

V–47. Tanta vitam ruris laude dignaris, tam letam fecundamque[493] depingis, ut amorem non modo[494] et desiderium infuderis michi sed medullitus infixeris. Et iam piget non esse quod audio; sed unde queat securitas optata contingere, cum scateant omnia furore bellorum?

P–47. Hominum vitio, non ruris, bella excandent. Sic rure vitam probo, ut illud quoque in pacis regione constituam. Sed ab initio invaluit pravitas, ac per hoc urbes menite[495] et fossis aggeribusque munite[496] sunt quatenus vel aliena improbitas arceatur, vel propria defendatur. Si enim uspiam fuit vel esse innocentia fingi valet, menia armaque bellica frustra sint. Quippe inter bonos nec claustra nec tela necesse est intervenire; sed malignorum causa velut tormenta civilia sic defensionis excogitata sunt instrumenta. Quid, inquies, luporum ferarumve sevitia? Nonne insiliant ultro rebusque partis officiant? Ita Deus omnipotens hominem conditis prestare animantibus voluit, terrorique esse iussit, ut non modo conventum sed solitarium quidem, sublata causa necessitatis, fera non ausit impetere. Verum ne infantibus ac pecudibus insidiosa fames obesse compellat, quo se inviminet[497] villicus tegetes oviliaque obseptet, ultro villa suppeditabit. Moriferi,[498] preterea, fossata, rubi, spina rosifera, pruni, aliave arbusta, ambitu silvescente vallabunt.[499] Quid canes, vigilia fidelis? Provida certe hominum natura apposuit unde noxia queque vitari et parari conferentia valerent. Quemadmodum enim bos ad

---

493. letamque fecundam V.
494. meo V.
495. mente P.
496. immunite V.
497. inviminet: apparently coined.
498. moriferi: apparently coined.
499. valla habet V.

family, position. What prince, what city-dweller could possess more readily, happily, or securely all things that life could require? Such a life as this, then, in my opinion, if any temporal life can be happy or imagined to be so, seems preferable, since it is innocent, tranquil, carefree, and supplies all wants spontaneously.

V-47. You deem the country life worthy of so much praise, you depict it as so happy and productive, that not only have you infused love and longing for it in me, but you have fixed it deep into my heart! And now I regret that what I hear does not exist; but from what source can this desirable security arise when all the world is ravaged with the madness of war?

P-47. It is through the faults of men, not of the countryside, that wars flare up. I am so much in favor of life in the country that I even define it as the region of peace. But from the beginning wickedness has prevailed, and therefore the cities have been walled and fortified by trenches and mounds so that outside evils might be warded off or inside ones defended. For if innocence existed anywhere or could be imagined to exist, fortifications and the arms of war would be useless. Surely there is no need for bars nor weapons between good men; but because of the wrongdoers, just as political tortures have been devised, so have weapons of defense.

You may say, what of the savagery of wolves or wild animals? Do they not leap up of their own accord and harm things that have been created? Omnipotent God has willed man so to surpass all established living things and has commanded him to be such a source of terror that except out of necessity a wild beast would not dare attack him, not only when he is with a group but even when he is alone. But lest the threat of starvation compel a beast to attack children and domestic animals, the farm will readily furnish the farmer means to build huts and fence up the sheep pens. Furthermore, the mulberry trees, the ditches, the bramble bushes, the thorny rosebush, plum trees, and other trees growing wild all around will provide protection. What about the faithful watchdogs? Nature, provident of men, has put at hand all means by which harm can be avoided and help acquired. For as the

utilitatem agrestilem, sic ad tutelam ortus est canis, efficax prorsus arcere luporum insidias ac vulpium, et si quid aliud infestum obrepat.[500] Reliqua[501] vero indomite feritatis animalia ceu leones, pardos, tigres, dracones,[502] eminus a mortalium frequentia providens divinitas amovit.[503] Itaque rurestris vite sanctimoniam bella ferarum haud turbabunt, quo, minus cessantibus malignantium conatibus, iocunditate[504] fruatur ruris amator.

V–48. Lepide adeo copioseque ad postulata respondisti ut dubitavisse[505] non pigeat! Sed iam persuasum habeo dignam prima laude ruricole sortem, qui suum rus exerceat bove suo, vite suppeditans, nec necessitate sed iudicio et voluptate villam incolat. Quam vero huic proximam ducis, glisco, dum adhuc superat iter, evolvas.[506]

P–48. Aperire dudum meditor quem proximo in genere civilis felicitatis collocem. Primam constitui, ut usu[507] loquendi beatam velut obvios bonos homines vocitamus, eorum qui ruris ubertate ac libertate potirentur. Sed ab hac in urbem demigremus. Difficile primum explicare formulam beati civis ac longe, arbitror, difficilius invenire. Sed velut anteposui, magis compositos presens intentio complectitur. Sunt igitur quos vulgus miretur, quorumque faciem fortune veneretur et expetat.[508] Sed ut vulgi iudicium sic vota caligant, nec beata sors quam predicant nec beati ipsi continuo si adipiscantur quod exoptant. Unde haud ab iure Anaxagoras, seu quisquis fuit e sapientibus, percontanti quisnam felix esset: "Nullus eorum," inquit, "quos reputas." Neque illa quoque sententia aspernanda, felicitatem esse presentibus contentari. Si animum ratio componat conformetque, fortune dictio vera

500. obreptat V.
501. relique V.
502. dracos PV.
503. amonuit P.
504. iocunde PV.
505. *ex* dubitavisset *corr.* P.²
506. evolvat V.
507. usum V.
508. expectat V.

Country versus City Life

ox exists for its usefulness on the farm, so does the dog for the protection it affords and its efficiency in warding off the ambushes of wolves and foxes and any other dangerous creatures that might come by stealth. But other animals of unconquerable ferocity like lions, leopards, tigers, and snakes, have been removed from the communities of mortals by provident divinity. Thus the sanctity of rural life will not be disturbed by battles with wild beasts, and therefore, though the attacks of the wicked do not cease, the lover of the country enjoys happiness.

V-48. You have replied to my questions so charmingly and copiously that I do not regret having had doubts! But I was already persuaded that the lot of the country-dweller is worthy of the highest praise, the man who works his own farms with his own ox, making provision for his livelihood, and who does not inhabit a country home out of necessity but through good judgment and preference. What life do you consider next to this? I am eager for you to tell me, while we are still on our journey.

P-48. I am just now planning to disclose what man I would place in the next class of civic happiness. I determined as first in happiness, or blessed, as we say in common speech, just as we call affable men good, the life of those who partake of the abundance and freedom of the country. But let us move from this to the city. First, it is difficult to define the formula of a happy citizen and, I think, far more difficult to find one. But as I have explained before, my present intent concerns those who live more orderly lives. There are men, to be sure, whom the common people admire and whose fortune they revere and covet. But as the common people's judgment is clouded by their desires, the lot that they praise is not a happy one, nor are they themselves consequently happy if they obtain what they long for. Hence Anaxagoras, or some one of the philosophers, was not incorrect when he replied to a person asking him who was a happy man, "Not one of those whom you think."[111] Nor is this other saying to be scorned, that happiness consists of being contented with what one has.[112] If reason guides and shapes the mind, the true meaning of fortune

est[509] que sapientium asseveratione fulcitur. Hoc igitur modo eam quam[510] optandam in civitate indagamus lanio pariter senatorque contingat, verum haud isto limite ratiocinatio cepta decurrit. Sed de eo potius qui[511] virtute subnixus[511] externorum quoque[513] successu instruitur, animadvertendum sane primum quo sit loco radicatus. Neque enim exigua est bene vivendi portio locus, proximum qualis in loco conditio. Omnis namque turba forensis, mercenarii, sordidarumve artium ministri a civili honore sequestrantur; nec, Aristotile teste, pars civitatis habetur qui a civili munere segregatur. In primis igitur hunc de civili corpore statuamus. Mox ei proventus ex prediis ad rei familiaris opportunitatem annua fecunditate[514] respondeant. Redditus namque fundani non tantum patronos instruunt sed honorant. Ad hec animi virtute sit[515] preditus : per hanc dico habitum quendam quo aliquid[516] operari valeas cum velis. Artes enim non tantum quatenus vite incommoda arceantur, verum ne situ torpeat adinvente. Quodque vix credibile audiatur, ipsa quoque vitia ad utilitatem universi et pulchritudinem redigunt.

V-49. Inauditum michi[517] prorsus, et ni doceas, incredibile. Nam qui fieri queat vitiorum bonus ut usus extet? Quid ergo? Omnis preceptio, leges omnes, omnisve coercio tantopere vitiosa adversatur. Minime secus atque ex nichilo aliquid fieri vitio fructum meti perpendo.

P-49. Qui ex nichilo que bona sunt condidit, ex malis quoque hominibus, quoniam aliquid sunt, bonum novit elicere. Sed prius de urbensi expedire cepta pergamus. Huic virtutem seu habitum quendam inesse paganas ultra facultates, velut premonui, ne vacet opere pretium est. Atqui omnes artes sordidas que artificum suorum corpora inficiunt, vel externam circa[518] materiam laborantes

509. et PV.
510. tamquam P.
511. quam V.
512. subnixius P.
513. que V.
514. fecunde V.
515. sit virtute V.
516. quid PV.
517. michi *om.* V.
518. contra V.

is the one that is affirmed by the philosophers. With this consideration, then, the life in the city that we are seeking as desirable can be attained by a butcher as well as a senator. However, the line of reasoning we are following does not deal with that limitation, but rather concerns a man who not only relies on virtue but also is fortunate in his possession of externals. Now, first it must be noted in what place he has put down his roots. For not a small part of living well is the location, and after that, what sort of condition prevails in that location. For all the marketplace rabble, the mercenary soldiers, or the practitioners of paltry skills live without civic honors; and, according to Aristotle, the man who is separated from civic duties is not considered a part of the city.[113] First of all, then, let us choose our man from the civil body. Then let him have produce from the farms in yearly abundance for his personal benefit, since farm revenues not only provide for their patrons but do honor to them. In addition to this, let him be endowed with strength of mind, by which I mean a certain character by which one can accomplish what one wishes. Indeed, the arts have been devised not only so that inconveniences of life may be prevented, but so that a man may not grow sluggish through idleness. And (a fact that scarcely seems credible) the arts turn even vices themselves to the usefulness and beauty of the universe.

V-49. Certainly this is a thing I have never heard of and cannot believe, unless you explain it to me! For how can it happen that a good result can come from vices? Every teaching, all laws, and every restriction vehemently oppose sinfulness. Just as I do not think that something comes from nothing, so I do not think that good fruits are harvested from evil.

P-49. The One who created from nothing things that are good also knows how to elicit good from evil men, since they are something. But first let us continue relating what we have begun about the city-dweller. It is worthwhile that there be in him a virtue or a certain characteristic beyond rural faculties, as I have previously mentioned, lest he be unoccupied. But we remove from our honorable citizen all the mean occupations that corrupt the bodies of the workmen or afflict those engaged

afficiunt, honorato civi subducimus, quamquam harum nonnulle respondentibus prediis sic adiciunt, ut illos sepe qui ampliore preire fortuna iudicantur ubere familiari precellant. Sed volo hunc honeste alicuius negotio vocationis[519] detineri, ex quo et fama et honor et utilitas comparari queat, velut iuris scientia, medicina, philosophia, seu aliqua liberalium, maximeque rhetorica, ex qua est oratoria et tueri et iuvare amicos peropportuna. Sunt et publica munera, senatorium, consulare, pretorium, censorium, questorium, in quibus qui laude versantur reverendi carique civibus evadunt. Forenses item occupationes, iudiciaria, assessoria, advocatoria, procuratoria, tabellionaria, cum honore et utilitate geruntur.

V-50. Miror apprime qui Palatinorum huiusmodi officinam[520] hominum probare videaris, quod locus ille nequissimos alit et instruit. Quam enim adversantur insanum forum, ut[521] nosti, poeta nominat ei sani hominis conversatio; tute decernis.

P-50. Nequaquam infitior, nec valeam si velim, locum illum pessimorum septum existere, ubi armatur nequitia legibus. Docentur emunturque mendacia, et offuscatur veritas; falsitas ipsa fucatur. Sed nunc addo, si minus dixi, quem conscientie perversitas disicit beate neminem vivere; propterea cuius vitam probare instituo, hunc ipsum a nefandorum factione seiungo. Talem ergo forensibus astituo officiis qui non auri sed equi potius amore feratur, adeptaque viris peritia,[522] innocentiam tueri, violentis obstare malit, quo nimirum studio non opes modo sed hominum dilectio predicatioque conflatur. Preterire libet pleraque munera civitatis ceu thesaurariam,[523] questoriam, vectigariam, edilicium, annonariam,[524] ceteraque paria, que, tametsi antelatis subsistant,[525] valent nichilominus cum laude et honore tractari. Quanto scilicet administratio ipsa frequentiore nonnumquam hominum turba versatur. In hoc igitur vite gradu determinatum

519. vacacionis PV.
520. huius medioficinam V.
521. ita PV.
522. periticia V.
523. thesauriam P.
524. armonariam V.
525. subsidant PV.

in nonintellectual activities, even though some of these occupations make such an addition to the farm income that their practitioners often surpass in personal wealth men who are supposed to be superior with greater fortune. But I wish our man to be engaged in some honorable vocation from which fame and honor and profit can be acquired, such as the law, medicine, philosophy, or some one of the liberal arts, in particular rhetoric, from which comes the oratorical skill that is so useful in protecting and helping his friends. There are also public offices—senatorial, consular, pretorian, censorian, questorian—in which men who are concerned with honor emerge revered and beloved of the citizens. Likewise the forensic offices—those of judge, assessor, advocate, procurator, notary—are held with honor and profit.[114]

V-50. I am greatly astonished that you seem to approve of this workshop of palace officials, because it nourishes and educates the most wicked of men. For both the poet[115] and any sane man by his way of life proclaim, as you know, how they oppose the mad forum. But you be the judge of this.

P-50. I do not deny, nor could I if I wished, that that place contains the worst of men, where wickedness is armed with laws. Lies are taught and bought, and truth is concealed; falsity itself is disguised. But now I add, if I have not said it, that no one lives happily who is torn apart by a wicked conscience. And particularly do I separate from the class of evil men this man whose life I intend to approve of. Therefore, I place in public office the kind of man who is impelled by love not of gold but rather of justice, and who prefers, when his experience has acquired strength, to protect innocence and oppose the violent. In pursuit of these activities, indeed, not only is his wealth, but the love and praise of men are increased. We may omit mention of the many offices of the city like those of treasurer, questor, collector of revenues, edile, tax collector, and similar ones, which, although inferior to those before mentioned, can be held with praise and honor. To be sure, administration itself is often engaged in by far too many men. Therefore, in this degree of life I would consider it worthwhile to undertake, as I have said, a limited and fixed

quippiam certumque ad quod animus urgeatur munus subire, ut dixi, opere pretium duxerim. Enim vero egritudinum casus sicut ad lectionem repetit medicum, ita iudicem causa speculari iura compellit. Par de ceteris ratio, quorum professionem cura indicti muneris equa castigat. Alioquin lectio vaga non solida quevis[526] faciet, non nutriat ingenium. Sic hominum vita, nisi cohibeatur actione laudabili, languet deviave fluit.

Intuere locupletes, quos certa rei nullius administratio, iussa ultrove suscepta coercet, sese non ferre, dies horasque habere infestas, fora, vicos, templa nequiquam obire, egredi[527] tempestive, sero domum regredi, et tamquam limen perosos, dum licet, effugere. Atque hoc ideo quod nullum sui usum norunt et humani ea vis animi est ut inactuosus esse non queat. Nam ceu ferrum tergitur et splendet attritu, rubiginem situ contrahit, sic animus ipse exercitio nitet, otio cariat. Ac per hoc otiositas, cunctorum voce sapientium, summopere declinanda censetur. Nedum, spiritus quiescere nescius ad meliora non erigitur agendo vel cogitando in damnabiles cogitationes actionesque labatur. Numera otiosam iuventutem vicos et porticus metientem, scorta solicitantem, infestantemque aliena connubia. Quid veterani?[528] Annon atria, fana, compita primi complent? Dumque otio negotiosi consident, vagas infantiliter nugas[529] serunt, aut versant aleas, aut versantibus assident? Cur ita? Quoniam certum eos aliquid[530] agere nullum tempus adigit. Rursum, quam vagum vanumque sit nulla actione constringi levitas popularis ostendit. Cum festa lux indicit ab actione vacare, quid nisi passim insaniunt? Pars prostitutas inquirunt, pars cauponas implent, alii turgent crapula, nonnulli avia lustrantes qua inebrientur fustium tegularumve iactu turmatim pecuniam sortiuntur. Profecto, nisi providentissima ratio tantis

526. queve PV.
527. egredique V.
528. veteram P.
529. ruigas V.
530. quid PV.

office to which the mind may be directed. For just as cases of sickness bring a doctor back to his studying, so a legal case compels a judge to investigate the laws. The same principle holds for other men whose professions are bound by equal responsibility in their appointed duties. Moreover, cursory reading will not produce sound results nor nourish wisdom. In this way the life of man, if it is not regulated by laudable activity, will languish or flow aimlessly.

You perceive that the rich, who are not constrained by the constant management of their affairs, either forced upon them or undertaken voluntarily, do not endure themselves. The hours and days weigh upon them; they visit the marketplaces, streets, and temples without purpose; they go out early and return home late, avoiding their own threshold while they can as if they hated it. These things have no use in themselves, yet they do them because there exists a force of the human mind that is not able to be inactive. For just as iron is rubbed and grows bright with the rubbing, but rusts from disuse, so the mind itself shines with exercise and decays with neglect. Hence idle time, in the opinion of all wise men, is adjudged a thing especially to be shunned. Even more, the spirit, not knowing how to be motionless, when not raised to better things by doing or planning, slips into wicked thoughts and actions. Count the young men with time on their hands, treading the streets and colonnades, soliciting harlots, imperiling the marriages of other people. And what about the veterans? Are they not the first to fill the courtyards, the shrines, the crossroads? And when, busy with free time, they sit down together, do they not like children converse in aimless nonsense, or play dice, or sit over other players? Why do they do this? Because time does not urge them to do anything definite. Again, how aimless and fruitless it is to be unoccupied is shown by the instability of the populace. When a holiday proclaims cessation of activities, what do people do except go mad all over the place? Some look for prostitutes, some fill the taverns, some grow bloated with drunkenness; others go in bands through back alleys where there are drunks and with blows of clubs or tiles take their money. Certainly, if providential design

vite necessitatibus hominem alligavisset, plurimi ritu pecudum segnes agerent nichilque preter voluptates et otium expeterent. Hoc igitur instituto, in urbana conversatione predicare sortem eius audeo qui suo lare continetur, suo rure alitur, et ultra civili quopiam privatove munere astringitur,[531] unde honos et quotidiana sentitur accessio. Rursusque, hominum familiaritas ipsarum rerum tractatione fovetur.

V–51.   Ita michi profecto videtur. Qui artis aut preceptionis vocatione[532] exercentur otio ac secordie locum adimunt, virtutem usu augent vel conservant; dumque adepta studia civilem ad utilitatem recte accommodant, cari urbibus reverendique visuntur. Adde, cum plures sepe eventus in agrestili reditu familiare negotium nummarium[533] pecunia conturbent, diarius ex virtute fructus emergens temperabit incommodum. Ex hoc sepenumero evenire cernimus ut artis fructu quam arvorum feracius paratiusque[534] vivatur.[535] Ex rure namque artes pascuntur urbane, contra vero ruris opere urbis artibus instruuntur. Ideo vehementer assentior cui ad uber agrorum arte secunda contingat seu virtute successus, hunc ipsum et cuicumque ex negotio census redit absolutioris vite conditione, felicem. Sed festino, ut vitia bonum parere ceu[536] pollicitus es, dum pariter adhuc imus, expedias.

P–51.   Morem tibi geram et dietam hanc largiar. Verum ne sic[537] arbitreris bonum ex vitiis evenire tamquam eos qui sunt

---

531. abstringitur V.
532. vacacione PV.
533. numali PV.
534. peraciusque V.
535. iuvatur P.
536. ceu *om.* V.
537. sit V.

had not bound mankind to so many necessities of life, most, like cattle, would work sluggishly and would seek nothing except pleasure and idleness. Therefore, since this has been established in city living, I dare to praise the lot of that man who stays at his own fireside, is supported by his own fields, and in addition is engaged in some civic or private occupation from which he realizes honor and daily profit. And too, friendly relationships between men are encouraged by the management of affairs.

V-51. It certainly seems so to me. Men who are busy with a vocation in a profession or teaching lack opportunity for idleness and indolence; they increase or preserve their talents by use; and when they apply what they have learned to civic usefulness, they are loved and revered by their cities. Even when frequent mishaps in farm production put the family financial condition into economic confusion, the day-by-day benefits of their skills will temper the inconvenience. From this we can see that often one lives more abundantly and better provided for by the fruits of a profession than by the fruits of the field. For city professions are fed from the country, but on the other hand the productions of the country are supported by the skills of the city. Therefore, I wholeheartedly agree that that man is happy to whom there comes, in addition to the fertility of his fields, success in a favorable skill or talent, and also the man whose wealth from business arises from his condition of a free life. But I am being quick, so that you can show me that vices produce good, as you promised, while we travel together.

8. Vices as Sources of Virtues

P-51. I shall comply with your request and make you a present of this day's journey! But do not think that good comes from evil, as if I were claiming that wicked men are good because of their very wickedness, although even wicked men

vitiosi ipso vitio bonos affirmem, quamquam et ipsi quidem scelesti in creaturarum ordine bonum et sunt et haberi debent.

V–52. Mallem hoc quoque, perdiscere malos bonum esse.

P–52. Dominum Deum creatis omnibus imperare non dubitas.[538]

V–53. Nequaquam. Et quis alius rerum esse dominus quam Deus ipse valet?

P–53. Potentissimum hunc fore ac sapientissimum censes?

V–54. Quia Dominum[539] existere confessus sum, potentissimum quoque esse ac sapientissimum consequitur. Nam duo ista potissimum ei qui vere Dominus extet inesse convenit, quatenus potentia coerceat si quid eius refragatur imperio, sapientia vero ut que moderatur ordinata permaneant efficit.

P–54. Exiguam mihi residuam esse operam[540] puto, huiuscemodi abs te veritate percensita, ut que audire expetis mox tute deprendas. Sed rursum rogo num[541] cui[542] rerum summam assignamus bonum etiam fore ambigis.

V–55. Nichil prorsus. Imo optimum quidem arbitror. Atque hoc ipso quod optimum est, omnia diligere diligique[543] ab omnibus ratio convincit.

P–55. Recte sentis, et fore ita necesse est. Is namque sanctarum velut testimonio litterarum omnia in mensura, numero, et pondere condidit, ita[544] sue lege bonitatis ad bonum regit ac dirigit, creatureque sicut naturam qua esset sic, ne otiosa quoque maneret, virtutem indidit. Ergo nos omnes bonus autor ad bonum edidit, verum alii serviliter, filialiter alii ad bonum convertimur, quare aut servi omnes aut filii sumus. Quicumque igitur, ut docet apostolus, Dei filio recte vivendo conformatur, erit ipse confilius cum ipso unigenito inter multos fratres. Contra, autem, impie agendo quisquis opido a filii imagine deformatur, computabitur in extima sorte servorum interque vasa ire et in contumeliam deputata.

---

538. dubitat V.
539. dominus V.
540. operam residuam esse V.
541. non V.
542. qui P.
543. diligitque V.
544. ita ut P

both are and ought to be considered a good thing in the order of creatures.

V-52. I should also like to learn that wicked men are a good thing.

P-52. You do not doubt that the Lord God commands all creation?

V-53. No, indeed. Who else can be Lord of creation except God Himself?

P-53. Do you think He is most powerful and wise?

V-54. Since I have confessed that He is Lord, it follows that He is also most powerful and wise. For it is agreed that those two qualities particularly are innate in the One who is truly the Lord, so that His power may apply force if anything resists His commands; but His wisdom brings it about that what He governs remains well controlled.

P-54. I think that there is very little work left for me, since you have thought out this sort of truth, to make you quickly understand the things that you ask to hear. But now I ask whether you doubt that the One to whom we attribute the totality of things is also good.

V-55. I do not doubt it at all; on the contrary, I think Him certainly the most good. And because of this very fact, that He is best, reason convinces us that He loves all and is loved by all.

P-55. You understand correctly, and it is necessarily so. For according to the testimony of sacred literature, as He has established all things by measure, number, and weight, so He rules and directs for good by the law of His goodness and has given His creatures a virtuous nature, by which they might be thus and not also remain useless. Therefore our good Maker has made us all for good; but some of us are directed to the good like servants, others like sons. Wherefore, we are all either servants or sons. So as the apostle teaches, whoever conforms to the Son of God by living rightly will himself be a son in company with the only-begotten Son in the midst of many brothers.[116] On the other hand, whoever by living wickedly does not conform to the image of the Son will be reckoned in the lowest rank of servants, fated to go among the vessels and

Dragmalogia

Quotiens itaque fiunt bella, cedes, rapine, ceteraque facinora furoris hostilis, que sapiens providentia iustissimum coercet[545] in ordinem, servorum ministerio utens, vel filios exercet vel devios corripit vel reprobos punit. Nam in ordine temporali, alios rex sue iocunditatis consortio dignatur, alios moderandis gentibus constituit, quosdam procurandis regni opibus[546] dispensat. Nonnullis, quatenus coerceant inquietos, arma gladiosque tamquam satellitibus tradit, indignum ratus[547] quos in usum familiaritatis ascisset eis satellicium severitatis indicere. Ita bonitas divina electos suos quos testimonio prophetico abscondit in abscondito faciei sue a conturbatione hominum inquietare parcit officio nefarios puniendi. Sed malos et[548] homines et angelos adversum eos quos vel deprimi vel exterminari iustum est uti nequitia permittit. Nam iustus nec odio nec avaritia nec ambitu effertur;[549] idcirco nec gladios tractare, nec iniuria quemquam afficere, indebitove grandescere honore letatur. Iniquus autem est pernix[550] ad ferrum quia sponte odit, pernix ad rapinam quia fervet habendi libidine, ad opprimendum quosque improbat[551] quia stimulatur aculeo superbie. His nequam spiritibus eas divina maiestas vices sinit quas electos implere nefas arbitratur.

In quo rursus Brixiam propono exemplum notum ac recens, que, civili odio conflagrans, intestina seditione vicinos populos venenavit et dux et fomentum Gallie urbibus furoris extitit. Horum ergo superbiam malignique spiritus contumaciam dum iustitia superna puniri statuit, Euganeum ducem estuantem dominandi ardore suscitat; quos dum res novas moliuntur, facile intercipit. Laxataque Guelfis, quorum factione Brixiam recepisset, seviendi licentia, cunctos vicatim Gibelinos insatiabili crudelitate

---

545. cohorcet V.
546. obibus V.
547. raptus V.
548. et *om.* V.
549. fertur V.
550. pernox PV.
551. improbus PV.

Vices as Sources of Virtues

into disgrace.[117] Whenever, therefore, wars occur, or slaughter, pillage, and other crimes of hostile madness, which wise providence confines to a very just category by using the help of servants, that same providence disciplines the sons or chastises wrongdoers or punishes the wicked. For in a temporal situation, the king deems some men worthy of participation in his pleasures, puts others in charge of governing peoples, entrusts still others with looking after the wealth of the kingdom. To some, so that they may control the restless, he gives armor and swords as if to guards, thinking it unworthy to impose a harsh duty of guardianship upon those who have been admitted to the pleasure of his friendship.

In the same way the divine goodness refuses to distress with the duty of punishing the wicked its chosen ones whom, according to prophetic evidence, it has hidden in the hiding place of its face away from the confusions of men. But it permits the evil, both men and angels, to employ their wickedness against those who justly ought to be overcome or destroyed. For a just man is influenced by neither hatred nor avarice nor vanity; therefore he does not rejoice in wielding swords or doing injury to anyone or growing great through undeserved honor. But the unjust man is quick to the sword because his hate is spontaneous; he is quick to plunder because he seethes with the desire of possession, and quick to oppress whomever he condemns because he is pricked by the goad of pride. To such wicked souls the divine majesty permits those duties which it thinks wrong for the chosen ones to carry out.

In this regard now, I offer as a well-known recent example, Brescia, which, burning with civil hatred, poisoned with internal sedition the neighboring peoples and became the leader and fomenter of madness for the cities of Gaul.[118] Therefore, when the supernal justice determined to punish the pride and stubbornness of these men's evil spirit, it aroused the Paduan leader, who was aflame with the ardor of conquest, and he easily forestalled those who were plotting revolution. The unbridled savagery of the Guelphs, the party by means of which he had taken Brescia, was given free rein, and they pursued all the Ghibellines through the streets with insatiable

persecuntur, nisi qui fuga salutem quesiverunt omnes ad unum
cesos. Tali nempe victima Paduanus Brixie dominium auspicatus
est. Quis tandem exitus? Nimirum par auspiciis. Nam abeunte
ilicet re profecti superstites Gibelini Guelfis pari feritate vicem
impietatis rependerunt. Atque sic utrinque suo veneno, suo ferro
populus nocens ruit.
Recense divine potentie iustitiam, qua serie, quo ordine malas
hominum voluntates per malos hominum punit affectus. Ex hac
item serie procedit ut dum procelloso dominandi estu[552] Carriger
bello vicinos infestat, merita vicissitudine bello ipse prematur
recipiatque quod fecit, plena et coagitata ac supereffluente mensura,
ut qui pacem contempsit exoptet et careat. Quare cedes, rapine,
excidia populorum iustitia et Dei ordo putanda sunt.[553] Nam si
occiditur noxius, iustitia est; si rapitur ab iniquo possessore quod
habet, equitas est. Si emigratur de tabernaculo suo qui noluit
intelligere ut bene ageret, et dilexit malignitatem super benigni-
tatem, iustum est, et utique bonum est. Iusta igitur permissione
facit iniquus unde alterius iniquitas afficiatur. At si huiusmodi
adversis improbi probos torqueant, aut humanis oculis probi visuntur et non sunt, aut ad meritum exercentur. Quid ergo? Ista
mala sunt quia perverse fertur agentis intentio, bona vero quia a
iusto ordine non discedunt. Sic dignitas celestis nec affici iniuria
qui non debet nec voluntatem hominis, quamquam scelestissimam,
fini debito inofficiosam[554] sinit. Nequam igitur homo, quia natura
est, bonum est; eius autem nequitia,[555] quia nature corruptio est,
mala est.[556] Quare mala voluntas hominis et demonis, etiam
nesciens nolensque, divino ordini famulatur, dum perverso
desiderio id exequitur quod causa equissima temperatur.

---

552. estu dominandi V.
553. reputanda est V.
554. inofficiosam que V.
555. eius autem nequitia *om.* V.
556. natura corupcione mala est V.

cruelty; and except for those who found safety in flight, all were killed to a man. With such a sacrifice did the Paduan enter upon the domination of Brescia! For when the affair was drawing to a close, the surviving Ghibellines, returning with equal ferocity, retaliated against the Guelphs for their treachery. And so on both sides a destructive people fell prey to their own poison, their own swords.

Consider the justice of the divine power, with what an orderly plan it punishes the evil desires of men through the evil dispositions of other men. As a result of this same plan, when Carrara, in his stormy passion for domination, attacked his neighbors in war, he himself was overwhelmed by war in merited retribution, and received what he had meted out, in full, compressed, and overflowing measure; so that the one who scorned peace now longs for it and lacks it. Therefore, the murder, rapine, and destruction of the people must be considered to be the justice and design of God. For if a harmful man is slain, there is justice; if possessions are seized from an iniquitous possessor, there is equity. If a man is cast out of the tabernacle who has been unwilling to learn how to act rightly and has loved doing evil rather than good, it is assuredly a just and good thing.[119] Therefore it is with righteous permission that the evil man commits acts by which the wickedness of another is punished.

But if wicked men torment good men with this sort of mischief, either the good seem upright to human eyes when they are not, or they are disciplined for merit. What then? Such deeds are evil because the purpose of one who acts wrongly is carried out, but they are good because they do not deviate from the just order. Thus the heavenly greatness does not permit injury to befall one who does not deserve it, nor permit a man's will, however wicked, to work contrary to its proper end. Therefore, a bad man is a good thing because he exists through nature; but his wickedness is evil because it is a corruption of nature. Thus the evil will of man and the devil even unknowingly and unwillingly serves the divine order, when with wrongful desire it pursues an end that is controlled by a righteous cause. From this source arises the

Hac radice oritur mirum illud quod, dum mali adversum malos furunt, iniuste quod fieri iustum est agitur. Olim pecuniam sancto viro Bernardo missam obvius predo corripuit; sed dum non sua rapiendo iniustum facit, iuste ab impedimento seculari servum Dei nolens absolvit. Cuncta igitur si penitus animadvertantur, vel ea ipsa que flagitiosissima apparent in boni alicuius exitum vergunt. Atque hoc fit quia omnis[557] creatura sic Domino Deo subiecta est ut statuti ordinis nullatenus limitem queat excedere. Ac per hoc quicquid a creatura ipsa, vel indebite operando, geritur ita ligatur in serie ut sine fructu in rerum universitate non existat.

V-56. Opido iuvat premisse continuatio narrationis. Iam liquet in rerum eventibus ut mortales iniuste sepe moveantur, cum in his divinum potius iudicium laudari debeat et timeri. Sed exple, queso, reliqua.

P-56. Id pergo dudum absolvere, quo patefiat nichil prorsus dempta utilitate, siquidem universi ad pulcritudinem referas, vel ab ipsis quidem improbis geri. Quid superbia importabilius? Quid damnabilius? Quid Deo adversius? Tamen fructu non caret, preeminere enim dum superbi certant,[558] attritis interdum plebeisque sordibus abstinent; viderique magni[559] cupientes magno ore magna resonant, magna iactant, maiora etiam plerumque viribus aggrediuntur. Qua[560] consuetudine pertinaci tenor quidam clarioris altiorisque vite gignitur. Queque prius fuerat vitium, species virtutis evadit. Quid quod liberales, dativos efficit?[561] Nam dum coli

---

557. omis V.
558. errant P.
559. magis V.
560. quam V.
561. efficitur V.

remarkable fact that, when the wicked rage against the wicked, an unjust deed accomplishes a just purpose. Once a robber, meeting the holy man Bernard, stole some money that had been sent to him; but when the thief performed an unjust act by taking what was not his, without willing it he justly freed the servant of God from a secular impediment.[120] Therefore if all things are thoroughly examined, even those which appear most disgraceful tend to result in something good. And this is so because every creature is subjected to the Lord God, with the result that it can in no way exceed the limit of the fixed order. For this reason whatever is done by the creature itself, even working without a just cause, is so bound in an orderly sequence that it does not exist in the universe without value.

V-56. The additional facts of your explanation are certainly helpful. Now it is clear how in many events mortals are often moved wrongly, although the divine judgment in these ought rather to be praised and feared. But continue, please, with the rest.

9. Value of the Seven Deadly Sins

P-56. I shall proceed in explaining this, so that it will be obvious that, in reference to the beauty of the universe, nothing is done without usefulness even by evil men themselves. What is more unbearable than pride, more reprehensible, more opposed to God? Nevertheless, it does not lack value; for when the proud are struggling to prevail, they in the meantime refrain from trite, petty meannesses. Since they desire to seem great, they pronounce great words in a loud voice, they boast of great undertakings, they even frequently attempt deeds greater than their strength. From this persistent habit a certain distinguished and lofty way of life is born. What had previously been a fault emerges as a species of virtue. Consider this effect, that it makes men liberal and inclined to give. For when a proud man

studet elatus inferioribus largitur, tribuit, dispergit; ipsoque arrogantie morbo se predicabilem reddit. Quotiens preterea salutem populis, quotiens libertatem urbibus peperit?[562] Impatiens namque superioris sepe[563] tirannos, sepe iniquos dominos exterminavit. Insuper ad meliora complures erexit, qui tum oratoriam, tum medicinam, aut ius civile perdiscere conati sunt, quatenus gloriosi adepta virtute civibus anteponantur qui, sublata ambitione, sicut nichil ducerent anteferri, sic laborare studio noscendi meliora negligerent. Quid eos memorem qui vera virtute, qua carent, nequeuntes assurgere ad honores, quos intentione superbissima calcare videntur, ambiunt adumbrata. Intonsi namque et squalidi cultu ac vocibus spectantium oculis sanctitatem obiciunt, intrinsecus autem, ut ait veri doctor, lupi rapaces. Quot exempla recte vivendi simplicioribus anteponunt?[564] Quot pios monitus auribus instillant,[565] et humilitatem dum predicant, flatu scientie tument audituri quandoque[566] veritatem illam; dicunt enim et non faciunt. Suo tamen langore intuentibus prosunt, pares gazellis, quarum[567] subinguinale ulcus proximos odore delectat, illas[568] prurit.

Similis prorsus ratio de vanagloria. Nimis multi cupidine laudis et glorie, in dictis factisque, etiam rerum contempta iactura, servavere constantiam, equitatem, modestiam viteque decorem. Et usus ipse laudabiliter agendi tandem penitus ita componit ut quod agebatur virtuose amore laudis fiat mox laudabilis actio, amore virtutis.

Ceterum velut iactantie morbum insequitur sic proximas ei vices habet invidia. Haud est tamen ea ipsa sine fruge; imo ferax quidem emulatio enim calcar est mentibus, quo alios anteire stimulantur, fervent studia litterarum, fervent artificum. Unde

---

562. peperitur V.
563. seu V.
564. anteponuntur V.
565. instilantur V.
566. quandocomque V.
567. quorum V.
568. illos V.

is eager to be venerated, he is generous to his inferiors, he makes them gifts and bestows largess; and by the very disease of his arrogance he makes himself praiseworthy. Besides, how often has pride created security for the people, how often freedom for the cities? For, being impatient of a superior, it has often exterminated tyrants, often unjust rulers. It has raised up to greater heights many men who attempted to learn oratory, medicine, or civil law, so that, glorying in their acquired accomplishments, they might be preferred to citizens who, lacking ambition, placed no value on advancement and so failed to work hard with a desire to learn something better. Let me mention those who, being unable to rise to honors by means of true virtue, since they lack it, pretend to spurn those honors with a very lofty purpose and go around with a feigned virtue. For, unshorn and foul in dress and speech, they show sanctity to the eyes of beholders, but inwardly, as the Teacher of Truth says, they are ravening wolves.[121] How many examples of righteous living do they offer simpler men? How many pious warnings do they drop into ears? And when they preach humility, they swell up with the haughtiness of knowledge, as if they are at some time going to hear that truth; for they speak it and do not practice it. However, even with their own inactivity, they benefit the onlookers, like gazelles in whom an inguinal sore attracts by its odor others nearby and makes them lascivious.

There is a similar reasoning concerning vainglory. Very many men, through desire for honor and glory, even disdaining the loss of their possessions, have retained in their words and deeds constancy, righteousness, and a pleasing modesty of life. And the very habit of acting in a praiseworthy fashion finally alters them deep within so that what they used to do virtuously through love of praise soon becomes a praiseworthy action through love of virtue.

Now since it follows the disease of boasting, envy has the next turn. Envy itself is not without value. On the contrary, fertile rivalry is a spur to minds, by which they are stimulated to excel others. The study of literature is carried on briskly and likewise the development of skills. From what source

nisi invidia? Nichil eque generose indolis pueris ad scientiam et ad mores prodest quam emulatio comparis; quare hanc imprimere[569] discentium mentibus summopere anniti instructor debet. Iam vero in publicis muneribus singulus quisque urit ne pregravet felicius agendo collega; nec tantummodo meliora conari sed damnabilia quoque vitari invidentia ipsa compellet. Nam dum morsus delatoris imminere sentimus, vivere sine reprensione molimur. Ac per hoc quo purius vivatur, conducit cum emulante versari. Hic sane stimulus Themistoclis[570] somnos excutiebat, hoc Pirrum gloria Romanorum, hoc Romanos Cartaginensium exuscitavit. Semper fuit et perstabit, emula virtute, ut discrimina subeantur et probra vitentur. Quodsi ceteris vite in studiis livor prodesse sentitur, in aula certe, ubi regnat, potissimum liquet. Siquidem tiranni assistentium invidia durant, regnant, tuti sunt. Nam dum emulo quisque nixu placere studet, plenius servit; et rursus dum invidet quisque ac socium metuit, fit ut non timeat qui dominatur quos dissidere cognoscit, hisque etiam liberius imperet, quorum unionem fatiscere nec unam fore sciat temperiem animorum.

V-57. Haud illo mentem verteram, sed nimirum constat vite humane partibus conferre non minimum esseque tum ad urbana, tum ad incrementa bellica urgentissimum calcar.

P-57. Sic pariter reliqua. Porro ira iustitie satelles est, nec damnabilis quam aut[571] odium crudele ulciscendive libido, sed recti zelus[572] emendandique disciplina comitatur. Qualis indignatio Moysis qua ydolatram populum cecidit, qualis Phinees, cui desevisse in sacrilegos reputatum est ad iustitiam usque in sempiternum. Age, homini irascentiam[573] detrahe; imbellis et contumelie manceps erit. Neque item castigatio familiaris, neque

---

569. imprime V.
570. Themistodis PV.
571. haud PV.
572. zelo V.
573. irascibilem PV.

except envy? Nothing is of so much benefit for knowledge and character to boys of good quality as the rivalry of a companion. Therefore an instructor ought to strive earnestly to impress this upon the minds of his pupils. Now, indeed, in public offices each individual is on fire lest a colleague have more influence than he by performing with more success; and his very envy drives him not only to attempt better deeds, but also to avoid censurable ones. For when we feel that the bites of an informer threaten us, we try to live blamelessly. So in order to live a purer life, it is profitable to stay around those who are envious. In fact, this stimulus inspired the dreams of Themistocles, through it the glory of the Romans was a spur to Pyrrhus, and the glory of the Carthaginians roused up the Romans.[122] It always has been and always will be true that by virtue of jealousy dangers are undergone and shameful deeds are avoided. Now if in other pursuits of life envy is perceived to be helpful, surely in the court, where it reigns, this is particularly clear. Indeed, tyrants last by means of the envy of those around them; through this they rule and are secure. For when each man eagerly strives to please in a rivalry, he serves completely; and when each one envies and fears his companion, the result is that the ruler does not fear those who he recognizes are in disagreement. He also rules boldly over men whose unity he perceives is cracking and whose temper of mind is not unanimous.

V-57. I had not paid attention to that point, but certainly it is agreed that envy is no small benefit in areas of human life and is the most urgent incentive to the growth of cities as well as to the growth of wars.

P-57. It is the same with other vices. Anger is a companion to justice, not the censurable anger that is accompanied by savage hatred or lust for revenge, but that which is accompanied by zeal for the right and by the discipline of correcting. Such was the indignation of Moses through which he destroyed an idolatrous people, such that of Phineas, to whom it was imputed that he raged forever against the impious with regard to justice.[123] Now then, take away from a man his ability to grow angry; he will be unwarlike and a target for insults.

iniuriarum depulsio, ira languente, procedet. Quid est homo, dempta ira, nisi insensibile animal ad nocentia? Si tollis iram, nec scelus penam, nec disciplinam negligentia pertimescet. Quippe lenitas contemnitur, severitas formidatur.

Ceterum, quemadmodum ira exuscitat animum, ita sopit ignavia, que nimirum, in viro turpis et arguenda, ita sine laude versatur in vita ut vix discernatur quid ad universi ordinem conferat. Confert tamen, nam, dum intra otii ambitum residet, nec ipsa sibi inquieta nec proximis improba sentitur. Quanta pax interdum populorum et urbium, quanta rerum quies et successus imbellia presidentium sequitur. Atque utinam noster iste plus segnitiei et minus animi habuisset ad bella! Felix ipse profecto, felices eius quoque aura victuri. Longe itaque prestitisset tepenti[574] spiritu intra sue possessionis metas deliciari, quam elato vicinos infestans sibi hostes acerrimos irritare. Quanto felicius Mantuanus, qui, suis letus finibus, nec suos quotidie in alveandis fluminibus, cavandis fossis, vallandis bastitis aut fugandis aut fugiendis hostibus inquietat, nec vicinorum odia concitat, ignavum licet imbellemque gliscentes arma diffament. At certe sine metu sui populi, sine solicitudine certi letique, familiaribus studiis impendent. Preterea indemnes agricole, rura culta, inviolate pecudes notis saltibus aluntur.

Deperiret profecto humana societas siquidem atrocior quisque vicinum subdere, quam socium pati mallet. Sed ignari vere laudis inclarescere belli furore et vi quacumque magnificari pulcrum ducunt. Quanto satius sanctiusque nomen paratur in posterosque dimittitur habita reformando et iustis artibus exornando honestisque studiis excolendo, velut olim Franciscus prior, vivus[575]

---

574. tempenti P.
575. vir PV.

He will also neither chastise his family nor revenge injuries if his anger is weak. What is a man without anger except a creature unfeeling toward harmful things? If you take away wrath, then crime does not fear punishment, nor negligence discipline. Truly, leniency is scorned, but severity is respected.

As anger stirs up the mind, so indolence dulls it, which, being base and reprehensible in a man, has so dishonorable a place in life that one can scarcely discern what it bestows upon the order of the universe. It does, however, have some value, for since it resides within the sphere of idleness, it is not felt to be distressing to itself nor troublesome to those nearby. Meanwhile, what a great peace among peoples and cities, what a great calm and happy issue follows when leaders are unwarlike! If only that leader of ours had had more slothfulness and less spirit for war! He himself would surely be happy, as would also those destined to live in his aura. It would have been far better to take his pleasures with a mild spirit within the bounds of his own possessions than with a haughty spirit to harass his neighbors and rouse up fierce enemies against himself. How much happier is the Mantuan, who, content in his own borders, does not disturb his people daily by changing the beds of rivers, digging trenches, and walling up fortifications either to put enemies to flight or to escape them; nor does he incite the hatred of his neighbors, even though men who greatly love arms malign an inactive and peaceful man. But certainly, without fear, his own people, being secure and happy and free from care, apply themselves to their personal interests.[124] Moreover, the farmers are secure from loss, their fields are cultivated, and their cattle graze unharmed in familiar woodland pastures.

Surely human society would perish if everyone preferred to subdue his neighbor savagely instead of permitting him to be a comrade. But men ignorant of true honor consider it a fine thing to become famous through the madness of war and to be glorified through any sort of violence. How much more satisfying and decent a name is acquired and handed to posterity by reforming and adorning one's character with proper skills and cultivating it with honorable studies. Formerly,

adhuc, Paduam urbem ornavit et auxit, imo, ut ita dixerim, recreavit, non quidem bellis sed virtutum cunctarum studio, ut primariam sapientie ac iusti principis gloriam in omni Latio reportaret. Extinxit autem fulgorem nominis et amisit felicitatem simul bellandi ardor incessit. Deinceps Nicolaus Estensis, nonne venerabilior fuit et clarior, paci et litterarum otio studens, eo amplitudinis Ferariam promovendo ut ex asseritia latericiam faceret? Nulla certe vicinarum pro magnitudinis portione formosior hodie neque opulentior habetur.[576] Ipse nimirum defunctus in hominum celebri laude versatur magis eiusmodi animi lenitate quam si feroci spiritu, clade, et ruina, bellorum gloria[577] flagrans et sua profligasset et esset vicina demolitus. Quo turbine dum se minime temperavit gener eius, nec acquisivit externa que possidere certabat, nec sua retinuit que possidebat.[578] Prestitisset nempe, reside spiritu, Euganeis fruendo deliciis, terminos suos indulgenter excolere[579] incolumesque servare quam niti aliena iniuria nomen imperiumque magnificare. Quietum enim principem boni omnes laudant; turbulentum ferroque gaudentem improbi tantummodo secuntur et colunt. Michi vero presideat malim qui, pusillo contentus animo, priscorum ambitu, propria fovere quam magno impatientique spiritu provehere hominum se rerumque[580] strage festinare.[581] Quemadmodum ita habentis animo segnities officit, sic laborem dum fugit, a turbulentissimis interdum motibus quiescit.

V–58. Ita est procul dubio. Magnanimes dum sese ferre nequeunt, eo sepe efferuntur, unde sua crebro et aliena ruendo prosternant. Quare tranquillius feliciusque michi videntur urbes ac populi remisso quam furenti rectore gubernari.

P–58. Talem de lentescente[582] fructum metimus. Quid irrationalis illa motio carnis que libido appellatur? Num[583] in mundana

---

576. habeatur V.
577. gloriam PV.
578. nec . . . possidebat *om.* V.
579. extollere V.
580. reorumque V.
581. festinat PV.
582. delendescente V.
583. non V.

Francesco il Vecchio in his lifetime ornamented and beautified the city of Padua, in fact, I might say, remade it, not by wars but by his love for all virtues, so that it attained the highest fame in all Italy for learning and its just prince. But it extinguished the brightness of its name and lost its prosperity as soon as the ardor for war appeared. Then, was Niccolò d'Este not revered and famed because through his interest in peace and literary studies he raised Ferrara to such a degree of excellence that he made it a city of brick from one of tile?[125] Surely no neighboring city today is considered more beautiful or wealthy in proportion to its size. Indeed, after his death, he is now widely praised by men more for the gentleness of his mind than if with fierce spirit, destruction, and ruin, and eager for the glory of war, he had wasted his own possessions and destroyed those of his neighbors. When his son-in-law did not restrain himself from these agitations, he neither acquired the foreign possessions that he was striving for nor kept the ones that he owned. To be sure, it would have been better, by enjoying the pleasures of Padua with a quiet spirit, to cultivate his own lands tenderly and keep them from harm, instead of trying to make his name great and reign by doing injury to others. For all good men praise a peace-loving prince; only the wicked follow and cherish one who is tempestuous and delights in the sword. For my part I would prefer a ruler who, being content with a limited outlook and a display of old-fashioned virtues, takes care of his own belongings, instead of hastening with a great and impatient spirit to advance himself by the destruction of men and property. As slothfulness hampers the mind of such a one, so when he is avoiding labor, he is in the meantime free of turbulent upheavals.

V-58. Yes, there is no doubt of it. When high-spirited men cannot control themselves, they are often beside themselves with passion; hence they frequently destroy their own and others' goods in their downfall. Cities and peoples, it seems to me, are ruled more quietly and happily by a remiss ruler than by a rampaging one.

P-58. Such a harvest do we reap from a lax ruler. What about that irrational excitement of the flesh which we call

re publica, Deo regulante impuros hominum actus, fructu caret? Quid? Laudabimus adulteria, stupra, incestus, quod ex his aliquando minime spernendus sequatur effectus? Nequaquam probra enim sunt, supplicio digna non laude. Nichilominus infitiari non possumus, damnabili plerumque complexu id nullatenus intendentibus, interdum etiam nolentibus, qui flagitium patravere, gigni tales, quorum vita laudabilis et tum in re publica, tum privatis quoque muneribus merita probarentur. Ita inimicus homo vicini plerumque culture tendit seminare zizania et frumentum[584] nesciens serit. Haud secus libidinis opera, dum enim succensa voluptas optata specie fruitur, nequiter vel invita spargit in carne subiecta quod dispensatione celesti in fructum utilitatis exuberat. Nam quot damnato concubitu editi tum scientie, tum religionis, tum civilis ac bellice virtutis excellentia clari evasere? Quot etiam salutem stupris, quot adulteriis sortiti sunt? Adulterium Paridis Troiano excidio vindicatum est; inde exorta sunt Romane magnitudinis elementa. Alcibiadem apud Lacedemonas exulantem, cum invidiam odiumque virtute contraxisset, ab imminenti exitio regii thori adultera vindicavit. Par facinus Massilienses ab Ligurum insidiis et solvit et victores fecit. Ita divina celsitudo ex humanis fructum legit erroribus.

Sed quid pervetusta exuscito? Accipe rem exiguam sed veram. Ludovicus Ravennas, absumptis[585] rebus patriis, ad vestram olim urbem egenus divertit, famulatuque, cum nichil artium litterarumve nosset,[586] se addixit. Ilicet dominum auspicatus apud quem opes et coniugium repperit, quippe adulterio domine non quidem famulantis sed filii, cum pater non esset dominus, partes in domo gerebat. Quid tandem? Obiens herus puellam pietate Christiana filialiter educatam famulo uxorem larga dote, id prestruente

---

584. furmentum V.
585. assumptis V.
586. noscet V.

Value of the Seven Deadly Sins   213

lust? Surely in a worldly commonwealth, where God regulates the base acts of men, it does not lack rewards. Why? Are we to praise adultery, debauchery, incest, because from these there sometimes is an outcome that cannot be despised? Indeed, they are shameful acts and worthy of punishment instead of praise. Nevertheless, we cannot deny that frequently from a sinful embrace, when the perpetrators of the sin plan no result and even sometimes do not wish it, there are born men whose laudable lives and merits are highly esteemed, not only in public affairs but also in private positions. Thus an unfriendly man intends to plant tares in his neighbor's plowed field and often unknowingly sows grain.[126] So it is in the operation of lust; for when burning desire enjoys the wares it has longed for, in its licentiousness it, even when unwilling, bestows upon the subject flesh what through celestial dispensation becomes an abundant harvest of benefits. For how many men born of a sinful union have turned out famous for their excellence in learning, religion, or civil or military worth? How many also have acquired prosperity as a result of debaucheries, how many from adulteries? The adultery of Paris was avenged by the destruction of Troy, and from that arose the first elements of Roman greatness.[127] When Alcibiades was in exile among the Lacedemonians, after he had attracted envy and hatred because of his abilities, the adulteress of the royal bed saved him from imminent death.[128] A similar deed rescued the people of Marseilles from the ambushes of the Ligurians and made them victors.[129] Thus does the divine greatness pluck rewards from human waywardness.

But why bring up ancient examples? Listen to this insignificant but true story. When Luigi da Ravenna had consumed his inheritance, he once visited your city as a pauper; and since he had no skill or learning, he went into service.[130] Right away he found a master at whose home he acquired both wealth and a wife. In fact, by committing adultery with the mistress, he played the role in the household not merely of a servant but of a son, though the master was not his father. How did this come about? When the master lay dying, he chose as wife for this servant a girl whom he had brought up like a

coniuge, destinat. Sed adultera iam vidua et gravis etate, seu conscientia seu pudore, a prioris vite culpa prorsus abhorruit; queque pelex fuerat se parentem socrumque mecho exhibuit. Tantus adulteralis commercii fructus extitit ut, defuncto Ludovico et uxore, infantulos superstites, cunctorum patrocinio destitutos, sola susceperit, officiosissime aluerit, educaverit, instruxerit. Nunc et facinora hominum iudica! Iuvenis peregrinus et inops Venetias appulit; civis orbus liberis externam alumnat; peregrinum famulatu asciscit[587]; famulus adulterio uxorem, opes, et superstantibus matris instar nutricem liberis comparat.[588] Vagari per exempla[589] valere, sed hoc tam domestice abunde liquere potest quanta nonnumquam carnali turpitudine tum rebus, tum hominibus opportunitas conflata sit. Quot nuptarum viduarumque stupris ad litterarum, ad civiles honores adiuti[590] evectique sunt?

Nec illud quoque omiserim quod duorum corporum illa coitio, cum omnino sit probrosissima[591] atque immundissima, nichil pene studiosiore mundo queritur. Lectus siquidem nitidissimus illecebrique apparatu sternitur, quam etiam lautissimus quisque comprendi certat. Adde respersos odores aquarum, pigmentorum; preterea in vestibus primus nitor, in ore vernantia coloris, in crinibus ordo, decor in habitu paratur vel fingitur. Iam vero quanto ingenio tum mores, tum verba componit, quatenus amans placeat amato! Cura hec insuper iuventutem canere, sonare vota, affectusque metrorum ligare modis instruit. Tum denique vera vel ficta probitate digni nituntur ostendi strenuique, liberales, ac magnifici comparere, que deinceps adulta cum etate consuetudo in omni vita observata est. Solebat Antonius Mutinensis, iuris peritus, affirmare nequaquam sibi displicere externo uxorem paulisper amore perstringi, quod eius rei causa accuratior cultu,

587. ascisit V.
588. extra P.
589. extra P.
590. adiucti V.
591. pudorosissima PV.

daughter in Christian piety, with a generous dowry, all of which his wife had arranged beforehand. But the adulteress, now a widow and of advanced age, through either conscience or shame, henceforth revolted from the sin of her previous life; and so the woman who had once been his concubine now appeared as parent and mother-in-law to the adulterer. There was so great a benefit from the adulterous connection that, when Luigi and his wife died, she alone took in the surviving children, bereft of the protection of all, cared for them most dutifully, brought them up, and educated them. Now pass judgment on the sins of men! A poor foreign youth has arrived at Venice; a childless citizen is bringing up a daughter not his own; he takes the foreigner into his service; the servant acquires by adultery a wife, riches, and a nurse like a mother for his orphan children. It is possible to ramble through more examples, but in this homely one we can see fully how great an advantage both to possessions and to persons is sometimes produced by carnal sinfulness. How many men have been helped and advanced to literary and civil honors through the defilement of brides and widows!

Nor, in addition, should I omit that even when the union of two bodies is wholly shameful and unchaste, almost nothing else causes a woman to pay more attention to her toilet. The couch is splendid and decked with enticing magnificence, and strives to appear the most elegant one possible. Add the scattered fragrances of perfumes and cosmetics. The lady also arranges and fashions shining neatness in her clothing, youthful color on her lips, and a nice hair style, and affects a charming mien. Indeed, with what great cleverness the lover arranges both her manners and her speech in order to please the beloved! On the other hand, love teaches the young man to sing, to give musical expression to his hopes, to express his emotions through the rhythmic measures of poetry. Then, finally, with either real or feigned honesty, both attempt to seem worthy and to appear lively, generous, and noble—a habit that afterwards in adulthood is preserved in the life of each. Antonio da Modena, a lawyer, was accustomed to claim that it was not at all displeasing to him for his wife to be involved temporarily in an

vultu iocundior, gestibus motuque agilior versaretur. Quibus ita se habentibus, esse perspicuum valet quid boni tum ad artes, tum ad mores et vite iocunditatem vitiosa libido in rerum universitate conferat. Vix michi persuaderi queat aut ingenio aut vite facetiis prestare qui amans numquam fuit! Acuit enim vis illa ingenium, disertum efficit, excolit[592] mores, et conversatione lepidum reddit.

V–59. Assentior, inquam, et in nostra civitate maxime liquet. Nam alternis placere dum studiis viri femineque decertant, nusquam molliore cultu iuventus[593] et cura nixuve operosiore compti, tersi, depilesque incedunt, ut nostrorum instar reliquarum urbium agrestes[594] spectent.

P–59. Exornata, fateor, et augusta pubes vestra! Verum haud tam libido ipsa quam summa divitiarum inconcussaque libertas pompe spectabilis fertur occasio, sed morbus est cunctorum ad quod quisque anelat sese magnopere effingere.[595]

Verum ad residua humane pravitatis vitia, gulum et avaritiam, quid conferant, si valeam, asseverare iam propero. In primis gule voluptatem sequi detestabilem fateor servitutem. Quid enim abiectius quam ventris ferri mancipium? Tamen huiusmodi cupido in salutem cessit interdum, nam evenit, seu colerali[596] motu cessante seu instante flegmatico, vim appetitivam plerumque fatiscere, desiderioque sepulto eum qui langueat allatam pastionem fastidire. Sed dum quam valens ardebat refectio propinatur, fertur animus, ipsaque aviditate virtutem exuscitat progressumque iniciat sanitati.

Quid ingenia ad cocturam escarumve condituram, ad sapores, ad colores, ad odores multifarios atque sumptu et arte operosissimos? Ipsa profecto castrimargia, ut putant, non extendit sed utilitas

---

592. extolit V.
593. inventus V.
594. agrestiles PV.
595. fingere V.
596. colerali: apparently coined.

extramarital affair, since on this account she became more painstaking in her dress, more cheerful of countenance, and more lively in gestures and movements.[131] Since matters are thus, it is very clear what good is conferred not only upon the arts, but also upon manners and pleasantness of life by wrongful lust, in the overall scheme of things. I can scarcely be convinced that a person who never was a lover is outstanding in either wit or the pleasantries of life! For that force sharpens the wit and makes it eloquent, refines the manners, and makes one charming in conversation.

V-59. I surely agree; and in our city it is particularly obvious. For when men and women vie to please with mutual zeal, nowhere do the young people parade around with more delicate grooming, or combed, scrubbed, and shorn with more painstaking care and trouble; with the result that the uncultivated folk of other cities strive for the appearance of our people.

P-59. Your young people, I admit, are elegant and grand. Yet not merely lustfulness itself, but also the amount of wealth and the constant freedom of remarkable display are said to be the cause. But it is a disease of all men to model themselves after what each one greatly desires.

As for the remaining vices of human depravity, namely, gluttony and avarice, I now hasten to demonstrate what they confer, if I can. Particularly do I aver that to pursue the pleasure of gluttony is a detestable form of slavery. For what is more lowly than to be owned by the belly? Yet desire of this sort sometimes results in health. For when the movement of the bile ceases or the phlegmatic motion oppresses, the strength of the appetite generally decreases; so with his desire buried the sick man has a distaste for the food brought to him. But when he is served the refreshments he craved when well, his spirit is revived, and through his very greed he gets back his strength and initiates progress to health.

Think of the cleverness used in the cooking or seasoning of foods, the flavoring, the coloring, the many fragrances demanding expense and painstaking skill. Surely gluttony itself, as is thought, is not the reason for their popularity, but rather

potius atque necessitas. Nonnulla sunt enim absque[597] condimento nocitura, vel minimum profutura; alia facile nature imperio non obtemperant; que ars admota prestare docet obsequium. Tempus item alia, alia sumentis etas valitudoque aliter atque aliter flagitat. Propterea sapores et conditure honesto ex fonte prodierunt, verum quemadmodum penes[598] cetera insolens culpa a laudando seduxit improbandum[599] ad usum. Nam dum voluptas[600] ratione utilitatis assumitur,[601] rectus est usus rerum; cum autem causa voluptatis utilitas non iam usus sed abusus potius esse censetur. Nichilominus quamvis anteponat naturalis intentio utilitatem, plerumque tam[602] opprimitur ipso carnis vitio ut voluptati et iactantie magis obsequatur industria. In quo nimirum studio omnis Secana tenus Gallia et simul Rheni Histrique barbaries fervet, quos nostri velut in omni sapientie commercio facile in hoc quoque iam exuperant. Sed quamvis illa coquinandi[603] peritia saporandique alimentum inserviat culpabiliter voluptati, nichilominus non tantum delectatur ea sensus sed iuvatur. Nam haud pauci, valitudine minus integra aut senio aut imbecilli natura deliciarumve consuetudine, quorum ingenti iactura succederet interitus cum minime valeant communibus refici conditis, arte vixere; factumque est ut quemadmodum in ceteris, Deo in usum singula redigente, res improbanda exitio multis fuit, rursus multis salutaris existeret.

Adde quod plura tum venatico, tum aucupio, tum etiam piscatione ad vite opportunitatem, cupedia instigante, mortales attulere, que, ceu castrimargis mensas infarciunt, ita plerumque pauperes ditant.[604] Quot ex agris aquisve pretio ingenti veneunt, et venditorum incommoda, dum luxuria non parcit impensis, levant? Rumbum electum salmonemve piscario sors offeret, bistardam pariter aucupi. Ni quispiam, ut dici assolet, gutture piloso compareat,[605] quis frugi emat? Verum indigentie captoris providentia succurrens edacem astituet, et unde culpabiliter[606]

597. asque V
598. pene PV.
599. improbandum seduxit PV.
600. voluptates V.
601. assumuntur V.
602. tamen PV.
603. cocimandi PV.
604. dictant V.
605. compereat V.
606. *ex* culpapiliter *corr.* V.

usefulness and necessity. For there are some foods which without seasoning will harm or be of no help; others do not easily conform to the command of nature, yet when art is applied to them, they are taught to give compliance. Likewise the season of the year demands some things, and the age and health of the consumer others. Furthermore, flavorings and seasonings have come from an honest source; but, just as in other matters, excessive fault-finding has misled people from praising to disapproving their use. For when pleasure is received through concern for utility, there is a correct use of things; but when utility develops from concern for pleasure, this is no longer considered use but abuse. Nevertheless, though nature's intent prefers utility, generally it is so overwhelmed by the vice of the flesh that our industry gives more service to pleasure and ostentation. Indeed, all Gaul up to the Seine, and also the barbarian region of the Rhine and Danube, is assiduous in this pursuit. However, our people easily surpass them now in this respect also, as well as in all matters of wisdom. But although that skill in cooking and seasoning does blameworthy service to pleasure, nevertheless it not so much delights the senses as does them good. For not a few people, either because of unsound health, old age, a weak constitution, or habitual use of delicacies, who would die in great numbers since they cannot thrive on foods prepared in the ordinary manner, have lived by means of culinary skills. So, as in other matters, since God makes each thing for a use, a disapproved practice has been harmful to many but also healthful to many others.

In addition, hunting, bird-catching, and fishing have brought mankind many things for the advantage of life and to satisfy a taste for delicacies, foods which, as they load the tables of gluttons, usually make poor men rich. How many things are sold from the fields or waters for a large price, relieving the harsh circumstances of the sellers, since luxury spares no expense! Chance will offer to the fishmonger a choice turbot or salmon, or a bustard to the fowler. Unless someone, as is customarily said, appears with a shaggy throat, what frugal man could buy it? But providence coming to the aid of the poverty of the catcher will bring a glutton to him; thus what will bring

delectabitur cui deus venter est, inde[607] utiliter iuvabitur cui familiaris egestas molesta est. Ad hec minime pauci cultiora tardicordes coquinali[608] ministerio rem domesticam absque angustia duxere. Alii fortunatis dum placuere conditura pulmenti, opibus et honore provecti sunt, ceu nescio quem ferunt condimento[609] anseris a soldano Damasci prefecturam meruisse.

Sed poscit tempus a castrimargia aggredi castra philargyrie,[610] que tanto maius quanto spiritualius crimen est. Sententia cunctorum, nec ab iure, avaritia damnatur. Tamen quia in rerum universitate nichil ordine carens valet existere, hanc, velut adulteram matronam crebro ancille pudice comitantur, sic quedam laudabilia post ambulant, dum cogit avarus unde cui Deus disposuit accedat, attestante scriptura, quod peccatori dedit Deus curam et afflictionem supervacuam ut addat et congreget et tradat ei qui placuerit Deo. Id quotidianis patet eventibus ex avarorum nempe thesauris[611] collegia, hospitalia, ecclesie, theatra, portus erecti constructique sunt. Plures quoque egenorum nuptie supplete, et sicut Antistenes Kifisidotum tirannum "lacrimam turis" appellavit, ita par est de avaro censere. Tus namque incendio, proximis deflagrat[612] avarus, autem moriendo pluribus prodest. Superbi in celum domos erigunt, struunt palatia, ornant urbes, et hoc quidem in iactantiam viventes. Avari autem dum obeunt posteros iuvant. Quantus preterea locus pateret ignavie, quot artes obsolefierent, quantus ministeriorum immineret defectus nisi avaritia impingeret ad laborem? Quin etiam[613] huius pestis utilitas ad res usque divinas protenditur. Per eloquentiam siquidem predicationis[614] enitere laborant qui questuosam faciunt pietatem. E regione specta[615] navitas, calones,[616] cementarias carpentariasque operas, ac mercenarios turbe forensis, quorum ad manus nequiquam, nisi obtemperare adigat lucelli dulcedo, recurras.

---

607. in V.
608. coquinali: apparently coined.
609. condimine PV.
610. philagie PV.
611. thesaurus V.
612. defragrat PV.
613. esset V.
614. predicaciois V.
615. spreta V.
616. *ex* colones *corr.* V.

blameworthy delight to the man whose god is his stomach will prove a real benefit to the man who is burdened by his family's poverty. Furthermore, many slow-minded persons have brought their domestic affairs out of financial difficulties by their culinary performances. Others, by pleasing the rich with their preparation of sauces, have been advanced in wealth and honors; they say someone or other earned the prefecture of Damascus from the Sultan because of his seasoning of a goose.

But time demands that we leave gluttony and approach the camp of avarice, which is a greater sin because it pertains more to the spirit. In the opinion of all, and not unjustly, avarice is condemned. Yet, since in the universe nothing can exist without order, just as frequently chaste handmaidens accompany an adulterous matron, so certain laudable results go along with avarice; a greedy man gathers riches to add to what God has granted, as Scripture attests, because God has given the sinner this worry and needless affliction so that he may add and collect and pass on these riches to someone who has pleased God.[132] It is obvious from daily occurrences that from the treasuries of the avaricious, corporations, hospitals, churches, theaters, and harbors have been erected and built. Many weddings for the poor have also been provided. Just as Antisthenes called the tyrant Cephisodotus "the tear of incense," so the same thing can be thought concerning an avaricious man.[133] For incense is consumed by fire, and the avaricious man is consumed by his fellow men; but in dying he is useful to even more people. The proud raise houses to the sky, build palaces, adorn cities, and all this indeed to vaunt themselves while alive; but the avaricious help their descendants when they die. Furthermore, what opportunities for slothfulness would exist, how many arts would grow obsolete, and what a shortage of services would threaten us if greed did not compel men to labor! What is more, the usefulness of this disease extends even to divine matters, for the men who make piety profitable work hard to distinguish themselves through the eloquence of preaching. On the other hand, look at sailors, soldiers' servants, stonecutters, wagonmakers, and hirelings of the marketplace crowd: you would run to these groups in vain if the sweetness of a little profit did not compel them to accommodate you.

Nec rere angustia domestice paupertatis dumtaxat ad servitia trahi, quandoquidem plerique, tamquam in cloacas aurum mergunt ac velut minime sentientes, esuriem et erumnam ferunt. Hi profecto quod volunt[617] et acervant simul perdunt. Verum quoniam habendi ardor exurit et cogit ad lucrum, circum fora, portus, emporia, apum instar[618] perstrepunt unde opportunitas urbana suppletur. Quid cetarios[619] tanto labore viteque iactura pisces persequi et macellarios nundinas seductasve plagas lustrare, nisi lucrandi estus impellit? Nonne ad Assirios, ad Tanaim Mauritaniamque navigatis? Flandriam Anglosque aditis? Quid tanto itinere tantove discrimine quam aurum postulatur? Qua quidem in re si nichil aliud dignum laude foret, opere pretium est quod multarum rerum, morum, regionum, magnum ad prudentiam adiumentum instructi notitia redditis.

His igitur satis innotescere potest quales in usus improbos hominum actus affectusque celestis sapientia convertat. Ex quo etiam bella ipsa bellantiumque facinora non tam queri quam equanimiter ac bene de Domino Deo in bonitate sentiendo tolerare mortalium debet humilitas[620] et extimare sic celitus iuste decerni. Hisce nimirum cladibus aut plures exterminantur iniqui, aut molestia adversorum exercentur electi, aut temporalium illecebris virtute[621] torpentes rerum amissione revocantur. Superna quippe benignitas, ut equum est, reprobos ruere nequitie pondere sinit, amatoribus vero iustitie in mediis quoque turbinibus vel assistit protegendo vel educendo custodit. Sepe iustus, inops incomitatusque, exulabit. Expende finem : videas liberationem a procellis instantibus extitisse non fugam.

V–60. Profecto circa tuum illum Ravennatem, divina protectio misericorditer intenta comparuit, ab imminentibus angustiis evellendo.

P–60. Quanta mortalium caligo! Cum potissimum odisset vota bellantium, mussabat tamen merebatque decedere; inde locorum

---

617. vivunt PV.
618. instrar P
619. ceptarios PV.
620. utilitas V.
621. a virtute PV.

Do not think that the difficulties of domestic poverty are peculiar only to the servant class, since many, as it were, throw gold into the sewers without noticing it, and suffer hunger and hardships. What they wish for and amass is simultaneously squandered. But since the ardor of possessing burns them and urges them on to gain, like bees they buzz around the market-places, harbors, and shops where opportunities are to be found in the city. Why do the fishmongers pursue fish with such great effort and loss of life, and the meat-sellers traverse the markets and distant places, except that the desire for gain drives them on? Do you not sail to the Assyrians, to Tana and Mauritania? Or go to Flanders and England?[134] What do you seek by so long a journey and at such great danger except gold? In fact, if nothing else is worthy of praise, it is worthwhile that in acquiring the knowledge of many events, customs, and regions you bring back great additions to wisdom.

Therefore, by these facts one can adequately learn to what sort of uses the wicked deeds and affections of men are converted by celestial wisdom. And for the same reasons the humility of mortals ought not so much to complain of wars and the crimes of warriors as to endure them with equanimity, thinking well concerning the Lord God in His goodness, and to consider that thus all is rightly decided in Heaven. In fact, in these calamities either many wicked people are destroyed, or excellent ones are kept busy by the troublesomeness of their adversaries, or those sluggish in virtue because of the enticements of worldly goods are called back by the loss of their possessions. To be sure, the supernal loving-kindness, as is just, permits the wicked to fall with the weight of their wickedness; but it also aids with its protection the lovers of justice in the midst of storms, or saves them by leading them out. Often a just man, poor and without companions, will triumph. Consider the result: you can see that freedom from threatening storms has come about, not flight.

V–60. Concerning that Ravennate of yours, the divine protection has very evidently been inclined to mercy in rescuing him from imminent dangers.

P–60. How great is the blindness of mortals![135] Although he hated exceedingly the aims of those making war, yet he kept

hominumque consuetudine allectus, diu multumque ancipiti sententia nutavit. Nichil mestius fecit, nichil secundius cessit. Homo omnium maxime bella tristesque bellorum vices perosus, quietis ac solitudinis queritans, laboribus civium meroribus, damnis, tediis, iniuriisve contabuisset.

V-61. Auspicato se Venetias contulit, gentium nusquam melius collocandus: urbem, Latialium amplissimam matrem asillumve lassorum,[622] felicem inquam opibus, frequente numero gentium, rebus quas usus exposcat completam omnibus.

P-61. Aliter ipsum audires et loquentem et optantem! Haud talia animi eius parvitas exoptat. Rusculi et colliculorum virorem suspirat, et non marmorata aurataque palatia visere gestit. Quod notis ipse minime siluit, Aquilegiam sepe portumque gruarium,[623] humilia contemptaque loca, adivisse aut quemvis solitudinis[624] perpetue[625] secessum maluisse testatus. Quandoquidem ibi purius celum, vagatio iocundior, et per rura, per prata, per frondentium umbras arborum meditatio tranquillior; quia minus hominum, minus turbarum, minus etiam improbandorum morum occurreret, ac studioso sedatoque spiritui aptior sedes longeque minore impendio comparanda.

V-62. Perversum hominis votum, cum innumerabilis multitudo ex omni orbe confluat, huic uni minime cum ceteris multoque prestantioribus in civitatis laude convenire!

P-62. Imo, laudat et ita ut est magnificat. Sed ita est homo affectus, et singulari rapimur singuli voluptate. Quis civitatem et

---

622. lapsorum V.
623. gruarum V.
624. soli PV.
625. perpetui PV.

silent and gained permission to leave; then, attracted by familiar habits and people, for a long time he wavered greatly, his mind not made up. Nothing was sadder for him to do, but nothing was more fortunate than for him to depart. A man hating above all things wars and the unhappy events of wars, desiring the pleasures of quiet and solitude, he would have wasted away in the hardships of the citizens, their grievances, losses, weariness, and injustices.

10. Criticisms of Venice

V-61. He arrived in Venice at a fortunate moment, and could nowhere in the world be better located: a city that is the wealthy mother of the Italians, an asylum for the weary, happy in its riches, well populated, and filled with all the things that comfort demands.

P-61. You could hear the man himself both saying and wishing otherwise! The humbleness of his mind does not desire such things. He sighs for the verdure of the country and little hills and does not long to see palaces of marble and gold. This fact he himself has not concealed from his friends, attesting that he has often gone to Aquileia and a harbor for cranes, lowly and despised places, or that he has preferred any retreat of constant solitude.[136] Indeed, there the sky was purer and strolling more pleasurable, and through the countryside, the meadows, the shade of leafy trees, meditation was more tranquil; because there he came across fewer men, fewer crowds, and also fewer wicked customs, and found a home more suitable for a studious and calm spirit attainable at far less expense.

V-62. It is a perversity in the man, when countless multitudes are streaming together from all the world, to be the only one not concurring in praise of the city along with other much more outstanding persons!

P-62. On the contrary, he does praise it, and he calls it glorious, as it is. But thus is the man disposed, and we are

amplissimam quidem et exornatissimam vicinarumque prestantem expertus infitiabitur? Sed avaro quisquis ingenio, lucri estu agitur, huc ruit et libens mansitat. At sapientie studio contractis nec mores nec dexter est locus. Tam mehercule ubi fervet cura nummalis scientie defervet, quam in litterarum sacrario divitiarum honos postponitur. Vos haud aliter quam piperis crocive negotium sortimini litterarum. Emisso pretio omnis ea congressio familiaris ilicet evanescit. Nequaquam ita par est in docendi discendive commercio, quod utique felicius dilectione quam pretio conditur. Quandoquidem, ceu filius, alter erudientis vocem suscipere debet; ut pater, alius discenda propinare. Ac sic, dum alter alterius presentia delectatur, dicendi audiendique munus intenta prosperitate perficitur.

Iuvenes autem vestri nec accedunt ut filii, nec velet discipuli reverentur, quia vix discunt ut sciant, nec ideo scire volunt ut que didicere colant. Hoc ideo quia tanta extat spes et fiducia divitiarum ut totus vite laborisque fructus illo conferatur. Cum igitur solido nulli iudicio confederentur, similes huc et illuc temere volitantibus muscis[626] preceptores alternant. Ideo numquam proficiunt quia, dum negligunt instructores, negliguntur, ac per hoc tepidius instruuntur; quia nature morbus est, dum despici animus se conspicatur, eum qui despiciat negligere vel odisse. Eruditio nempe velut omnia familiaritate liberalique studio confovenda est.[627] Trita est apud nos dictio[628] prodire de laribus litteras. Quid? Nimirum officiis domesticis sedulitatem eius qui doceat confoveri.

At vel si cupiatis, liberales fore[629] nequitis, cuncta enim ex labore, ex ingenio, ex periculo possidetis, et tenaciter servatur quod discrimine acquiritur. Nobis autem terra, fruges, vinum, altilia, ceteraque

---

626. muscis *om*. V.
627. est *om*. P.
628. dicio V.
629. fore liberales V.

differently affected by different pleasures. What person who knows the city will deny that it is the richest and most elegant and outstanding of all its neighbors? However, everyone who is driven by a greedy nature and eagerness for wealth rushes here to Venice and gladly remains. But for those united by the desire for wisdom neither the customs nor the place is right. By heaven, where love for money flourishes, not only does interest in knowledge die out, but also the honor of riches in the shrine of literature is less esteemed. You Venetians deal with learning as a business just as you do the pepper or saffron trade. Once the money is paid, all that friendly association at once disappears. This is not the case in the relationship of teaching and learning, which certainly is based more felicitously on love than on money. Indeed, like a son one ought to heed the words of the teacher, and he like a father should furnish the material to be learned. And so, when each is happy in the presence of the other, the duties of speaking and listening are performed with vigorous success.

But your young men do not approach as sons, nor show reverence as pupils, because they with difficulty learn in order to know, and for this reason they do not wish to know in order to cherish what they have learned. This happens because there is so much hope and faith in wealth that the whole harvest of life and labor is conferred upon that. Since therefore none are united by sound judgment, like flies flitting aimlessly here and there they keep changing teachers. Hence they never profit, because in neglecting their instructors they are themselves neglected, and consequently are instructed but indifferently; for it is a disease of nature, when the mind perceives itself despised, to ignore or hate the one who despises it. Certainly learning like everything else must be fostered by intimate acquaintance and liberal studies. It is a well-worn saying among us that literature is born at the hearthside. What does this mean? That the thoroughness of the teacher is encouraged by family duties.

Yet, even if you wish you cannot be generous, for you own everything as a result of hard work, intelligence, and dangers; and what is acquired at a risk is held on to tenaciously. But

usui opportuna ultro respondent,[630] gratisque videtur acceptum quod ubertate annua reportatur. Ex hoc non minus facile donatur cuius fecunditas sine impendio sentitur. At denarius vobis denarium parit. Et cui non est contractior[631] manus ad nummum? Facile donabimus par caponum, tritici modium, et vix crumenam ad solidum recludemus. Adeo aurum presens blanditur, ut sincerius cum non videtur emittatur. Hinc dominatores urbium liberalius effundunt, quia nec contingunt nec oculis intuentur que donant. Cum autem ad ratiocinium liberalitas revocatur, contrahitur. Quoniam igitur apud vos pecunia geruntur cunctur, largitas coartatur.

V-63. Hoc veto obicias! Advenarum enim ceterorumque[632] vel questu vel fortuna vagantium confugium ac hospitium sumus, humaniter cunctos favorabiliterque civitas suscipit. Nec uspiam locorum pecunia liberalius in egenorum usus erogatur, nec eruditoribus pretium amplius exolvitur.[633]

P-63. Multi, fateor, et multigeni[634] illo divertunt, quos libertas loci mercaturaque allicit; et difficile quemquam, innumerosissima multitudine, tantis ac tam variis adminiculis indigente vita, nisi segnis ultro maneat, sine fructu consistere. Quod autem dexter exteris liberque pateat, necessitas prudens admonuit. Nam plantati septique pelagi[635] lacunis sicut rerum cunctarum advectione, sic mortalium adventione prorsus indigetis. Et vestro rursus studio populi adiacentes indigent. Quare Dei opera et munus civitas Venetica fuit, quoniam ab ortu solis ad occasum quicquid est iocundum visu et utile usu congeritis, unde omnis Europa instruitur et ornatur. Per vos enim familiare Latiis gentibus mare, per vos oriens atque occidens commercii facultate iunguntur. Ita ergo conducit ad amplitudinem rei publice ut, sicut externorum indiget, sic respiciat presentius adventantes. Atqui ad elemosinariam[636] quam iactas largitatem, respondere suffecerit quod magne opes

---

630. respondet PV.
631. contracior V.
632. ceterorum V.
633. exolvit V.
634. multigene PV.
635. pelegi V.
636. elimosinariam V

for us the earth, its crops, wine, fowls, and other things suitable for use come of their own accord, and what is produced in annual abundance appears to have been received without cost. Hence we give readily from the plenteousness that is felt to be without expense. But a penny brings forth a penny for you. And whose hand does not close tighter around a coin? We will easily give away a pair of capons or a measure of grain, and yet we will with difficulty open our purse for a coin. Ready gold is so cherished that it is let go more cheerfully when it is not seen. Hence the rulers of cities pour out more liberally because they do not touch nor see with their own eyes what they give. When, however, generosity is referred to an account book, it shrinks. Since, then, among you all things are represented by money, generosity is straitened.

V-63. I forbid you to reproach us with this! For we are a refuge and shelter for strangers and others who are wandering about in search of gain or fortune, and the city receives them all courteously and kindly. And not anywhere in the world is money paid out more generously for the benefit of the poor, nor is a higher price paid for teachers.

P-63. I admit people of many kinds go there who are enticed by the freedom of the place and by its trade; and it is difficult for anyone not to make money in such a large population, when life needs so many varied provisions, unless he remains lazy of his own volition. But it is prudent necessity that has recommended that the city should lie readily open and free to strangers. For just as you need the importation of all sorts of goods through the lagoons of your artificially dammed-up sea, so do you also need the immigration of human beings. And, again, the adjacent peoples need your zeal. Therefore, the city of Venice has been the handiwork and gift of God, since from east to west you gather whatever is pleasing to see and convenient to use; and from this all of Europe is provided and ornamented. For through you the sea is familiar to the Latin nations, through you the East and West are united by means of trade. Therefore it is useful to the growth of the commonwealth, since it has need of foreigners, to have a high regard for those timely arrivals. As for the charity that you boastfully call

sine magno peccato non congeruntur, magna vero peccata magnopere conscientiam quasi Titii iecur iugi morsu vultures urgent. At conscientia stimulis agitata effusione opum sese prodiga redimit.

Porro autem stipendia que ingentia monitoribus iuventutis tribui memoras haudquaquam[637] largitati datoris[638] sed loco potius imputanda, qui veluti cetera sic[639] hanc quoque mercem pretio maiore vindicat. Ei sane qui liberorum vestrorum instructor et fictor accipitur pactam mercedem semel[640] redditis, verum cunctis deinceps familiaritatis indiciis destitutum tamquam ethnicum vobis publicanumque nescitis, minus advertentes quotidianis officiis hominum studia enutriri, ubi desinant, situ oblivioso[641] evanescere. Ceterum in Euganea imo, ubicumque cura est iuventutem instrui, qui natos eruditum iri mittunt annalis stipendii impensa liberalitatem non claudunt, frequentato sed officio monitorem natis emereri moliuntur. Preter enim corporalis opere pretium, quevis ferme[642] ebdomada[643] suo munere curam domesticam memorat, neve torpeat docentis labor instigat. Quare nichil ei magis qui discere laborat procuranda est opera quam illius qui docere debet affectus. Qui vero negotium docentis emi, contempta dilectione, satis arbitrantur, emunt quidem operantis ministerium non doctrinam, ubi, quoniam alterum impense, laboris alterum piget, fit ut ille segniter colat, sero iste fructum metat. Unde parare instructoris voluntatem quam servitium magis opere pretium est; quia vero hand setius doctrine munus atque[644] mercenarias operas licemini, evenit ut scientie negotium subsidat,[645] et quo defervetis divitiarum urbes vicinas pregravatis.

Quid de aere disseram,[646] quem meus ille sue saluti noxium criminatur? An non crassus impurusque sentitur dilucularibus

---

637. haud quamquam V.
638. *ex* dataris *corr.* V.
639. si V.
640. simul V.
641. obluoso V.
642. firme PV.
643. ebdomeda V.
644. aut V.
645. subsidas V.
646. differam V.

generosity, it will be sufficient to answer that great wealth is not collected without great sins; but great sins strongly beset the conscience, as the vultures constantly beset the liver of Tityus with their beaks.[137] Then conscience, when pricked by goads, redeems itself by a prodigal effusion of wealth.

But, furthermore, the large salaries that you say are paid to the teachers of the youth are by no means to be attributed to the generosity of the donor but rather to the place, which, as it does other things, acquires this merchandise, too, at a rather high price. You give once, to be sure, a stipulated fee to the man who is accepted as instructor and molder of your children; but afterwards he is denied all signs of friendship from you, as if he were a heathen and tax-gatherer.[138] You ignore him, not realizing that the studies of men develop with daily activities and that they disappear at the cessation of these tasks, because of the inactivity that produces forgetfulness. But in Padua, on the contrary, wherever care is taken for young people to be instructed, those who send their sons to be educated do not end their liberality with the payment of an annual salary, but by frequent employment of the teacher they attempt to gain his favor for their sons. For in addition to the value of physical work, almost every week with its own tasks reminds the student of domestic responsibility; the exertions of the teacher prod him along lest he grow dull. Therefore no service is more worth acquiring by one who is laboring to learn than the good attentions of the one who has to teach. But those who think it satisfactory to buy the efforts of the teacher, scorning his affection, buy indeed the service of a workman, not education, where, since one begrudges the expense and the other the labor, the result is that the teacher cultivates apathetically and the student reaps a harvest too late. Hence it is more worthwhile to acquire the good-will of the instructor than his service. But because you evaluate the performance of teaching as a hired service, the result is that activity in learning subsides and you surpass the neighboring cities in the riches for which you are ardent.

What shall I say about the air, which that friend of mine charges is harmful to his health? Is it not perceived to be

horis quando necdum nocturnos sol radiis aut extenuavit aut exhausit vapores mundi, alitum expurgans?[647] Putidus certe odor animeque officiens nocte concretus exalat. Nimirum tot cloacis, tot latrinis,[648] tot excrementis hominum, rerum, pecudum redundantibus, que nisi fluxus refluxusque ille Neptunius vicissitudine verrat ac temperet, quis ferat? Quis non langueat? Quemadmodum calcem lateresque spiritus flans, ita mortalium artus exedit et angustat[649] anelitum. Unde id, nisi quia superficiem sali radens ventus salsedine inficitur et uredine quicquid illinit demolitur. Quo valuisse[650] arbitror ut seri stratis et cubiculis evadatis, quousque sol ortus mephitem noctis absolverit. Sapora, queso, lineam supellectilem candentem, licet et mundam,[651] si non sapore et odore sensum offenderit, quoniam circumfluens aer, lacunari alitu infectus, contactu rebus quibus inheret suam indit qualitatem. Nec abnue complexionem suopte genio raram ac tenuem eiuscemodi salsi vaporis acritudine[652] offendi, pinguescentem forsan temperari, sed nec minorem fortasse effectum animalibus motibus ingigni. Quippe salubri impermixtoque aere sanguis ac inde purior spiritus creatur, quo anime acies liquidius rerum species haurit et discernit cuditque conceptus vehementiores, crasso autem haud aliter atque ocularibus fertur oculus in obiecta.
V–64. Culpas aerem. Iurene id inuriave nescio. Illud tamen vehementer contradicit nusquam numerosior nec varia adeo populi multitudo; taceo iuventutis florem et senii dignitatem.
P–64. Id non infitior, sed indigenis consuetudo non officit, cuius vis adeo ut animantium feculentis lutosisque sedibus alia

647. experire PV.
648. lacrimis V.
649. angusciat V.
650. moluisse P inoluisse V.
651. immondam V.
652. aredine PV.

thick and impure in the hours of dawn when the sun has not yet with its rays thinned out or drained off the night vapors of the world, cleansing the exhalations?[139] Certainly a fetid odor, damaging to the breath, thickens at night and seeps out. Indeed, with so many sewers, so many latrines, so much excrement from men, things, and animals overflowing, who could endure the pollution if it were not for that alternate ebb and flow of Neptune's tides which sweep it out and keep it under control? Who would not be ill? Like an exhalation blowing on limestone and bricks, it eats away the strength of mortals and constricts their breathing. What is the cause of this, unless that the wind, grazing the surface of the sea, is tinged with its saltiness and blights with burning itch whatever it passes over? For this reason I think it has been important for you to be late emerging from your bedcoverings and sleeping chambers, until sunrise has broken up the noxious vapor of night. Smell, I ask you, your white bedlinens, even though they are clean, to see if they do not offend your senses with their odor and scent, for the air flowing around, infected with exhalations from the lagoons, infuses by contact its own characteristics into the things to which it adheres. And do not deny that a physical constitution that is spare and feeble is damaged by the sharpness of this kind of salt vapor, while one that is fat is perhaps tempered. Yet it may be that a greater effect appears in mental activities. Indeed, by an admixture of healthful air the blood and then the breath are purified, by means of which the acuteness of the mind takes in and discerns more clearly the appearance of objects and forges more vigorous concepts; but when the air is thick, it is like the eye's being focused onto objects by means of eyeglasses.

V-64. You blame the air, but whether you do this rightly or wrongly, I do not know. However, nowhere does the existence of a larger and more varied multitude of people vehemently contradict that, not to mention the flower of youth and the dignity of old age.

P-64. I do not deny this; but because the native born are accustomed to the situation, they are not damaged. The strength

proficiant, quo si transtuleris alia deficiant. Addunt preterea delicie vestre et cultus operosus ad speciem. Advenam vero exigui mora temporis non inquinat. Ex hac namque impuritia crebro pestifera lues plebem afficit, quam[653] nisi frequens navigatio eduxerit vicatim languens ruat. Otium quippe, male sanus victus, aer tabidus, aqua impura, cuncta morbos pariunt faciuntque contagium.

V–65. De aeris qualitate ignarus, phisicalium[654] rationum non facile habeo quid contra hiscam. Sed aquam inhibeo criminari, quoniam salubris fertur et medentium autoritas pluviam probat.

P–65. Sed colluvie nulla[655] infectam, nullius coloris nulliusve saporis emulam, qualem, exquisita licet cura, vix in vestris ebibes. Quid quod nichil est vivacis adeo prestantisque nature, quod contracto forinsecus morbo vel tempore saltem non senescat ac vitium patiatur? Cisternarum aqua, assentior, laudabilis vulgatur et est, sed minime qualis a plebe vestra passim potatur.[656] Nam pluvii sepe humoris congeriem quanta sordicies impurat. Immundi nempe vagantium gressus canum, puerorum mictus,[657] ac egestio anserum quoque et gallinarum, sucularum, equorum, ceterorumve animalium que vel[658] utilitatis causa vel voluptatis retinentur fedant. Que superficie quidem herentia per meatus licet angustos, aque insudanti permiscentur, mixtamque commaculant. Esto adhibita spurcitiam diligentia coerceat, harena ipsa que ad eliquandum imbrem sepelitur, vetustate, quemadmodum orta omnia[659] alterantur,[660] corrumpitur, et a qualitate propria terre convertitur. Num[661] insuper circumstantis vicinia telluris humorem per ambientis crete poros negabimus insudare, et quod repperit impurare?

V–66. De sabuli[662] corruptione subterraneove[663] sudore nec sentire nec dissentire[654] facile auserim.[665] Verum ex te audita

653. qua V.
654. phiscalium V.
655. nullam V.
656. a plebe . . . potatur] plebem vestram . . . potat PV.
657. minctus V.
658. ulla V.
659. anima V.
660. alteratur PV.
661. nam V.
662. *ex* sauuli *corr.* P.
663. *ex* subterraneo *corr.* V.

Criticisms of Venice 235

of habit is such that some living things do well in impure and muddy abodes, yet if other things are brought there, they will die. Furthermore, your charming and active way of life adds to your fine appearance; in fact, a short stay does no harm to a newcomer. From this impurity often a pestiferous plague afflicts the common people, who would fall fainting in the streets if frequent voyages did not take them abroad. In fact, idleness, unhealthful food, polluted air, and impure water all bring forth disease and cause contagions.

V-65. Being ignorant of the quality of air, I do not have any convenient reasons from physics to put up against your argument. But I refuse to blame the water, since it is called healthful, and the authority of physicians approves of rainwater.

P-65. But they approve only when it is infected with no impurities and is free from color and odor, the kind that you are not likely to have to drink among your people, no matter how careful you are! Remember that there is nothing of so lasting and excellent a nature that it does not waste away from disease contracted from without, or at least from time, and become flawed. The water from cisterns, I agree, is commonly pronounced excellent, and it is, but not the sort that is generally drunk by your populace. For often how much filth defiles the collected rain water! Indeed, the dirty feet of stray dogs, the urination of boys, and the voiding of geese, chickens, pigs, horses, or other animals that people keep either for use or pleasure, cause fouling. These impurities clinging to the surface, although going through very narrow passageways, are intermingled with the water that seeps in, and they contaminate it when mixed. Even though the application of diligence may control the defilement, the sand itself that is buried to filter the water is corrupted by age, as all created things are changed, and it is converted from its proper characteristics to earth. In addition, we surely will not deny that, because of the nearness of the surrounding earth, the water seeps through the pores of the encompassing clay and defiles what it comes upon.

V-66. I would not readily dare either to agree or disagree about the corruption of the gravel or underground seepage. But what I have heard from you will make me more careful in

accuratiorem[666] me studio reddent, cisterne domestice ambitum, quantus est, ab omni labe servare[667] perpetuum.

P–66. Scite id quidem, nam quod eliquatur aquam harenamque contaminat, atque infecte plures usu aque morbent, quorum deinceps contagio serpit in proximos.

Quamquam nichilo secius putrescentium rerum ceu fructuum, carnium, farine esus et usus infirmitates creant. Ceresa namque, crisomula, ficus, Persica, pira, ceteraque eiusmodi mansa vel recens lecta obesse feruntur quanto magis stativa. Adde quod semotis in regionibus immatura leguntur, et confertis invecta navibus primum imponendo et exponendo eliduntur. Elisa demum et ipsa exacervatione compressa concalentiaque vicissim sese tabificant, ac fiunt de malo cibo deterior.

Nec de animalibus absimilis ratio. Nam e virentibus pascuis, latis saltibus, ab aperto fragrantique solo, a fluentis irriguis, navali includuntur angustia, ubi estu, gelu, inedia, siti, ac situ ipso stercoribus urinaque olente, denique statione perpetua, solitarumque rerum defectu egrent, febriunt, et penitus absumuntur.[668] Quis est adeo intrepide sanitatis qui talibus coartatus et affectus incommodis navigans non alteretur et infirmetur? In qua re, cum percuntabundus lanionem ex vestris quonam pacto edos eminus advectos alerent rogarem, "Quomodo," inquit, "lactantes[669] alamus? Ieiunos etiam quinque diebus plerumque servamus." Que vita usque adeo tenax ut non in semet deficiat et exorbeatur, nedum hec lactans[670] et tenella? Quid de bubus et arietibus reris? Nunc hisce vesci carnibus quibus, alimento cessante, nec salus nec sapor suus nec odor suppetit; sed mandentem potius gustu conturbant, contracto vitio contagiant. Pullos forsan probas? Conditione pari vitium criolis ac stiis infarti capiunt. Animal siquidem vagum et quietis nescium, carcere obtrusum

664. discentire P.
665. ausim V.
666. accuracione V.
667. asservare V.
668. absumittitur V.
669. lactentes P.
670. lactens PV.

my efforts to preserve the entire circumference of my cistern at home, as large as it is, free of all defects!

P-66. This would indeed be wise, for what is filtered through contaminates both the water and the sand, and many people become ill from the use of polluted water; then the infection spreads from them to their neighbors.

However, the eating and use of rotting foods such as fruit, meat, and grain create just as much sickness. For cherries, quinces, figs, peaches, pears, and other fruits of this sort, when eaten, even though recently picked, are said to be hurtful, and more so if they have been standing around. In remote regions, furthermore, they are picked green, and when brought in on crowded ships they are bruised first by being loaded and then by being unloaded. Then, damaged and mashed by piling up, they grow warm, they rot, and from bad food become worse.

There is a similar problem with animals. For, taken out of green pastures, broad groves, from open and fragrant land and streams full of water, they are closed up in the confines of a ship, where because of heat, cold, hunger, thirst, and the place itself reeking of manure and urine, finally, because of the constant standing and the lack of conditions they are used to, they become sick, develop fevers, and are destroyed from within. What creature is of such unshakable good health that, if confined and afflicted by such inconveniences on board ship, it does not become changed and weakened? Concerning this, when I inquired of a meat merchant of yours and asked how they fed the young goats that had been brought from a distance, he said, "How are we to feed nurslings? Usually we keep them even for five days without food." What life is so strong that it does not fail within itself and drain out, not to mention a tender nursling? What do you think of oxen and rams? Now you eat this flesh which, since its nourishment has ceased, has neither healthfulness nor its own flavor and odor; but rather it upsets the eater by the taste and infects him with the harm it has contracted. Do you perhaps like young chickens? Under similar conditions, stuffed into traps and coops, they become infected. Certainly a freely

compressumque cum multis, socio pariter cum calore et fetore[671] contabescit. Nec escam nec tempestivum recipiens potum, aere item libero et motu[672] carens, squalore mutuo inficitur, unde insuavis odore ac gustu caro et nequaquam vite salubris invenitur. Quos[673] vivaria pisces carcerarunt repudias.[674] Nec advertis[675] altilia peiori[676] conditione morbescere exque loco trahere et angustia contagium? Cristas liventes deciduasque videbis et carceraneo senties plumas squalore putrescere. Quale pariat alimentum morbida infectaque materia?

At vero compensamini quod vina electe propaginis ex Meroe, Tiro, Creta, atque Motono,[677] rursus et Dalmatia, Sanio, Piceno, e vicinis oris, Flaminio, Gallia Cisalpina, Foro Iulii, Sinuque Tergestino, atque ex omni demum superi maris plaga convehuntur. Cuius omnes ferme ad humores emundandos, ad alimonie temperiem moderandam, sanguinem depurandum, spiritumque gignendum, ac vires anime reficiendas usum tempestivum et laudant periti et experiuntur imperiti. Piscarios namque vallestres, exalatu palustri quotidianoque piscium alimento de[678] aeris ac cibi colluvie ipsis testantibus, vinum quo[679] infarciuntur sanos valentesque preservat. Quamobrem huiuscemodi[680] nature beneficium tamquam parabile vulgareque antidotum extimari valet. Ac vobis in primis, limoso septis ambitu, opportunum vite salutique suffragium, cuius quidem rei nusquam[681] tanta varietas tantave prestantia.

Quid de oleribus dicam? Quorum non usque modo ad innumerabilis turbe sed vicinorum quoque indigentie explementum exuberat copia, eaque vobis e litorali cultu Mediterraneorumque[682] locorum fecunditas redit. Quid de fructibus quorum incolumitas annali diuturnitate non variat? Adeo presens abundantia vos instruit quam si nusquam[683] alias gentium nascerentur.

671. fectore V.
672. mutu P.
673. quo P.
674. repudiatis PV.
675. advertitis PV.
676. peiora V.
677. metonio V.
678. ab PV.
679. quoque V.
680. huiusmodi V.
681. nuspiam PV.
682. Meditanneorumque P.
683. nuspiam PV.

wandering animal, unused to keeping still, if thrust into a pen and crowded in with many others will waste away with the accompanying heat and stench. Receiving neither food nor regular drink, also deprived of free air and movement, each is infected with the filth from the others, as a result of which the meat is found to be of unpleasant odor and taste and not healthful for life. You would refuse the fish that the fishponds contain. And do you not notice that the fowls grow sickly because of worse conditions, and contract illness from the location and confinement? You will see that their combs are bluish and drooping, and you will perceive that their feathers are decaying from the squalor of their cages. What sort of nourishment can be produced by sickly and diseased substances?

But you Venetians are compensated because wines from choice plants are brought from Meroe, Tyre, Crete, and Modon; also from Dalmatia, Sanium, Picenum, and from neighboring shores, Flaminium, Cisalpine Gaul, Friuli, and the Tergestine Bay, finally from all the region of the upper sea.[140] Nearly all men who are experienced with it praise the seasonable use of wine for purifying the humors, tempering the mixture of foods, cleansing the blood, raising the spirits, and renewing the vigor of the soul; and those who have been inexperienced put it to the test. For fishmongers in the lowlands, where the swampy vapors and a daily diet of fish are evidence of a vile medley of air and food, are kept sound and healthy by the wine with which they are filled. Therefore a blessing of nature such as this can be valued as an easily procured common antidote. And to you particularly, being hemmed in by a muddy surrounding area, it is an opportune aid to life and health. Nowhere else, indeed, is there so great a variety or such excellence of this article.

What shall I say about vegetables? Of these there is an abundance to supply not only an innumerable populace but also needy neighbors, and this bounteous crop comes to you from the cultivation of coastlands and of Mediterranean regions. What about the fruits, whose excellence does not vary the whole year long? Their ready abundance provides for you as if they grew nowhere else in the world.

Incassum memorem aromata pigmentaque et quicquid exotice mercis ad usum voluptatemque delicie necessitasve humana frequentat. Quorum alibi mercatura, hic pompa et miraculum est. Hinc omnem per Italiam, Germaniam, Hunnos, universamque barbariem redundant.

Ex quo quidem liquido, quam paulo ante perstrinxi, avaritie sese fructus explicat. Quippe ea pruriente, undique exaggeratis unde per universum defectus et voluptas suppleatur. Quare auro predivites estis et inhabitantium numero urbes Latias anteitis. Tum, vallati quoque obice lacunali a predonum aliorumve nefariorum improba hominum cupiditate, illesi inoffensique constatis. Commoditas itaque rerum, quarum est vobis undequaque pervius commeatus meraque vivendi libertas, cunctos elicit, et populo annumerat.

At illud multo largius quod, clarum licet ac prepotens prepollensque opibus, imperium summopere tamen paci studet, nec minorem premere intentat et mavult hostem placare quam perdere. Ex hoc itaque honestissimo vestra civitas et sanctissimo pacis cultu princeps vicinarum urbium, exornatissima, frequens, ac felix, cunctarumque rerum dexteritate letissima spectatur. Hinc ad eam totius humani generis fit coitio.[684] Adeo pax dulciter et libertas auditur. Nempe qui externa grandescere conantur[685] iniuria aliena sternunt et profligant sua pariterque hominum odiis subiciuntur. Quibus olim efferventibus vel ruunt imperia vel turbulentissime possidentur. Una siquidem pax est, sine qua nec fructuosa nec iocunda potest vita contingere. Christus Deus hanc munus hereditarium piis liquit, hanc sperat et precatur ecclesia, hec denique premium celeste spondetur. "Posuit," inquit, "fines tuos pacem," et rursum Ysaias "Sedebit," ait, "populos meus in

---

684. occucio V.
685. nituntur V.

It would be needless for me to mention the spices and cosmetics and all the exotic merchandise that human enjoyment or need uses frequently for convenience and pleasure. These things are purchased elsewhere, but here is the display and marvel of them. And from here they flood all Italy, Germany, the regions of the Huns, and the entire barbarian world.

From this, indeed, as I touched upon a little while ago, the reward of avarice is clearly revealed. Since avarice is an itch to you, you heap up on all sides the means of supplying needs and pleasures throughout the world. Therefore you are very rich in gold, and you surpass all Latin cities in the number of inhabitants. Protected also by your barrier of lagoons from the wicked greed of robbers or other nefarious men, you remain unharmed and unattacked. Thus the benefit of goods that come easily to you from every direction and the pure freedom of your way of life allure all men and increase the size of your population.

But that system of government is much more bountiful which, though famous and strong and potent in its wealth, nevertheless earnestly strives for peace, does not threaten to oppress an inferior, and prefers to appease an enemy rather than destroy him. Therefore, it is because of this honorable and pure cultivation of peace that your city is the leader of the neighboring cities, the most elegant, populous, and fortunate, and is seen to be the happiest because of its prosperity in all things. Hence to her there gathers all the human race. So sweetly do the words peace and liberty fall upon the ear! Indeed, those who attempt to grow great by doing injury to others destroy the property of other people and waste their own, and at the same time incur the hatred of men. Since these hatreds have been seething for a long time, governments are either falling in ruins or are in tumultuous upheaval. For peace is the only thing without which men can have neither a fruitful nor a happy life. Christ the Lord has left peace as an inheritance for the pious; it is what the church hopes and prays for and what is finally promised as a heavenly reward. "He has made your territory peaceful," he said, and also Isaiah

pulcritudine pacis et in tabernaculis fiducie et in requie opulenta."
V-67.   Rem solide veritatis enuntias. Venetus nimirum principatus studio cultuque pacis tam amplus et perpetuus, tam decorus magnificensque visitur. At Padua, dudum frequens numero magnificentiaque civium et potentia incolarum magnifica et opibus splendens, vestrorum ducum inquiete imperandique libidine deformis et comminuta ac prope in nichilum versa est. Et tam se orbam civibus quam viduata colonis rura deflet, in similitudinem posita gentibus; quod pacis studio urbes florent, evertuntur belli, ruuntque in perditissimam servitutem, quam velut malorum extremum adeo civitas nostra semper exhorruit, ut summa rerum incommoda ac vite discrimen[686] sepe subiverit. Transeo pervetusta; quod nostram turbavit etatem repeto. Nam secundo bello Euganico, adversum conspirantibus undique hostibus et deserentibus sociis, spe, subsidio, et rebus exhausti, angelis et hominibus spectaculum fuimus, omnia perpessi que dura, que aspera, que misera forent. Tantus erat libertatis amor in pectoribus singulorum, qui utique si usquam est gentium nos sumus illi.
P-67.   Clarum est nomen libertatis, carum etiam et dulce, quin altero anno vocula ipsa complures in Etruria, Piceno, Flaminioque urbes movit, et ab ecclesie dicione[687] subduxit; exercitus cum ducibus aut contempsit aut stravit. Sed quamquam linguis frequentata, scita nichilominus notaque a paucis est.

---

686. discrimine V.
687. dictione V.

said, "My people will sit in the beauty of peace and in the tents of trustworthiness and in abundant rest."[141]

11. The Nature of Liberty

V-67. You express a sound truth. Certainly, the Venetian state is seen to be not only rich and constant in its desire and cultivation of peace, but also beautiful and magnificent. But Padua, recently teeming in the numbers and excellence of her citizens, outstanding in the great influence of her inhabitants and splendid in her resources, has, because of the restlessness of your leaders and their lust for power, become unattractive and diminished and brought almost to nothing.[142] And she mourns that not only is she bereft of citizens but that her countryside is stripped of its peasants, and she has been made a byword among the nations,[143] for cities flourish when zealous for peace but are overthrown when zealous for war. They fall into the most desperate slavery, which our city has always so much avoided as the worst of evils that we have often suffered very great hardships and perils of life. Omitting ancient examples, I shall mention an event that has thrown our age into confusion. For in the second Paduan war, with the enemy conspiring against us on all sides and our allies deserting us, being drained of hope, aid, and resources, we were a spectacle for heaven and earth, suffering every experience that was harsh, cruel, and wretched. So great was the love of liberty in the hearts of all individuals! If indeed that love is anywhere in the world, it exists among us.

P-67. The name of liberty is famous, beloved too, and sweet. Even more, during another year the name itself stirred many cities in Etruria, Picenum, and Flaminium, and led them away from the control of the church; it either defied or overthrew armies along with their leaders. But although frequently on men's lips, it has nevertheless been experienced and known by few.[144]

V-68. Qui amari adeo optarive queat, si nescitur?
P-68. Quandoquidem tantopere nomen diligitur, coniecta quantopere res ipsa placeret. Plus dixerim ita parum intelligi ut pluribus servitium libertas videatur.
V-69. Amabo, an[688] non est libertas vivere posse quemadmodum velis?
P-69. Haudquaquam,[689] sed que iure ac lege dirigatur.
V-70. Quot populi, quot nationes nec ipsum quidem iuris aut legis nomen audivere et liberi tamen vivunt?
P-70. Nemo sine iure[690] oritur; legem nescire potest, ius non potest. Duo sunt nature iussa que propheta vidit et cecinit: "Declina a malo et fac bonum." Omnis[691] quippe lex divina et humana hoc sonat. Cuncta volumina que iam nimis multa vix leguntur huiuscemodi scaturigine gemina emanant. Aut enim docent quomodo fiat bonum aut quomodo quod malum est fugiatur; et qui scripta lege caret profecto conscientie lumine[692] impressa non caret. "Testimonium," inquit apostolus, "reddente eis conscientia ipsorum, qui ostendunt opus legis scriptum in cordibus suis." Nullus enim sui compos non pungitur conscientia flagitii, quamquam placeat dum perpetratur. Idcirco Titii iecur a vulturibus edi poetica memoravit autoritas, quod quisque nequam suos vultures patiatur. Adeo liber iste conscientie? Nature ius est ut irrationalia quoque non sinat expertia. Canes et muricipes, quorum mores familiaritas docuit, si facinora[693] fecerint, ceu conscientie aculeo perculsi, ultro secedent et territi comparent. Alui corvum fraudosumque notavi. Insiliebat mensam paratam et, circum speculabundus si observator afforet, nemine circumspecto, fialas deiciebat; e vestigioque evolans eminus astabat, nec nisi blanditiis, quasi data fide, vocatus accedebat.[694] Vulpes quoque feruntur, qua mansitant indemniter, observari.[695] Quid hoc nisi conscientie

---

688. an *suprascript.* V.
689. haud quamquam V.
690. iure sine PV.
691. omis V.
692. volumine P.
693. fore PV.
694. accederat V.
695. obversari P.

The Nature of Liberty

V-68. How can liberty be so loved and desired if it is not known?

P-68. Since indeed the name is loved so greatly, consider how very pleasing the reality itself would be. I would say, furthermore, that liberty is so little understood that it seems to many a servitude.

V-69. Please tell me: is liberty being able to live just as you wish, or is it not?

P-69. It is not. It is what is guided by justice and law.

V-70. How many peoples, how many nations have not even heard the very name of justice and law, and yet live free?

P-70. No one is born without a sense of justice. He can be ignorant of law but not of justice. There are two commands of nature that the prophet saw and sang of: "Turn from evil and do good."[145] In fact, every law both divine and human proclaims this. All the volumes that now are so numerous that they are scarcely read emanate from this twofold source. For they teach either how good comes about or how evil is avoided; and the man who lacks written law certainly does not lack the law that the light of conscience has impressed upon him. The apostle says, "Their conscience bears witness for those who show that what the law requires is written on their hearts."[146] For no one with control over himself is not pricked by the consciousness of evil, however pleasurable it may be while it is being committed. Hence poetic authority has recorded that the liver of Tityus was eaten by vultures, because every wicked man suffers his own vultures. Is he so free from conscience? It is a law of nature that irrational beings are also not permitted to be without a share. When dogs and cats, whose characteristics are familiar to us, have done wrong, they will voluntarily draw back and appear terrified as if struck by the pangs of conscience. I brought up a raven and noticed he was deceitful. He would jump upon a table that had been set, and, looking around to see if there was an observer nearby, if he perceived no one he would knock over the cups; and immediately flying off he would stop at a distance and not come near, unless called by soothing words that reassured him. Foxes also are reported to show themselves in a like manner,

morsus? Hoc itaque iure multo artius nos, prediti[696] ratione, obnoxii tenemur. Libertas ergo non est agere posse quod velis nisi previa ratione. An si mechari, si predare, si minorem opprimere cum velit iniquus valet, liber tibi videatur?
V–71. Haud intelligo de[697] libertate peccandi, sed cum nulli subditus homo se et suis velut cupiat uti potest.
P–71. Et quis est iste, et laudabimus eum? Tali certe formula libertatis pauci quidem liberi sed servi potius multi. Taceo quod omnis vita aut vitium sequitur aut virtutem. Utrobique servitus : honesta et secundum naturam virtutis, fedissima vitii. Unde apostolus "Cum," ait, "servistis peccato, liberi fuistis iustitie. Nunc autem iiberi a peccato, servi facti estis iustitie." Quis nempe sic habet pro voto fortunam ut se quisque rebus uti pro arbitrio queat? "Sufficit," ait Veritas, "diei[698] malitia sua." Et cui aut diei[699] malitia aut cupiditas aut ambitio aliave instantia de libertate non subtrahat, ut quod velit minime valeat efficere? In civitate vestra ubi tantam asseris libertatem, quis sic agit ut vult, imo quis non agit et tolerat multa que non vult? Duxne vester an summatum quisquam eorum qui rem publicam gerunt in ea quam tibi[700] tute descripseras libertate censetur?
V–72. Non, mehercule—cui vix hora quidem libera vacat! Quin, meo iudicio, si demas honorem, ut ita dixerim, cunctorum servissimus est.[701]
P–72. Recte iudicasti. Num[702] cives amplissimi et divites? Campana magistratus et ordines citat. Negotia, voluptates, otia studiosa interrumpenda sunt, omne seponitur studium, acceleratur, hinc ambitu, hinc emulatione, hinc simultate pulsante. Artes vero artifices vindicant, ut quelibet se frui non sinunt. Dicit scriba, dicit medicus : "In civitate sum libera; liber sum, nulli servio, nemo instat michi." Quid est ergo die tota[703] prostas et scribis?

696. predicti V.
697. quod V.
698. dici V.
699. dici V.
700. tibi quam P.
701. est *om.* V.
702. non V.
703. tota die V.

safely in their lairs. What is this but the pangs of conscience? Therefore, we, being equipped with reason, are held under obligation much more stringently by this law. And so liberty is not being able to do what you wish, unless your wishes are guided by reason. If a wicked man is able to commit adultery, to steal, to oppress an inferior whenever he wishes, would you consider this freedom?

V-71. I do not mean the freedom to do wrong; but when a man is subject to no one, he can do what he wishes with himself and his belongings.

P-71. And who is that man, and are we to praise him? To be sure, with this definition of liberty few indeed are free, but instead many are slaves. I need not mention that every life pursues either vice or virtue. On both sides there is a servitude: the honorable and natural one of virtue and the base one of vice. Thus the apostle says, "When you were slaves to sin, you were free of righteousness. But now being free from sin, you have become servants of righteousness."[147] In fact, who has fortune so favourable to his wishes that he can act and use his possessions at will? The Truth says, "Sufficient unto the day is the evil thereof."[148] And for whom does the evil of the day, or greed, or ambition, or other pressing matters not detract from liberty, so that as a result he cannot accomplish what he wishes? In your city where you claim so much freedom, who does as he wishes, in fact, who does not do and tolerate many things that he does not wish? Is your leader, or any one of the highly-placed officials who run the commonwealth, thought to be in that condition which you have defined for yourself as freedom?

V-72. No, by heaven! For the leader scarcely even an hour is free. Even more, in my opinion, if you take away the honor, he is, so to speak, the most enslaved of all.

P-72. You have concluded rightly. Is it not true also of distinguished and prosperous citizens? The bell summons the magistrates and the senators. Their business affairs, pleasures, leisure hours for study have to be interrupted, and every pursuit is set aside. They scurry about, driven here by ambition, there by jealousy, there by rivalry. The arts lay claim to the

Et diluculo[704] medicus exiens, nisi quatenus reficiatur, limen non repetit? Quid obire gementes et nolentes[705] horis omnibus imperat? Pransabit uterque, quiescet; appellat egrotus quem rigor invasit, appellat volens testari notarium continuo. Mensa lectusque deseritur; exit, ad operam festinat uterque. Quis adeo improbe dominatur ut alimonie ac somni servis tempus vacuum non indulgeat? Cernis quod servit uterque, tirannum habet, calcar sentit. "Volens," inquit, "facio." Volens itaque servus es. Sic tirannis aulici ultro subduntur et titulo venustant blandiore servitium. Non adeo nisi caros. Quosnam? Quos nimirum fecit pretium et facit! Non urget inquam amicitia, sed timor ne congestus minuatur acervus, vel amor ut grandescat.

Quid de studiosis litterarumve cultoribus? Num[706] liberum tempus habent et se fruuntur? Pallet et aret iuris[707] consultus inter codices defossus. Sic orator, sic philosophus, sic poeta, dum inveniat aut cudat nova inedia, cura vigiliaque tabescit. Omnes vite sibi commoditates voluptatesque eliminat. Atqui poetarum, philosophorum, et ceterorum qui sapientie desiderio sese negligunt servitus est que corporis sucum exorbet, extenuat membra, pallorem inducit, calorem extinguit, sed laudabilis quidem; eorum vero miserabilis quibus par est servitus, intentio par non est. Quis suis temporibus Butrigario studiosior[708] Bononie? Huius olim consultum vicarius Conventus Fratrum Minorum pro causa flagitavit. Spopondit Butrigarius et "Cras," inquit, "dabo." Astitit mane vicarius brevique papiro paucas lineas accepit. Et, viginti quinque ducatos Butrigario deposcente, "Ubinam est," ait vicarius,

---

704. diliculo PV.
705. olentes PV.
706. non V.
707. iuri P.
708. studiosi V.

The Nature of Liberty

artisans, for they are not permitted to enjoy themselves. The scribe says, or the doctor says, "I am in a free city. I am free, I serve no one, no one is pressuring me." Why is it, then, that you stand all day in public and write? And why does the doctor, going out at daybreak, not return home except for meals? What compels them to go forth, complaining and unwilling, at all hours? Suppose they are eating or sleeping: a sick man calls who is having an attack of rigors; a man calls who needs at once the witness of a notary. The table or bed is abandoned; each goes out, hastening to his task. Who is so cruel a master that he does not grant to his servants free time for food and sleep? You perceive that each man serves; he has a tyrant, he feels the spur. "Willingly," he says, "I do it." And so you willingly are a slave. Thus courtiers of their own accord subject themselves to tyrants and pretty up their slavery with an agreeable title. They would not act thus unless they considered their tyrants dear; and why are they dear? Why, because money made and makes them so! Friendship, I say, does not impel such men, but the fear that their collected pile be diminished or the desire that it be increased.

What of scholars or students of literature? Do they not have free time and do they not enjoy themselves? The lawyer is pale and dried up, buried among his codices. So are the orator, the philosopher, and the poet, who dwindle away with hard work and wakeful nights, while new starvation comes upon them or strikes them down. They eliminate all comforts and pleasures from their lives. The slavery of the poets, philosophers, and others who neglect themselves in their passion for learning is one that sucks out the moisture from their bodies, weakens their limbs, causes pallor, and extinguishes warmth, yet is praiseworthy. But others who are equally enslaved find their slavery miserable because the purpose is not equal. Who in his day was more studious than Bottrigari of Bologna? Once a vicar of the Convent of the Franciscans asked his advice on a legal case. Bottrigari promised, saying, "Tomorrow I shall advise you." In the morning the vicar appeared and was given a few lines on a small piece of paper. But when Bottrigari asked for twenty-five ducats, the vicar

"conscientia?[709] Unius hore scripturam tanti facis?" "Ista," respondit, "hora quinquaginta annos habet."

At Johannes de Lignano, vir plane doctissimus et qui litteris semper incumberet, cum sacerdos Faventinus responsum in lite deposceret, audita causa respondit cras redire. Profectus ille pro iussu nil reportavit nisi "Cras redi." Tertia luce rediens pariter audivit "Cras redi." Iterate vocis miraculo presbiter commotus amicis narrat, et mirabundus quid homo tanti nominis[710] se illudat queritur. "Haud est lusus,"[711] aiunt, "sed morbus animi. Fructum expetit. Auro posce, non ore." Ille, accepto[712] Johannis vitio, quot frater Butrigario persoluisset totidem tulit et apposuit. Confestim calamo accepto, parva mora sacerdotem voti compotem dimisit. Advertis quo migrat humanorum intentio studiorum et quare impendunt obstinatam adeo litteris servitutem.

Eque de ceteris prope hominum studiis argute discussioni licet attendere. Porro numerus bella sectantium non modo libertate caret verum continetur in miserrima servitute. Quippe iniuria demolumentoque[713] alieno semper alitur[714] horum instabilis incertaque conditio. Insonat tuba, nescios in que discrimina quosve labores aut facinora ducantur ire oportet per tenebras, estum, ac frigora, per ardua, per aspera, et queque invia; cumque ratione degentium communem ad utilitatem ars ac negotium referatur, isti dumtaxat in stragem exitiumque rerum atque hominum adhibentur, et evenit ut sicut vivunt brutaliter moriantur. Quare merito ipsa nequitia non servi tantum sed infelicissimi iudicandi sunt.

V-73. Nulla verior sententia. Quenam vita fore deterior potest quam que[715] semper venui patet, et numquam emitur nisi ad repellendum vel[716] inferendum mala, rapinam, damna, cedes? De quibus Salamon "Letantur," inquit, "cum malefecerint, et exultant in rebus pessimis." Quare velut numquam sui sunt, ita nec liberi putari debent.

---

709. conscientia vicarius PV.
710. hominis V.
711. lusus est V.
712. accepto ille PV.
713. demolumento: coined. Cf. note 23.
714. aluntur PV.
715. qua V.
716. et V.

said, "Where on earth is your conscience? Do you put so high a price on one hour's worth of writing?" The other replied, "That hour is fifty years old."

Giovanni da Legnano was a man exceedingly learned and always devoted to letters. When a priest from Faenza asked for his opinion in a lawsuit, he heard the case and answered that the priest was to return tomorrow. The priest, returning as ordered, received nothing except "Return tomorrow." Coming back the third morning, he again heard "Return tomorrow." Angered by this amazing repetition, the priest told it to his friends and wonderingly asked why a man of so great a reputation would mock him. "It is not mockery," they said, "but a disease of the mind; he wants pay. Ask him with gold, not with your mouth." Having learned this fault of Giovanni, he brought and offered him as much as the friar had paid Bottrigari. At once taking up his pen, Giovanni with little delay sent the priest away in possession of what he wanted.[149] You notice where the purpose of human studies tends and why men devote so determined a servitude to letters!

Similarly, one can have a lively discussion concerning almost all other pursuits of men. A number of those engaging in wars not only lack freedom, but are held in the most wretched kind of slavery. Their unstable and uncertain condition always feeds on the injury and destruction of others. When the trumpet blares, men who are ignorant of what dangers or labors or crimes they are being led into must go through darkness, heat, and cold, through harsh, difficult, and pathless places. While the skill and energy of those living rationally are being turned to the common usefulness, soldiers are concerned only with the slaughter and destruction of men and goods; and the result is that they die brutally just as they live. Therefore, because of their very wickedness, they deserve to be judged not merely slaves but exceedingly wretched ones.

V-73. Nothing is truer than that. What life can be worse than one that is always up for sale and never is bought except for fending off or bringing on troubles, pillage, losses, deaths! Concerning such individuals Solomon said, "They rejoice when they do evil and exult in wickedness."[150] Therefore, since they are never their own men, they must not be considered free.

P-73. Nimirum quo magis ipsa iniquitate fruuntur hoc infelicius serviunt, quoniam longius ab dignitate hominis deiciuntur. Sed quid de principibus? Similis ratiocinatio de libertate cepta nos[717] tenet. Quid, inquam, censemus? Aliis presunt, imperant. Num[718] ideo liberi sunt adeo ut nulla servitute premantur, et quicquid fieri cupiunt possunt?
V-74. Speciosa frons rerum et secunda conditio, mortalium etiam favor, liberos asseverare videtur, cum quicquid iubeant pareatur. Videre tamen videor defore nescio quid ad libertatem.
P-74. Haud dicas defore "nescio quid" singulariter, sed "multa" pluraliter, nam quo plura possidemus, pluribus indigemus. Quo fit quanto plura quis possit, plura quoque non possit, si[719] indigere est non habere quod[720] exigas. Mercatores nempe, medicos, iuris consultos, oratores, ceterosque suum quandoque negotium et cura occupat, coercet sibique subicit. De dominatibus par iudicium, nam regni metus et suspicio dubios efficit, solicitudo noxia repellendi et conferentia retinendi inquietos. Quid quod externis modo legationibus, modo veris fictisque rumoribus fatigantur? Modo etiam subiectorum querelas sopire aut obstare iniuriis adiguntur. Haud alia boni principis ac patris familiarum fore debet intentio. Singula circumspicere, emendare, salvare, dirigere, magnificum certe ac divinum opus, quod, quam sit mole, in suo quemque lare experiri coniecto. Quamobrem improbandi sunt asseverantes non omnia esse dominis referenda, quo ne molestia afficiantur. Dictitant enim : "Non est ut infirmes caput pro quaque re domino. Non inquietes. Sine quiescat." Ego vero equius fore duco nosse[721] cuncta qui debet emendare cuncta, quatenus dum nullatenus speratur latebra, iniustitia caveatur. Si dignum est recta queque

717. nos cepta V.
718. non V.
719. sed V.
720. quidem P.
721. nosce V.

P-73. Indeed, the more they enjoy their wickedness, the more wretchedly they are enslaved, since they are cast farther away from the dignity of man. But what about princes? The same reasoning about liberty with which we began still holds. What, I say, do we judge of them? They are in charge of others, they give the orders. Are they for this reason so free that they are burdened by no servitude and can do whatever they wish to be done?

V-74. The fine outward appearance of their situation and their fortunate circumstances, as well as the acclaim of mortals, seem to proclaim they are free, since whatever they command is obeyed. Yet I seem to see that something is lacking for freedom.

P-74. You should not say "something" in the singular is lacking, but "many things" in the plural; for the more we possess, the more we want. Hence it is that the more a man can have, the more also he cannot have, if lacking means not possessing what you desire. To be sure, whenever their own business and concerns occupy merchants, doctors, lawyers, orators, and others, they are held in restraint and put under subjection by these. The same holds true for rulers, as fear for their kingdoms and suspicion make them hesitant, while the burden of warding off evils and retaining advantages makes them restless. What of the fact that they are harassed on the one hand by foreign legations, and on the other by both true and fictitious rumors? They are also compelled to allay the disagreements of their subjects or prevent injustices to them. Such ought to be the aims of a good prince and fathers of families. To see to individual matters, correct, save, and direct them is truly a magnificent and divine work, which I suppose each man experiences in his own home, although it is difficult. Therefore those men are to be censured who claim that not all things should be reported to the masters, lest they be troubled. For they say, "It is not right for you to give your master a headache for every little thing. Don't disturb him. Let him rest." But I consider it better for him to know all since he has to correct all, so that at a time when no subterfuge is expected, precautions can be taken

cognoscere ad premium, cur non etiam inde recta[722] ad vindictam? Ideo ista librantibus solium servitio non vacat. Sensit hoc rex ille subtilis iudicii qui pondus diadematis aut damnavit aut horruit. Cessit Dioclitianus imperium.[723] Cur, nisi quia minus quietis quam laboris inesse cognovit?

Quanta illa quoque servitus qua[724] satellites, qua[725] ministros, tam varios quam multos, pandoces ac fallaces tenere et pascere coguntur! Quorum improbos mores non minus ferre molestum est quam explere insatiabiles voluntates. Nec parum servile rearis nichil privatum audere nec vesci posse, nec indui, nec otiare, nec deambulare absque nominis aut maiestatis iniuria. In quo vera profecto Annei sententia: "Omnis magna," inquit, "fortuna magna servitus est." Unde Cesarem Augustum queri solitum memorant quam multis dedisset vacationem sibi dare non potuisse. Quam firme[726] sententiam Franciscus Senior olim suo Ravennati instillabat, quod sorte liberiore frueretur et posset incomitatus qua ferret voluntas pergere, emere, et nundinari, amicorum edes tacitus lustrare, cenare, conversari, quorum nil sibi presens status licere permitteret. Nec quod[727] dicam ridiculum habe, non minus esse difficile bene imperare[728] quam obedire. Famuli sentiunt presentia dumtaxat, de futuro securi, alacrius mandunt, meracius rident, sincerius dormiunt. Domini autem et prepositi patres denique familiae intenti curiosique[729] sunt, presentibus uruntur, suspenduntur futuris. Stertentibus interdum quiescentibusque ministris, vigilant ac mente discurrunt, acta ruminant,[730] agenda discutiunt, quod gentium doctor vidit et monuit: "Qui preest," inquit, "in solicitudine."

V–75. Assentior utique locum superiorem sine servitio non fore. Expertus fateor. Coniunx, nati, servi, ac serve domestice letantur, risant, cantant, alto sopore somniant. Ego miser pro singulis

---

722. indirecta PV.
723. imperio PV.
724. quam V.
725. quam V.
726. ferme PV.
727. quid V.
728. imparare P.
729. curosique PV.
730. ruinant V.

against injustice. If it is worthwhile for him to know whatever is right to reward, why not also what is deserving of punishment? And so to those dealing with such matters their throne allows no cessation of their servitude. That king of subtle judgment perceived this, who either rejected or abhorred the weight of the crown. Diocletian gave up his empire. Why, unless because he knew there was innate in it less of ease than of hard work.[151]

How great, too, is that slavery by which they are forced to keep and support attendants and ministers, as varied as they are many, gluttonous and deceitful! It is not less hard to endure their wicked ways than to fulfill their insatiable desires. And do not think it is not servile to be unable to attempt anything in private, to eat, to dress, to relax, or to walk about without damage to one's name or majesty. Concerning this there is a true saying of Seneca: "Every great fortune is a great slavery."[152] Hence it is said that Caesar Augustus was accustomed to complain that he was unable to give to himself the free time he had given to many.[153] In past times Francesco il Vecchio firmly instilled this belief into his Ravennate, because the latter enjoyed a freer life and could go unaccompanied where his will took him, could buy, trade, quietly go to homes and dine and visit with friends, while his own status permitted him to do nothing freely.[154] Do not think my words foolish when I say that it is not less difficult to command well than to obey. Servants are conscious of present circumstances only, being secure in their future; they eat more eagerly, laugh more sincerely, sleep more lightheartedly. But rulers and fathers of a family are tense and full of responsibilities. They agonize over the present and are in suspense about the future. They lie awake while the servants are snoring and sleeping, and run over things in their minds, muse over what has been done, worry about what is to be done. This the teacher of the Gentiles perceived, and he admonished that "The man who rules must expect trouble."[155]

V-75. I agree certainly that a superior position is not without its servitude. I admit it, as I have experienced it. My wife, children, servants, and maids are happy; they laugh, sing,

vigilo, curas verso, uror, lectumque quantus est versatili motu perlustro. Quid? Omnium curator sum, cibum potumque omnibus provideo et comparo. Sed quantula cunctorum me portio contingit, ementem solventemque singula! Quam importabilis eorum existimari sarcina debet, qui familiam instar exercitus nutricant, quando tanta privati hominis patet! Omnis profecto familia et quo numerosior, tanto sarcina molestior est.

P-75. Magna certe, quamquam laudabile ac magni ducatur pro multis excubare, magnos sumptus facere, multa dispergere, multis dare. Sed in presentiarum non de magnificentia quae[731] in rebus principum[732] constet,[733] verum quomodo potius ipsi quoque mortalium communi servitutis necessitate colligentur intendimus. Et eo usque fando meandoque producti sumus, ut non modo quos conditio servire compellit, sed[734] qui preesse quoque putarentur, clareret suo famulatu non carere.

V-76. Ceterorum abunde qui sunt in hominum labore servitium docere conatus es; clericos taces. An mortalis eos servitus nobis equiperat, vel, uti proverbium est, vivis mortuisque fruuntur?

P-76. Nemo exors nascitur temporalis vite laborum. Mollior tamen evenit plerisque conditio. Dominus Deus sub lege obedientie hominem statuens in Paradiso locavit quatenus custodiret et operaretur. Quorum alterum quidem speculationi, alterum pertinet actioni. Finis enim creature est actio, quoniam adesse sequitur operari, ne quid lege divina in universitatis regno frustra et

---

731. quibus PV.
732. principium V.
733. consistet V.
734. si V.

sleep in deep slumber. I, poor wretch, stay awake over details, hash over my worries, become fretful; and as large as my bed is, I toss all over it in my turnings. Why? I am the caretaker for everybody, I take charge of and procure food and drink for everybody. Yet how small a share of everything is for myself, when I am buying and paying for everything! How unbearable must one consider the burden of those who support a family the size of an army, when the burden of a private citizen is obviously so great. Certainly the larger the family, the heavier the burden.

P-75. It is heavy indeed, although it is considered praiseworthy and characteristic of a great man to be vigilant in behalf of many, to have huge expenses, to disperse many things, and to give to many people. But at present we are not turning our attention to the greatness that exists in the circumstances of princes, but rather we are concerned with how they themselves are also bound by the necessity of slavery common to mortals. And we have been led to this point in our talking and rambling, namely, that it is clear that not only those whose condition compels them to be servants, but also those who are considered to be leaders do not lack their own servitude.

V-76. You have tried to show fully the slavery of others who do men's work, but you do not mention the clerics. Does human slavery make them equal with us, or, as the proverb goes, do they enjoy both the living and the dead?

12. Status of the Religious Vocation

P-76. No one is born free from a share in the work of temporal life. However, an easier condition obtains for some. The Lord God, in setting man under the law of obedience, placed him in Paradise so that he might keep and till it.[156] Of these duties one refers to observation, the other to action. For the end of a creature is action, since tilling follows being present, so

otiosum existeret. Illa itaque hominum portio que iudicatur a seculari famulatu sequestris paucioribus laqueis sed artioribus implicatur. Partim hominum serviunt Deo, partim mundo. Qui autem utiliter utrinque serviret, observaret Paradisum et operaretur, sicut iussum[735] est prime propagini. Atqui inter duo, ista Dei mundique servitia, interest; quod in terreno ad eum cui servitur utilitatis refertur intentio, Deo autem serviendo totus servitii fructus in servientem retorquetur. Quod[736] propheta cognoscens: "Deus meus es tu," ait, "quia bonorum meorum non eges." Quamobrem ea servitus appellari non debet, quoniam ipsa dignitas operis solius est famulantis. Sed quota portio Ierosolimam petit quatenus templo deserviat?

V-77. Etsi iamdudum exigua, nunc ferme[737] nulla. Omnes enim, ut eo usque querebatur apostolus, que sua sunt querunt, non que Christi Iesu. Quod per Malachiam quoque Deus[738] clamat: "Quis est," inquit, "ex vobis qui ostium claudat et accendat[739] ad altare meum gratuito?" Quis claustrum, quis presulatum gliscit ut pastor existat et non tonsor ovium Christi, et non supputat attentius prediorum fructum quam animarum? Quis lagene meri quam salutis subiectorum dispendio fraudari malit? Pompa et elatione vix secernuntur Levitica secularisque prelatio. Nulli hominum mollius, nec[740] apparatius, nec sumptuosius victitant, nec quibus adoratio maior fiat obsequiosiusque pareatur.

P-77. Haud est quicquam minus[741] ac faris. Possident agros, villas, nemora, saltus, pecuaria, domos, servos. Non fuit indultum possidere tam multa quo effluerent deliciarum illecebris, otiove torperent, aut luxu piorum erogationes[742] profligarent, sed quatenus, ab omni temporali necessitate soluti, Deo expeditius servientes, subiectas animas verbo et vita celo dirigerent. Sed versi in arcum pravum, contempta Dei, mundi servitute irretiuntur. Nam omnis ille ornatus, reverentia, apparatus, obsequium, famula-

---

735. visum V
736. quid V.
737. firme V.
738. Deus quoque V.
739. accedat PV.
740. ne V.
741. minus *om.* V.
742. erogacione V.

Status of the Religious Vocation

that by divine law nothing might be in vain or useless in the kingdom of the universe. Therefore that portion of mankind which is considered apart from secular servitude is enmeshed in fewer but tighter coils. Some men serve God, some the world.[157] But the man who would usefully serve both must keep and till Paradise, just as was commanded to the first of our race. And between the two, the service of God and that of the world, there is a difference, because in earthly service the intended advantage is directed toward the one served, but in serving God the entire benefit of the service is returned to the one serving. In recognition of this the prophet says: "You are my God because You do not need good things from me."[158] Therefore, this ought not to be called servitude, since the very value of the deed is for the servant alone. But how many seek Jerusalem in order to serve the temple?

V-77. For a long time a small number, now almost none. For all, as the apostle constantly complained, seek their own interests, not those of Christ Jesus.[159] God proclaims this also through Malachi: "Who of you is there," he says, "who will shut the door and kindle fire on my altar for nothing?"[160] Who yearns for the cloister, who for a bishopric, that he may live as a shepherd and not as a shearer of Christ's sheep, without reckoning more closely the harvest of his estate than the harvest of souls? Who would prefer to be cheated of the expense of a flagon of wine rather than of the salvation of his subjects? Because of their pomp and haughtiness, the Levitical and the secular prelacies can hardly be distinguished from each other. No men live more luxuriously, sumptuously, or elegantly, or receive greater adoration and more obsequious obedience.

P-77. It is exactly as you say. They own fields, farmhouses, woodlands, groves, herds of cattle, houses, servants. It was not granted to them to possess so many things in order to have an abundance of enticing delights, or to grow slothful with leisure, or to waste the monies of the pious in luxurious living, but in order that, being freed from all wordly needs and thereby serving God more easily, they might guide to Heaven by their words and lives the souls subject to them. But turning to an evil course they are ensnared by servitude of the world, scorning that of God. For all those embellish-

tus, opulentia, secularium servos efficit. Tanto quidem damnabilius, quanto abutentes[743] accepto munere, supernum famulatum in terrenum converterunt. Quare mundanis affecti nichilo setius quam ceteri secularis vite habendi sunt servi.

 Cardinales num[744] liberi tibi videntur? Quo maiore fulgent honore, hoc artius coercentur. Muscarum instar circumvolant, petentes, pulsantes, orantes, supplicantes quos nec repellere nec implere pervium est. Quod de seculi principibus dixi sentire de his licet. Quippe capellanos, cantores, auditores, scribas, vernas, pincernas, coquos, stabularios, et plura que piget evolvere, domi habent, quos omnes instantes hiantesque curare, explere, componere. Sine molestia spiritus extimas? Adde quod matutini urgentur ad pontificis atrium stare, sedere, audire, dicere minime suopte sed alieno[745] arbitrio in tedium usque plerumque ac nauseam[746] convenit. An summus ipse pontifex, quo nil admirabilius, quod ipsum indicat nomen, orbis adorat, exors forsan tibi videtur servitutis? At certe nulla vehementior, nulla angustior, nulla etiam fateor augustior. Quemadmodum namque extat super omnes, ita nec agere nec fari nec conversari sicut omnes valet. Omitto quam onerose quamque periculose villicatio illa suscipitur, vinee Domini Sabaoth; sed ea est vel ingentis conditio necessitatis ut, velut sanctus auditur, sic formam prebeat sanctitatis. Gregorio tribuunt quod prescribatur, "Servus servorum Dei." Verum profecto, quisquis fuit, sensit et protulit quam illa cathedra premeret insidentes, qui titulus haud tantum humilitatem sonat sed ipsam proprietatis officii veritatem. Nam si dixero "Deus Deorum," preeminentie exclusionisve signum prodo, ut intelligam Deum super omnes deos, et quod verius sit quam ceteri Deus. Tale est servus servorum Dei, quia cunctis Dei servis[747] preminet, seu quia verius ac plenius quam

743. abritentes V.
744. non V.
745. alieno sed PV
746. narisena V.
747. servus V.

ments, reverence, honors, obsequiousness, service, and wealth, make them slaves to secular interests. And they are the more to be criticized the more they abuse the office they have assumed by turning service of the divine to that of the earth. Therefore, being affected by worldly interests, just like other men they must be considered slaves of secular life.

Surely cardinals do not seem to you to be free? The higher the honors with which they are resplendent, the tighter they are bound. Like flies they flit about, attacking, nagging, entreating, supplicating; and there is no way of either fending them off or satisfying them. One can observe about them what I have said about secular princes. Indeed, they have at home chaplains, cantors, students, scribes, house servants, butlers, cooks, stable-keepers, and more, which it would be tiresome to relate, all of whom, demanding and eager, they must take care of, satisfy, and regulate. Do you think their spirits are without trouble? In addition, early in the morning they are urged out to stand at the courtyard of the pope, to sit and listen, to speak not in accordance with their own judgment but with that of another, to the point of tedium and often even of nausea. Does that high pontifex himself—than whom nothing is more admirable, a fact indicated by his very name, whom the world adores—does he perhaps seem to you free from slavery? Yet surely no slavery is stronger, none more restrictive, none, I also confess, more worthy of honor. For as he stands above all, he cannot act or speak or live like all. I do not mention how burdensome and how perilous is that parish he has undertaken, the vineyards of the Lord of Sabaoth; but this is a condition that greatly necessitates that, as he is called holy, he must show the appearance of holiness. Men attribute to Gregory the title "Servant of servants of God."[161] But certainly, whoever he was, he understood and made public how that papal chair oppressed those who sat in it. This title proclaims not only humility, but the real truth of the duty of its possession. For if I say "God of Gods," I produce a sign of preeminence or exclusiveness, that I know God is above all gods and that he is God more truly than the rest. Such a thing is the servant of servants of God, because he excels all servants of God and because he

alii servus est Dei. Hanc servitutem flevit sacer Gregorius, hanc quibus esset infensus Adrianus loco blasfemie imprecabatur. Norat uterque quante molis existeret simplici conscientie sedis illius ac nominis altitudo. Itaque siquidem singulos animadverteris,[748] suam cunctis reperies impendere[749] servitutem. Sed quid? Alii, obducta ratione, tamquam morbos frenetici, qua[750] premuntur nesciunt servitutem. Nonnulli, similes avibus quas esce dulcedo allicit in retia, ultro speciosis blanda titulis subeunt. Age, si verna regi discalceandi[751] fricandique prestet obsequium, quid distat a meo idem michi prestanti cum posco? Eadem servitus est, et forsitan durior illius qui timet vel odit habentem sue vite potestatem. Sed speciosum efficit ministerium conditio dominantis, tamquam referat, compedibus aureis, ferreis, ne quis coercitus pareat! Oneratur feno asellus, oneratur et serico —quid refert? Utrumque onus est. Sic vehit papam mulus, vehit et episcopum. Quid est nisi mulus uterque et nisi possidentis dignitate non differens? Ita qui propinat imperatori et militi non differunt munere sed fortuna.

Porro una ratio est que clarum valeat reddere famulatum, virtus et bonitas superioris. Nam queamadmodum sub optimo principe nasci felicitas est, ita glorie quoque tribuendum in optimi familia censeri, ad testimonium cedente laudis conversatione cum summis. Quo utique respectu satirus ait: "Principibus placuisse viris non ultima laus est." Sic Cassiodorus: "Non esse maius meritum quam gratiam invenisse regnantium"; non quidem cunctorum, sed sapientium, iustorum, mitium, rectaque amantium. Sub his, inquam, illustrior servitus, sed tamen servitus est.

748. animadvertis V.
749. impondere V.
750. que V.
751. discalciandi PV.

is a servant of God more truly and fully than the others. The holy Gregory lamented this servitude; Adrian invoked it, instead of blasphemy, upon those to whom he was hostile.[162] Each knew how great a burden for a simple conscience was the loftiness of that seat and name.

Therefore if you observe people individually, you will find that his personal slavery hangs over each. But what of it? Some, by suppressing their reason, just as madmen do not recognize their disease, do not recognize the slavery by which they are afflicted. Others, like birds that the sweetness of food entices into the nets, submit of their own accord to the blandishments of fine-sounding titles. See now, if a servant performs for a king the duty of taking off his shoes and massaging him, how does he differ from my servant who does the same thing for me when I request it? It is the same servitude, and perhaps harsher for the one who fears or hates the man with power over his life. But the status of the master creates a fine-sounding employment, as though it makes a difference whether one appears bound by golden shackles or iron ones! An ass is loaded with hay, or he is loaded with silk. What difference does it make? Each is a burden. Likewise, one mule carries the pope and one carries a bishop. What is each but a mule, differing in no way except in the rank of its owner? Thus the man who serves a general and the one who serves a soldier do not differ in duty but in fortune.

On the other hand, there is one consideration that can make servitude distinguished: the virtue and goodness of the superior. For just as to be born under an excellent prince is good fortune, so to be counted in the household of a very fine man is to be considered a glory, since association with excellent persons becomes a sign of honor. In respect to this, the satirist says, "To have won favor with the foremost men is not the lowest glory."[163] And Cassiodorus: "There is no greater merit than to have found favor with rulers"; not all, to be sure, but the wise, the just, the merciful, and those who love the right.[164] Service under such as these, I say, is illustrious; but it is still service.

V-78. Isto, inquam, pacto cuncti servimus. Dasne ulli uspiam libertatem?

P-78. Eodem[752] an non servimus cuncti? Nam preter eam servitutem quam externarum rerum memoravi, quis rationis compos non experitur infestam corporis servitutem? Volo discere et aliquam ad rem honestam lucubrare, et dormire caro iubet. Negotiari pro rerum exigentia non sinit exuries; sedere lassitudo compellit. Omitto concupiscentias carnales quot lacessunt telis spiritum repugnantem. Audi Paulum, audi sanctum virum Andream, quam gemat uterque sub carnis imperio. Ravennas ipse crebro lamentari solebat non pati quicquam[753] suo corpore infestius, cum senio iam gravis morbisque irruentibus[754] impediretur a familiaritate litterarum. Ita multis evenit, sed non sentiunt quidam morbo animi, ut dixi; ambitu quidam aut cupiditate pondus gemunt et ferunt.

At vero cum indeclinabili servitute nascamur, annitendum[755] ut famulatum conditionis accepte referamus, quo omnis exacte rationis molitur examen, quod tum incorruptibilis corone meritum sperare licet; alias, velut perituris servimus, perituro[756] sic premio fulcimur. Interea tamen conducit, quantum in nobis est, ut quam prestanti idoneos nos paremus, quoniam accepimus cuncti secundum mensuram, in acceptione gratiarum differentes,[757] quod nimirum in temporalibus liquet. In curia siquidem gerarche, impariter distributis muneribus, impariter[758] obsecuntur multi. Sic rursus in regia seculari alii scriptorum et rescriptorum, alii thesaurorum, alii equorum, hi canum, quidam herodiorum et asturum, ita diversi diversarum rerum custodie ministerium impendunt. Verum quia rationalis creatura prestantior est, speciosior cura ducitur hominibus preesse quam aliis. Sicut[759] moderans equos subulcis

---

752. eo dum PV.
753. quisquam P.
754. ruentibus V.
755. amitendum V.
756. parituro V.
757. referentes V.
758. pariter PV.
759. sic PV.

V-78. In that way, of course, we are all servants. Do you grant that anyone anywhere has freedom?

P-78. Do we not all serve in an identical way? For in addition to that servitude of externals which I spoke of, who possessed of reason does not experience the troublesome servitude of the body? I wish to learn and to work by night at some honest task, but my flesh orders me to sleep. Hunger prevents me from carrying on necessary business; weariness compels me to to sit down. I shall not mention how carnal lusts wound the spirit with their weapons, even though the spirit fights against them. Listen to Paul, listen to the holy man Andrew, how each groans under the command of the flesh.[165] The Ravennate himself was accustomed to lament frequently that he endured nothing more troublesome than his own body, when, burdened with age and suffering the onslaught of disease, he was kept away from the familiar joys of literature. So it happens to many. But some do not acknowledge this burden because of the disease of their spirit, as I have said; and some because of ambition or greed groan under the weight and endure it.

But, indeed, since we are born to inevitable slavery, we must seek a servitude of an acceptable sort, toward which every considered and accurate reasoning strives, because then we may hope for the merit of an incorruptible crown.[166] Otherwise, as we serve those who are destined to perish, we are relying on a reward that is destined to perish. Meanwhile, however, it is good to make ourselves as useful as we can to our superior, since we have all received according to measure, differing in our receipt of favors, as is certainly obvious in temporal matters. In the court of the archbishop, where the duties have been distributed differently, people perform them differently. Thus, too, in a secular court some are in charge of scripts and rescripts, others of treasuries, some of horses or dogs, and others of gyrfalcons and hawks. Thus various persons perform the duties of taking care of various things. But because a rational creature is superior, it is considered a superior responsibility to be in charge of human beings rather than of other things. As the horse-trainer is

antefertur, ita rationari etiam de artibus licet: titulo honestiore laborat orator quam sutor, et quam navita medicus sic dignior habetur, pincerna quam coquus. Porro in huiuscemodi tanta varietate ministeriorum et graduum hominis meritum levat aut ponit in suscepta fortuna laudabili actione versari.

Sed interdum equanimitatis serenum ambitionis et invidie cupidinisque vapor fuscat, nec sinit accepta sorte frui dum sociam miratur aut odit. Atqui in Levitica portione, ut pretuli, exoneratior[760] in parte et tranquillior vite conditio, nam preter quod multifarie a solicitudinibus seculi remittuntur, illa certe maxima, coniugis ac liberorum, absolvuntur.[761] Que quam[762] sit urens ac molesta, non siluit comicus: "Uxorem," inquit, "duxi. Quam miseriam ibi vidi! Nati filii, alia cura!" Quod advertens, vas electionis Corinthios monens "Volo," inquit, "vos sine solicitudine esse. Qui sine uxore est, cogitat que sunt Dei, quomodo placeat Deo. Et qui cum uxore est, solicitus est que sunt mundi, quomodo placeat uxori, et divisus est." Et subdit:[763] "Hoc ad utilitatem vestram dico, non ut[764] laqueum vobis iniciam, sed ad id quod honestum est, et facultatem prebeat sine impedimento Dominum obsecrandi."

Ita celestis sapientia tot vitam servitiis ascripsit quatenus, dum se mens cerneret necessitatibus subditam, sue prestantie[765] dignitatem non in rimoso perituroque carnis tabernaculo sed in augustiore parte intelligeret constitutam. Atque ob hoc[766] infra hominis se meritum sternit homo quanto corporeis illecebris mancipatur. Eius porro minor est servitus qui temporalia necessitate colit, non amore. Et ut non fallitur blandiente, sic non frangitur adversante fortuna. Nullius enim rei liberior est possessio quam que elapsa non premit affectum.[767] A servitio itaque vindicat conscientie puritas seculariumque contemptus et qui audit et vivit[768] ut docet apostolus: "Hoc, dico, fratres; tempus breve

---

760. exornacior V.
761. solvuntur V.
762. quamquam V.
763. suddit V.
764. ut non V.
765. prestatie P.
766. hec V.
767. *ex* effectum *corr.* V.
768. vidit V.

superior to the swineherds, so one can reason with regard to the professions: the orator performs under a more honorable title than the cobbler, and the doctor than the sailor; the butler is considered worthier than the cook. Furthermore, within the great variety of these offices and degrees, the merit of a man is heightened or established by his being engaged in praiseworthy activity in the career he has undertaken.

But sometimes the mists of ambition and envy and greed darken the clear sky of man's equanimity, and prevent his enjoying the lot that has fallen to him, since he wonders at or hates his accompanying fate. But among the clergy, as I have said before, the condition of life is in part less burdensome and more tranquil; for besides the fact that in many ways they are relieved from secular worries, they are freed from the one that is surely the greatest, that of wife and children. How annoying and troublesome this is, the comic poet does not hesitate to say. He says, "I married a wife. What a misery I found there! Children were born, another bother!"[167] Noting this, the chosen vessel, in admonishing the Corinthians, says, "I wish you to be without worry. The man who does not have a wife thinks about the affairs of God, how to please God. And the man who has a wife has concern for the affairs of the world, how to please his wife, and he is divided."[168] He also adds, "I say this for your benefit, not to put a restraint upon you, but for what is honorable and will give you opportunity to devote yourselves to the Lord without impediment."[169]

Thus heavenly wisdom vowed life to so many services, in order that, when the mind perceived itself subject to necessities, it might know that the worth of its excellence was based not in the flawed and perishable tabernacle of the flesh but in a more noble part. On account of this the merit of man decreases in proportion as man gives himself over to the enticements of the body. Furthermore, servitude is less for the man who tends to temporal matters out of necessity rather than love. And since he is not led astray when fortune is kind, he is not broken when it is adverse. For no possession is less restrictive than one that can be lost without causing regret. Therefore a purity of conscience and disdain for secular matters frees from servitude the man who hearkens and lives as the apostle teaches: " I say

est; reliquum est ut qui habent uxores sint tamquam non habentes, et qui gaudent tamquam non gaudentes, et qui flent tamquam non flentes, et qui emunt tamquam non possidentes, et qui utuntur[769] hoc mundo tamquam non utantur; preterit enim figura mundi huius." Ita instruit contra servitutem apostolus. Ita qui huiusmodi sapientia agit et graditur non, dico, omnino liber est in hoc mundo, sed minimum servus.

V-79. Qui cuncta sic [770] impromiscuo censeat indifferentique affectu possideat, si qua extat, libertate prorsus excellit. Sed quis est cui felicitas tanta contingat?

P-79. Cassa foret doctrina que non posset impleri. Non docuit apostolus quod impossibile esset imitari. Nec ego huiusmodi libertatem somnio potius quam scio. Esse enim in aliquos tales negandum non est, quamquam rarus iste nature sit partus. Unum letor vidisse, Thomam Gradensis,[771] ecclesie patriarcham, virum utique absolutissime sapientie. Cum ageret in claustro moribus et magnitudine animi supra cunctos erat. Deinde generalem in ordine vera humilitate infra omnes aspiceres. Factus est postea[772] patriarcha ac demum[773] cardinalis; non crevit dignitate sed magnificavit potius dignitates, spiritu idem et moribus claustralis ac pontifex. Dum opibus caruit non optavit; cum habuit non amavit, sed despexit; quodque una libertas est, animo numquam possedit. Ideoque nec novit umquam sed nec voluit nosse[774] quantum assumpta dignitas responderet, quantum emitteret. Is erat qui dignitatem et paupertatem iuxta penderet et calcare temporalia videretur. Cuncta assumpte religionis monumenta[775] ad finem usque perpetua virtute servavit, et quam semel vovit paupertatis normam constanti[776] mente coluit, et moriens secum tulit. Nam papa cum potestatem morituro testandi fecisset,[777] "Fratres minores," inquit, "testamentum nesciunt," et triduo quam moreretur se ad claustrum referri iussit; stratoque storio in cappa et capistro

---

769. ututuntur V.
770. scit V.
771. grandensis V.
772. poste V.
773. dominum P.
774. nosce V
775. momenta PV.
776. *ex* constant *corr.* P² constanter V.
777. fecisset testandi V.

this, brothers, time is short. It remains for those who have wives to be as if they had none, and for those who rejoice as if they did not rejoice, and those who weep as if they did not weep, and those who buy as if they did not own, and those who use this world as if they had no use for it. For the shape of this world is passing away."[170] Thus the apostle instructs against servitude. So the one who acts and moves according to this sort of wisdom is not, I say, entirely free in this world, but he is least a slave.

V–79. The man who judges all things so discriminately and possesses them indifferently certainly excels in liberty if it is possible anywhere. But who is there who has such great felicity?

P–79. That would be a useless doctrine which could not be implemented. The apostle did not teach what was impossible to imitate,[171] nor do I dream idly about this kind of liberty instead of having knowledge of it. That it exists for some people is undeniable, although that offspring of nature is rare. I am fortunate in having seen one, Tommaso da Frignano, patriarch of the church, a man surely of the most complete wisdom.[172] When he lived in the cloister he was above all in character and greatness of soul. Then you could see him as minister general of the order, below all in true humility. Later he became patriarch and finally cardinal. He did not grow because of the honor, but rather he exalted his honors. In spirit and character he was the same, whether monk or pontifex. When he was without riches, he did not wish for them; when he had them, he did not love, but despised them; and, which is the one freedom, he never possessed them in his heart. And so he did not ever know, nor did he wish to know, how much his acquired rank brought in or how much it paid out. He was a man who valued high rank and poverty equally and seemed to spurn temporal things. He preserved with constant virtue all the marks of his acquired religious beliefs up to the end, and once he had taken the vow of the rule of poverty he observed it with steadfastness and bore it with him till his death. For when the pope had given to him on his deathbed the power of making a bequest, he said, "The Franciscans are ignorant of wills," and ordered that he be carried to the cloister on the third day before his death. Dying on a spread rush

decedens quanti fecisset mundanam[778] gloriam ostendit. Loculum preterea corporis minime celato auratoque alabastro, columnis pilisve substantibus, eminenter conspicuum, sed humo plana superiecto saxo statui voluit, ut quam vivendo coluisset humilitatem haberet comitem moriendo. Eant modo qui vario lapide affabre decussata auroque micantia suspendunt monumenta, et innotescere miraculo artificii querunt. Thomas utique laudem vite memorem pro sepulcro habet. Horum vero dumtaxat frigida imago sculptumque nomen agnoscitur. Merita quidem vicissitudine ut cuius virtus nequaquam fulsit in vita prorsus solum nomen, teste petra, sciatur.

V–80. Si uspiam libertas est, fateor, sub huiusmodi forma[779] animi reperitur. Magni pretii Thomas extitit, et exitum audisse iuvat, quia patriarchatus in nostra urbe insolite virtutis et constantie exemplum se prebuit. Accepto quippe a Romano pontifice coercendi cleri mandato, dum sub religionis disciplina componere aversos moliretur, invidiam plurimorum contraxit, etiam ex summatibus patriciorum. Quorum insolentiam ac furorem alto usque adeo iudicio despexit, ut minas et iniurias, immutata vultus ac sermonis dignitate, nescire semper quam recipere videretur. Quare delectasti me opido eius redintegratione memorie.

Sed continuate quoque mulcedo ratiocinationis et socialis commeandi iocunditas letum ita intentumque rapuit ut ipsa oratio vehiculum fuerit et de producta via compendium fecerit. Sed ecce, vel minus animadversa itineris meta ultro moram poscit. At munus egregie cumulabis si quemadmodum ambulationis sic te quoque hospitii socium sodalemque donaveris.

P–80. Tuo parerem arbitratu nisi procedere iuberet. Bene vale.

Venetiis Anno Domini MCCCIIII.

---

778. humanam V.
779. foram V.

mat, in a monk's robe and cowl, he showed how much he had valued the glory of the world. In addition, he did not wish the coffin for his body to be outstandingly conspicuous with carved and gilded alabaster and supported by columns or pillars, but placed on the level ground with a rock above, so that the humility that he had cherished while living might be his companion in death. Let others go and erect monuments of colored stone, skillfully made in the shape of a cross and shining with gold, and seek to become famous by that miraculous work of craftsmanship! Tommaso surely has the memorable glory of his life as his sepulcher. But of these others nothing is known but a cold statue and an engraved name. Indeed, it is by a well-deserved fate that one whose virtue never shone in life is henceforth known only by a name on the testimony of a rock!

V-80. If there is freedom anywhere, I admit, it is found in the form of a spirit like this. Tommaso lived a very worthy life; and I am glad to have heard the description of his death, because the patriarchate in our city has shown itself as an example of unusual virtue and constancy. Indeed, when he received the Roman Pontiff's mandate to restrict the clerical order, and when he attempted to regulate by religious discipline those opposing him, he contracted the dislike of many, even of the highest-ranking patricians. He so despised their insolence and wrath, in his lofty judgment, that he appeared always to ignore rather than to receive their threats and injuries, keeping unchanged the dignity of his countenance and his speech. Therefore, you have certainly pleased me by refreshing my memory of him.

But also, my enjoyment in your discourse and the sociable pleasure of being in your company have borne me along, so happy and interested that your very conversation has been a vehicle and has made our long journey a short one. See, the end of our trip has come without our noticing it, and we have to stop. But you will make the favor complete if you offer yourself as a sharer and companion of my guest-house as well as of our walk!

P-80. I would comply with your request if personal affairs did not require me to go on. Farewell!

At Venice, A.D. 1404.

Notes to the Dragmalogia

The classical quotations are cited according to the texts and divisions of the volumes of the Loeb Classical Library, and, when the text is not available in that series, according to the Bibliotheca Scriptorum Graecorum et Romanorum Teubneriana. Further, in those instances when Giovanni's version departs from the accepted classical text, the accepted version is given in the note. The scriptural quotations have been checked with the Biblia Vulgata, 4th ed. (Madrid, 1956), and the Psalms have been cited according to the Vulgate numbering. For all other quotations, the edition used is given in the notes. For the historical allusions, the most useful and appropriate secondary studies are cited, as well as important primary sources when these would seem to be helpful to the reader.

1. Francesco Novello da Carrara, lord of Padua (1390–1405). At the time of the composition of this tract, Padua, defended by the Carrara lord and his garrison, was under siege by a Venetian army, which finally conquered the city in November 1405. In the *Dragmalogia* as in his other, later tracts, Giovanni da Ravenna manifests a strong penchant for the anachronistic use of classical place names. Hence he uses *Euganeus* for the more common late-medieval *Paduanus* or *Insubrii* instead of *Lombardi*. In the translation this affectation has been disregarded and the most common modern equivalent is used.

2. The Gallic disaster refers to the wars waged by Giangaleazzo Visconti, duke of Milan (1385–1402), against Florence and many other cities of northern Italy until his death in September 1402. The Gaul in question is Cisalpine Gaul, or the region of northern Italy between the Apennines and the Alps.

3. The leader of the Ligurians refers to Giangaleazzo Visconti, the expansionist lord of Milan who waged a series of wars to bring northern Italy under his domination. For a detailed account of the events of his life and rule, see D. M. Bueno de Mesquita, *Giangaleazzo Visconti, Duke of Milan (1351–1402), A Study in the Political Career of an Italian Despot* (Cambridge, England, 1941), and for a résumé of the political events during the two decades before 1402, Hans Baron, *Crisis of the Early Italian Renaissance*, 2 vols. (Princeton, 1955; rev. ed. in 1 vol., 1966), chap. 2.

4. Here Giovanni is implicitly comparing the versatile interests of Giangaleazzo with the strictly military orientation of Francesco Novello.

5. Here Govanni reaches the height of his anti-Florentine diatribe and also reproves the precipitous Venetian withdrawal from the League

of Bologna at the Truce of Pavia on May 11, 1398. Venetian aloofness from Italian politics is condemned several times in the course of the dialogue.

6. Giovanni is describing the Mantuan War of 1396–1398, in which the lord of Mantua, Francesco I Gonzaga (1382–1407), was nearly defeated by the armies of the Visconti.

7. The reference is to Rupert (Robertus in Latin) of Habsburg, who as an ally of Florence and the Carrara attacked the Visconti from the northeast and was decisively defeated near Brescia on October 21, 1401.

8. It seems that Rupert's predilection for wine was well-known among contemporaries. The canonist and later cardinal Francesco Zabarella makes a similar condemnation in Book 1 of his *De Felicitate Tres Libri* (Padua, 1655), pp. 13–14, written about the same time as the *Dragmalogia*.

9. Giovanni's Paduan is here uttering the common complaint that Italian factiousness led to unnecessary wars. The villains in the dialogue are Florence for its ambition and Venice for its failure to keep the peace despite its great power.

10. The Venetian refers to the death of Giangaleazzo Visconti on September 2, 1402, and the subsequent peace treaty negotiated by Venice between Francesco Novello de Carrara and the regent of Lombardy, Caterina Visconti, that autumn. See G. Romano, "La pace tra Milano ed i Carraresi nel 1402," *Archivio Storico Lombardo* 18 (1890): 841–57, which, after a careful weighing of the evidence, concludes that Francesco Novello was responsible for the prompt resumption of hostilities early in 1403.

11. Giovanni here is describing Francesco Novello's support of the Guelphs of Brescia against the Ghibelline rule of the Visconti in the summer of 1403. See B. and G. Gatari, *Cronaca Carrarese,* ed. A. Medin and G. Tolomei, *Rerum Italicarum Scriptores,* n. ed. 17, pt. 1 (Città di Castello and Bologna, 1909–1932), pp. 505–7, for a contemporary account. Cf. n. 118.

12. With this reference to the law of dialectical reasoning, Giovanni is probably alluding to the logic of material consequence, which utilizes argumentation by analogy. That Giovanni knew at least some of the standard logical texts of his day is proved by the tracts in a codex that he once owned and that is described in G. B. Mittarelli, *Bibliotheca Codicum Manuscriptorum Monasterii S. Michaelis Venetiarum prope Murianum* (Venice, 1779), cols. 324, 383–84, 1098, and elsewhere. The MS is now in Venice, Biblioteca Marciana, Lat. XIV 129 (4334). The treatises described in the columns cited above deal respectively with dialectics, fallacies, and suppositions.

13. The Venetian's speech is a condemnation of the policy of Francesco Novello from the two years following the death of Giangaleazzo Visconti in September 1402. During this period, the Paduan lord sought to reassert his hegemony in northeastern Italy through a war

against Visconti-held Verona and by meddling in the affairs of other nearby cities. The Venetian leader who finally responded to Paduan provocations was the Doge Michele Steno (1400–1413), who persuaded his state to declare war on Padua in the late spring of 1404. Venetian intervention eventually resulted in the overthrow of the Carrara rule over Padua in 1405. For a contemporary account, see B. and G. Gatari, *Cronaca Carrarese,* pp. 507–30, and for a detailed narrative based upon research in diplomatic sources, see I. Raulich, *La caduta dei Carraresi* (Padua, 1890).

14. Here the Paduan introduces the author, Giovanni di Conversino da Ravenna, into the dialogue as the Ravennate. In the next four speeches, the Paduan details the nature of Giovanni's service at the Carrara court and gives the reasons why he left the post of chancellor in the late spring of 1404.

15. The actual length of Giovanni's service was fifteen years in the period 1378–1382 and as chancellor 1393–1404. The period of forty years refers to the time elapsed from his first visit to Padua, probably in 1364, to his final departure in 1404. Giovanni made a similar claim in letters to Rudolfo da Carrara and Enrico Gallo in Z, fols. 143v/b, 145v/b, respectively. See R. Sabbadini, *Giovanni da Ravenna, insigne figura d'umanista (1343–1408)* (Como, 1924), p. 104.

16. Enrico Gallo and Michele Rabatta of Gorizia were two of the most important and trusted officials of the Carrara court. Gallo was licensed in law at Padua in 1371, served as vicar to podestà of Montagnana in 1373, and was an intimate of the last two Carrara lords from 1385 to 1405, except for a period of exile during the Visconti occupation of the city in 1388–1390. See A. Gloria, *Monumenti della Università di Padova* (1318–1405), 2 vols. (Padua, 1888), 1: 260–61. Rabatta served both as military commander and ambassador for the Carrara lords from 1378 until the downfall of the regime in 1405. See ibid., 1, nos. 126 and 138; B. and G. Gatari, *Cronaca Carrarese,* pp. 336–38, 395–419, 448–54, 525–28, 572–74; and F. Seneca, "Un diplomatico goriziano a cavaliere dei secoli XIV–XV: Michele Rabatta," *Memorie Storiche Forogiulesi* 40 (1952–53): 138–74.

17. Lombardo della Seta (?–1390) was the most famous native Paduan humanist of his generation and the learned continuator of Petrarch's *De Viris Illustribus.* Della Seta worked in rustic retirement at a country home in Sermeola in the Paduan suburbs. See G. Ferrante, "Lombardo della Seta Umanista padovano (?–1390)," *Atti del R. Istituto Veneto* 93 (1933–34): 445–87.

18. Seneca, *Agamemnon* 1. 287, "Pretio parata vincitur pretio fires."

19. The harm wrought by evil counsellors is a convention in medieval and early Renaissance political treatises. Perhaps Giovanni had in mind the letter, composed in 1373, of Petrarch to Francesco il Vecchio da Carrara on princely rule, *Qualis esse debeat qui rem publicam regit,* ed. V. Ussani (Padua, 1922), pp. 29–30, which makes a similar judgment on advisers.

20. Pliny the Younger, *Epistulae* 1. 10, gives this description of his duties as provincial administrator in a letter to Attius Clemens: "Nam distringor officio ut maximo sic molestissimo; sedeo pro tribunali, subnoto libellos, conficio tabulas, scribo plurimas, sed inliteratissimas litteras."

21. For the identity of Gallo and Rabatta, see above, no. 16.

22. In 1402 the commune of Udine offered Giovanni an appointment as teacher of grammar, but at that time he preferred to stay in Padua. Cf. R. Sabbadini, *Giovanni da Ravenna,* pp. 79, 230.

23. The allusion to the freeing and guarding from evil by God is probably derived from Psalms 33: 20–21 and 96: 10—11, though Giovanni's words do not reduplicate the scriptural passages in either case. The account-book refers to Giovanni's autobiography entitled *Rationarium vite,* completed in 1400, which presumably had not been circulated beyond intimate friends.

24. This description of Giovanni's first tenure in the Carrara curia parallels his epistolary tract of 1385, *De primo eius introitu ad aulam,* addressed to Marco Giustinian, in which he describes the hazing and harsh treatment of those years.

25. Terence, *Eunuchus* 1. 252: "negat quis: nego; ait: aio; postremo imperavi egomet mihi omnia adsentari."

26. Seneca, *De Ira* 3. 8. 6. M. Caelius Rufus (82–48 B.C.), a Roman orator and friend of Cicero, was noted for his biting invective.

27. Antonio Meneghino of Chioggia, a Carrara household official and intimate of Giovanni during his several years of service under Francesco il Vecchio, was tried in Venice for trading state secrets to the Carrara and was decapitated on May 5, 1385. See Sabbadini, pp. 60, 161.

28. Giovanni Bombossolo, a Paduan druggist who served at the Este court in Ferrara, and Gerundino da Ravenna, a favorite at the court of Guido III da Polenta, lord of Ravenna (1359–1389), seem to be known only from Giovanni's *Memorandarum rerum liber,* V, fols. 48/a–48v/b. The longer versions of the anecdotes are as follows:

Per eadem quoque vestigia quam im precipiti ac lubrico spes fortunatorum pendeant Johannem Bombosolum fortuna proposuit, quem ex apotecaria taberna eo splendoris provexerat ut in aula Ferarie primus haberetur, nedum ipsi marchioni precarus curieque prefectus, verum, ut ita dixerim, omnem prope modum urbem ipsumque marchionem pugillo continere videretur. Qui, reflante mox huius aura favoris, vulgari cum ignominia carcere diro trusus occubuit. Hoc minus Francisco miser, quod illum nascentem ubere blandissimo substulit. Bombosolo multam post servitutem illecebris vani favoris illusit.

Quam metuendus ad fastigia sublatis casus, quam minime desperandus tacentibus ad alciora successus, nostris Gerondinus temporibus utrunque posse fortunam hostendit. Cui cunctos per felicitatis numeros obsequentissimam so prebuit. Eo si impuberem metiare, quid abiectius aut turpius; quid humilius si genus; quid ignocius si parentes? Cumulato nichilominus

hunc favore indulgencia complexa que mortales mirantur et optant omni contulit. Nempe Guido, Ravenne dominator, cunctis honoribus adauxit, urbem eius arbitrio subdidit, ut imperium, honores, publica munera promiscuo nutu agerentur. Omne denique archanum ipsum quoque penetrat coniugale ei pervium haberetur. Insuper lusu alee Guidoni uxorive cum ludo frequens ipsa versabatur, socius hic semper erat, et astante marito et solus eciam cum sola pernox ludum agebat. Usque adeo tirampno de Gerondino persuasum erat! Quin, olim valitudine laborante rompi aule murus imperatur, qua pervius in edem eius que mox contra patebat aditus preberetur, unde nunc principis, nunc coniugis ad egrum visendum hortandumque frequens esset accessus. Cuius quidem valitudine consternata civitas adeo fuit ceu cuique non deforet quid in languente periret. Publicis crediderim votis Gerundinum suum Ravenne deos superstitum voluisse, qui deinceps continuato successu ex Ordelafis genere, utique ex omni Romandiola antiquissimo atque clarissimo uxore ducta, in ipso felicitatis velu moli gremio spiritum posuit.

Montorso di Montorso of Modena does not figure in the chronicles of the period but is recorded as a witness to a procuratorship granted by Francesco il Vecchio of January 22, 1373, Gloria, *Monumenti,* 2, no. 1345.

29. Bernabò Visconti, lord of Milan (1354–1385), was famous for his patronage of physicians, but not of the liberal arts.

30. Terence, *Phormio* 41–42: Quam inique comparatumst, ei qui minus habent ut semper aliquid addant ditioribus.

31. Ecclesiasticus 13: 23.

32. Aristotle, *Rhetorica,* 1361a39–b2. I owe this reference to my colleague Professor James H. Day.

33. Vergil, *Georgics* 4. 212.

34. I have not succeeded in identifying the quotation from the "comic author."

35. Isaiah 5: 20.

36. Matthew 6: 24.

37. Psalms 77, 33.

38. Montorso di Montorso of Modena, cf. above n. 28.

39. The conquest of Verona by Francesco Novello took place in March 1404.

40. Giovanni de Legnano (d. 1383) was a professor of law at Bologna who taught Giovanni in 1360–62 and served his commune as ambassador on several occasions, including one embassy to Galeotto Malatesta, lord of Rimini (1372–1385). The anecdote, however, is not recorded in other sources. See F. Bosdari, "Giovanni de Legnano canonista e uomo politico del 1300." *Atti e Memorie della R. Deputazione di storia patria per le provincie di Romagna,* 3d ser. 19 (1901): 1–135.

41. The particular Aldobrandino in question was perhaps the young Aldobrandino da Polenta of Ravenna, who was in Padua in 1399. See Gloria, *Monumenti,* 2: 341, no. 2047.

42. Malachi 1: 6.

43. The aphorism that it is better to be loved than feared derived utlimately from Cicero, *De Officiis* 2. 6–7. 23–24. In fact, much of Giovanni's description of the good prince and the evil tyrant is based on the ideas in Book 2 of Cicero's well-known treatise.

44. This verse is the beginning of the third stanza of the hymn *Gloria in excelsis,* which comes between the *Kyrie* and the Collect in the order of the Mass.

45. The lines are from Euripides, *Phoenissae* 524–25, and were known to Giovanni either from Cicero, *De Officiis* 3. 21. 82, or from Suetonius, *Divus Iulius* 30. 5, or from both.

46. Sallust, *Bellum Iugurthinum* 35. 10.

47. The old Carrara is Francesco il Vecchio, lord of Padua (1350–1388, d. 1393), whom Giovanni much loved and admired.

48. The writers are the three most important of the Augustan Age: Vergil (70–19 B.C.), Horace (65–8 B.C.), and Ovid (43 B.C.–A.D. 18), who together with Cicero were the most popular Roman authors among early Renaissance humanists.

49. The reference is to the East Roman Emperor Justinian (d. 565), who was famous as the codifier of Roman law.

50. King Robert the Wise of Naples (1310–1343) was proverbial for his learning and patronage of the arts. At various times his court was adorned by Petrarch and Boccaccio. For a contemporary appraisal surely known to Giovanni, see Petrarch, *Rerum Memorandarum Libri,* ed. G. Billanovich (Florence, 1943), pp. 183–86, 3. 96, and also the standard monograph, W. Goetz, *König Robert von Neapel, seine Persönlichkeit und sein Verhältnis zum Humanismus.* (Tübingen, 1910).

51. Bernardino da Polenta, lord of Ravenna (1349–1359) was as famous a patron of Boccaccio as his grandfather, Guido II, lord of Ravenna (1316–1322), was of Dante in his last days.

52. Giacomo II da Carrara, lord of Padua (1345–1350), provided a prebend for Petrarch as a canon in the cathedral chapter at Padua. After 1361 Petrarch took up nearly permanent residence in Padua and in 1370 moved to Arquà in the Euganean Hills into a house he built on land provided him by Francesco il Vecchio. There Petrarch remained until his death in 1374. See E. H. Wilkins, *Life of Petrarch* (Chicago, 1961), pp. 82, 219–21.

53. Niccolò II d'Este, lord of Modena from 1351 and of Ferrara from 1361 until his death in 1388, was the patron of Giovanni's favorite teacher, Donato degli Albanzani, and hence the recipient of special praise for his patronage of the arts. See F. Novati, "Donato degli Albanzani alla corte estense," *Archivio Storico Italiano,* 5th ser. 6 (1890): 365–84.

54. Among the doctors employed by Giangaleazzo Visconti, Giovanni probably had in mind his own friend the Paduan physician Marsilio da Santasofia, who attended the Lombard lord during his final illness in the late summer of 1402. See Gatari, *Cronaca Carrarese,* p. 491.

55. For a good discussion of the vernacular Venetian historiography that Giovanni was condemning, see A. Carile, "La cronachistica veneziana nel secoli XIII e XIV," *La storiografia veneziana fino al secolo XVI,* ed. A. Pertusi (Florence, 1970), pp. 75–120, and especially pp. 108–9, for a discussion of Giovanni's views expressed in the *Dragmalogia.*

56. Aristotle, *Politica* 1328b5–15.

57. Giovanni makes a similar case for princely rule in his tract addressed to Francesco Novello, *De dilectione regnantium.*

58. The old saying "Cui caput languet, cetera membra dolent" is recorded in H. Walther, *Lateinische Sprichwörter und Sentenzen des Mittelalters,* 5 vols. (Göttingen, 1963–1967), 1: 453, no. 3839, as going back at least to the twelfth century.

59. Ecclesiasticus 10: 2, "Qualis rector est civitatis, tales et inhabitantes in ea."

60. Giovanni knew of these mythical and pagan queens from one of the abridgers of late antiquity, Justinus, *Epitoma Historiarum Philippicarum Pompei Trogi.* Semiramis, a mythical queen of Assyria and widow of Ninus, is recorded in Justinus, 1. 1–2, and in Valerius Maximus, *Factorum et Dictorum Memorabilium libri IX,* 9. 3. ext. 4. Marpesia, a queen of the Amazons killed by barbarous tribes in Asia Minor, is recorded in Justinus, 2. 4, and Tamyris, a queen of the Scythians in the time of Cyrus, in ibid., 1. 8.

61. Suetonius, *Divus Augustus* 38. 3.

62. Louis, King of Hungary (1342–1382), was the patron of the author's father and hence much beloved by Giovanni.

63. This aesthetic view of lordship is common in humanist political tracts. Petrarch gives much the same praise to Francesco il Vecchio for his public works program in the letter cited above, n. 19. In general, see W. Berges, *Die Fürstenspiegel des hohen und späten Mittelalters* (Stuttgart, 1938), pp. 280 ff.

64. The tower of Chioggia very probably refers to the castle that the Venetian Senate voted to build at Lupa near Chioggia in 1384. The document in the Archivio di Stato di Venezia, Senato Misti, reg. 38, fol. 148, July 19, 1384, provides for "faciendo unum castrum ad portum Clugie ad Lupam pro manifesta bona securitate et conservatione dicte terre ad nostrum honorem, que fuit et est utiles." There is no record in the series of Senato Misti that the castle was ever completed, so this is perhaps the interminable building that Giovanni's Paduan had in mind.

65. Giovanni is referring to Niccolò II d'Este (d. 1388); the youth mentioned is Niccolò III d'Este, of whom Giovanni hardly approved.

66. Giovanni here alludes to the Visconti occupation of Bologna in the early 1360s and again in 1402, which curbed the civil strife of communal factionalism.

67. Strasbourg, a free city after 1262, fought against the emperors Charles IV and Wencelaus in the second half of the fourteenth century and, as a member of the Confederation of Marbach formed in 1402, against the Carrara ally, Rupert of Habsburg.

69. Giovanni's knowledge of ancient tyrannicide doubtless derives from Cicero's well-known remarks in *De Officiis* 2. 23 and 3. 82–83.

69. The antithesis between guide (*regere*) and oppress (*premere*) was a common one in patristic and medieval literature on the nature of leadership. Using the antinomy of *prodesse* (to be useful to, to be of service) and *praeesse* (to rule over), St. Augustine expressed a similar notion in his discussion of the duties of a bishop in *De civitate Dei* 19. 19, "ut intellegat non se esse episcopum qui praeesse dilexerit, non prodesse." The same antithesis is to be found in St. Gregory the Great, *Regulae Pastoralis* 2. 16, ed. Migne, *Patrologia Latina*, vol. 77, col. 34, and *idem, Moralia in Iob* 21. 15, in Migne, vol. 76, col. 203. Giovanni either owned or frequently cited all three of these early medieval works.

70. The notion that a prince should be noble because of his own achievements and not from inherited wealth or ancient lineage closely parallels Dante's definition of nobility in the *Convivio* 4. 3. 7–10, ed. G. Busnelli and G. Vandelli, 2 vols. (Florence, 1954), 2: 26–28.

71. This is an allusion to the biblical story of David and Saul meeting in the cave and of David's refusal to take the life of his father-in-law; see 1 Samuel 24: 7–21.

72. Romans 13: 6.

73. Romans 13: 7.

74. Giovanni is again alluding to the factional struggles of late-fourteenth-century Bologna, which were overcome by the establishment of the *signoria* of Giovanni Bentivoglio and later by Visconti occupation.

75. The anecdote concerning the modesty of Augustus in the use of *dominus* was recorded by Petrarch in "Re Modestia" 3, in his *Rerum Memorandum libri*, ed. G. Billanovich (Florence, 1943), p. 275, and derives ultimately from Suetonius, *Divus Augustus* 53.

76. Philippians 1: 9.

77. Terence, *Phormio* 454, "quot homines tot sententiae: suos quoique mos."

78. The anecdote derives from the Chioggia War (1378–1381) when Venice was nearly defeated by Genoa, the Carrara, and their allies. The Venetian aristocrat was probably Andrea Contarini, doge of Venice (1368–1382), but I have not been able to identify the silversmith Bartolommeo, and the anecdote appears to have been recorded by Giovanni alone.

79. The ancient notion of an age of Saturn may have been known to Giovanni both from Vergil, *Aeneid* 8. 314–27, and Ovid, *Amores* 3. 8. 35–44.

80. I have not been able to identify this quotation from the Roman historian Justinus.

81. John 13: 13.

82. John 13: 14.

83. Christ's praise of Mary refers to Luke 10: 38–42.

84. Boethius, *Philosophiae Consolatio* 1. Prosa 24–25.

85. For this prophecy of Daniel, see Daniel 12: 3.

86. Proverbs 20: 26–29.

87. Jean de Montreuil (1354–1418) was a well-known humanist who served as chancellor for King Charles VI of France. He exchanged letters with the Florentine chancellor, Coluccio Salutati (d. 1406), and was an ardent admirer of the classics and contemporary Italian humanists. See C. Salutati, *Epistolario*, ed. F. Novati, 4 vols. (Rome, 1891–1911), 3: 71–72n., and R. B. Donovan, "Salutati's Opinion of Non-Italian Latin Writers of the Middle Ages," *Studies in the Renaissance* 14 (1967): 185–201, esp. 187–89.

88. In placing the headquarters of the Knights Templar on the island of Rhodes, Giovanni was making a curious historical error. In fact, the Templars had been dissolved in 1312 by the Inquisition; rather, it was the Knights Hospitaller who had moved to Rhodes in 1309 and were under the rule of a "Gran maestro."

89. This allusion to Minerva's representing the triumph of wisdom over Juno, who represented wealth, probably derives from Giovanni's reading of the account of Troy's fall in *Aeneid* 2. 162ff.

90. "Servus servorum Dei," one of the papal titles, derives from the time of Pope Gregory the Great (590–604).

91. This definition of *pontifex* was current from ancient times, its earliest appearance being in Varro, *De Lingua Latina*, 5. 83.

92. The reference to St. Augustine's views on women derives from Possidius, *Vita Augustini*, chap. 26, in Migne, *Patrologia Latina*, vol. 32, col. 55. "Dicebat vero, quia etsi de sorore et nepotibus secum commorantibus nulla nasci posset mala suspicio; tamen quoniam illae personae sine aliis necessariis secumque manentibus feminis esse non possent, et quod ad eas aliae etiam a foris intrarent, de his posse offendiculum aut scandalum infirmioribus nasci." I wish to thank Professor Edward Synon of the Pontifical Institute of Mediaeval Studies at Toronto and Fr. Dennis J. M. Bradley, Rome Prize Fellow at the American Academy in Rome in 1970–71, for providing this identification.

93. The Venetian of the dialogue refers to the law of the Levites as described in Numbers 18. However, in Levitical law the priesthood was entitled to only a yearly tithe, not an annual doubling of income as the Venetian suggests was the practice of the contemporary priesthood in Italy.

94. Giovanni probably refers to Gozzardino di Simolino di Gabbione Gozzardino, a member of a Bolognese family active in communal politics during the fourteenth century. See P. S. Dolfi, *Cronologia delle famiglie nobili di Bologna* (Bologna, 1670), p. 380. The specific allusion, however, does not appear to have survived in contemporary records.

95. Giovanni here has the Venetian rehearse some of the usual criticisms that citizens of Venice leveled against the venality of churchmen. That the Paduan does not dispute the Venetian's anticlerical invective suggests that Giovanni himself may have in part at least agreed with the criticisms. See Sabbadini, pp. 81–84, who reports on Giovanni's dismay with the papacy formed during an embassy to Rome in 1400.

96. "Fat cows on the mount of Samaria" is from Amos 4: 1.

97. The story of Alexander the Great and the Gordian knot was probably known to Giovanni from Justinus, *Epitoma* 11. 7, as well as from the vast corpus of medieval Alexandrian legend.

98. The Venetian here refers to Giovanni's present employment as a schoolmaster in Venice.

99. The books are *De fortuna aulica* (1396), *De primo eius introitu ad aulam* (1385), and *De dilectione regnantium* (1399), all of which treat the hazards and duties of the courtier as well as Giovanni's autobiographical experience at the Carrara court.

100. Vergil, *Aeneid* 6. 278–79.

101. Philippians 3: 20.

102. Ecclesiasticus 23: 6.

103. Horace, *Epodes* 2. 4.

104. Diocletian's retirement from the emperorship in 305 is recorded in Eutropius, *Breviarium ab Urbe Condita* 9. 27–28, which was widely diffused and used as a text for Roman history during the Middle Ages and the early Renaissance. The contemporary allusion is to Louis of Hungary (1342–1382), who retired from the cares of state in his last days, according to Johannes Archidiaconus de Kikullew, *Chronica Hungarorum*, in *Scriptores Rerum Hungaricum*, ed. J. G. Schwandtner, 3 vols. (Vienna, 1746–1748), 1: 198.

105. Cf. the *Apologia* for a similar encomium of the country life.

106. Vergil, *Aeneid* 6. 129–31.

107. These sentiments are echoed in the *Conventio inter podagram et araneam*, which Giovanni wrote a few years later, in 1407, in retirement at Muggia.

108. Simone degli Statuti was a Paduan notary who was wealthy enough to endow and construct a church in 1383, dedicated to S. Maria Novella, near Porta Savonarola. See Gatari, *Cronaca*, p. 249 n.

109. Aristotle, *Oeconomica* 1: 1345a4–5. I am indebted to my colleague Professor James H. Day for this identification.

110. Steno remains unidentified but is perhaps Lanfranco Steno, a native Paduan, recorded in Gloria, *Monumenti*, 2, no. 1832.

111. Valerius Maximus, *Memorabilia* 7. 2. 121. "Nec parum pudenter Anaxagorus interroganti cuidam quisnam esset beatus 'nemo' inquit 'ex his, quos tu felices existimas, sed eum in illo numero reperies, qui a te ex miseris constare creditur.'"

112. The saying that "Felicitas sub sorte contentorum est" is recorded in H. Walther, *Sprichwörter*, 2, 44, no. 8926c.

113. Cf. Aristotle, *Politica* 1253a3.

114. Here Giovanni is comparing the public offices of ancient Rome with the judicial offices of contemporary communal governments.

115. Giovanni is alluding to the withdrawal from worldly affairs by such poets as Vergil and Petrarch.

116. Romans 8: 29.

117. For this allusion, see 2 Timothy 2: 19–21.

118. The reference is to the revolt of the Guelphs of Brescia against Visconti rule that was fomented by Francesco Novello da Carrara in the summer of 1403. Cf. n. 11.

119. Cf. Psalms 51: 3.

120. Giovanni derived this anecdote from Jacopo da Voragine, *Legenda Aurea,* ed. Th. Graesse (2d ed., Leipzig, 1850), pp. 531–32. "Quidam abbas pro uno coenobio construendo sexcentas marcas eidem [i.e., Bernardum] misit argenti, sed tota pecunia, dum deferretur, a praedonibus sublata est. Quo audito nihil aliud dixi nisi: benedictus Deus, qui nobis peperrict ab onore, sed et illis, inquit, qui tulerunt, levius est ferendum, tum quia hoc humana cupiditas sustulit, tum quia magna pecunia magnam iis tentationem ingessit."

121. Matthew 7: 15. The "teacher of Truth" is, of course, Jesus Christ.

122. These allusions to anecdotes from classical antiquity were known from Justinus, *Epitoma* 2. 15. 1–12, for Themistocles; and Cicero, *De Divinatione* 2. 56. 116, for Pyrrhus. Both stories are also recorded in Petrarch, *Rerum Memorandarum Libri,* p. 119, 3. 22; pp. 206–7, 4. 26, respectively, which Giovanni doubtless knew and after which he modeled his last, unfinished work of the same title. See Giuseppe Billanovich, *Petrarca Letterato. I: Lo scrittoio del Petrarca* (Rome, 1947), p. 341.

123. These famous Old Testament stories of Moses and Phineas are to be found in Exodus 32 and Joshua 22: 30–32.

124. This is a comparison of the peaceful pursuits of Francesco Gonzaga, who declined to expand his territory after the Mantuan War, and the siege of Padua brought on by the aggressive policies of Francesco Novello da Carrara.

125. This is another allusion to the programs of public works and patronage undertaken by Francesco il Vecchio in Padua and Niccolò II d'Este in Ferrara. The city of brick from one of tile is from Suetonius, *Divus Augustus* 38. 3.

126. The scriptural allusion is to the famous parable in Matthew 13: 24–30.

127. Cf. Vergil *Aeneid* 1. 19–33.

128. The story of Alcibiades' political success because of his seduction of the Spartan queen is in Justinus, *Epitoma* 5. 2.

129. From Justinus 43. 4.

130. Luigi da Ravenna was a relative of Giovanni's first wife, who came to Venice from Ravenna and made a fortune in the manner that the Paduan of the dialogue describes. See the account in the *Rationarium vite,* V, fol. 23–23v, of which an extract is published in Sabbadini, p. 146. At Conegliano in 1372, Luigi nearly succeeded in poisoning Giovanni with arsenic. See ibid., pp. 39, 151–52.

131. The lawyer Antonio da Modena does not appear in the published records of fourteenth-century Padua, such as Gloria's *Monumenti.*

132. The concept derives from Ecclesiastes 2: 26.

133. Aristotle, *Rhetorica* 1407a10. The context is Aristotle's discussion of unusual metaphors.

134. The place names accurately suggest the extent of Venetian trade at the beginning of the fifteenth century. The Assyrians is a learned, consciously anachronistic term for the Levant. Tana was the Black Sea port in Azor, where the Venetians purchased the products of central Asia, including slaves. Mauritania refers to North Africa, and England and Flanders to the active carrying-trade between Venice and the cities of northeastern Europe, especially London, Southampton, Antwerp, and Bruges.

135. A similar slogan, "Quanta premit mortale genus caligo," is recorded in Walther, *Sprichwörter,* 4: 99, no. 23,581a.

136. The reference is to Giovanni's repeated visits to the town of Aquileia from the time that his uncle Tommaso da Frignano was patriarch there in the 1370s. It seems that he even left his books there during some of his wanderings. See T. Klette, *Beiträge zur Geschichte und Literatur der italienischen Gelehrtenrenaissance,* 3 vols. (Greifswald, 1888–1890), 1: 24–25.

137. Cf. Vergil, *Aeneid* 6. 595ff.

138. Cf. Matthew 18: 17.

139. The notion that noxious vapors accounted for plague and disease was very common by the end of the fourteenth century. Cf. A. M. Campbell, *The Black Death and Men of Learning* (New York, 1931), esp. pp. 48–56.

140. Meroe, Tyre, Crete, and Modon were Venice's most important trading outposts and colonies in the Levant. Dalmatia, Sanium, and Picenum refer to the eastern shores of the Adriatic and the Marches in Italy respectively. Flaminium is the ancient region around Ravenna, Cisalpine Gaul the area of the Veneto, and Friuli the region of northeastern Italy. Tergestine Bay, or the Gulf of Trieste, is the northern part of the Adriatic Sea between Aquileia and Istria.

141. See Leviticus 26: 6 and Isaiah 32; 18.

142. The notion that a leader's lust for power is the chief cause of his downfall was a commonplace in medieval political thought. For the Christian origin of the idea, see St. Augustine, *De Civitate Dei* 3. 14.

143. Psalms 43: 15.

144. The Second Paduan, or Chioggia, War of 1378–1381 was the closest that Venice came in Giovanni's lifetime to suffering military defeat. See n. 78. The struggle of the cities of Tuscany, the Marches, and Emilia against the Church refers to the so-called War of the Eight Saints, which Florence, Bologna, and smaller cities of the Papal States waged against the papacy of Gregory XI in 1375–1378. Characteristically, Giovanni ascribes largely a propaganda value to the use of the word liberty by Florence and other cities. On the concept of liberty in contemporary humanist thought, see Ronald Witt, "The Rebirth of the Concept of Republican Liberty in Italy," *Renaissance Studies in Honor of Hans Baron,* ed. A. Molho and J. A. Tedeschi (Florence, 1971), pp. 173–99.

145. Psalms 36: 27.
146. Romans 2: 15.
147. Romans 6: 18.
148. Matthew 6: 24.

149. Giovanni da Legnano, former teacher of Giovanni and famed jurist and author, was one of the principal learned servants of the commune of Bologna until his death in 1383. See n. 40. The Bottrigari were a well-known Bolognese family of judges and lawyers of whom three members, Giacomo, Bartolomeo, and Lorenzo, are recorded among the professors and lecturers in civil and canon law at the University of Bologna in the fourteenth century. See A. Sorbelli, *Storia della Università di Bologna,* vol. 1 *Il Medioevo* (Bologna, 1944), p. 100. The particular anecdote, however, is not recorded except in the *Dragmalogia,* and it is not known which member of the Bottrigari family is mentioned here.

150. Proverbs 2: 14.

151. Another reference to Diocletian's retirement in 305. See n. 104.

152. Seneca, *Ad Polybium de Consolatione* 6. 5. "Magna servitus est magna fortuna."

153. Augustus's desire for leisure was known from Petrarch, *Rerum Memorandarum,* p. 6; 1. 6, and Seneca, *De Brevitate Vitae,* 4. ,

154. Giovanni records the affection and trust which Francesco il Vecchio held for him in other works, especially *De primo eius introitu ad aulam,* and his letter to Rodulfo da Carrara, which served as the preface to *Familie Carrariensis natio.*

155. Romans 12: 18.

156. The allusion is to the story of Adam as recorded in Genesis 2: 15 ff.

157. The distinction between service to God and that to the world is ultimately derived from St. Paul; see Romans 8.

158. Psalms 15: 2.

159. Philippians 2: 21.

160. Malachi 1: 10.

161. Giovanni properly credits Pope Gregory the Great (590–604) with the creation of the papal title *servus servorum Dei*.

162. Giovanni's knowledge of the slavery of Pope Adrian IV parallels the account in Petrarch, *Rerum Memorandarum Libri*, p. 183, 3. 95, which was derived from John of Salisbury's *Policraticus*.

163. Horace, *Epistulae* I. 17. 35.

164. Cassiodorus, *Variae*, ed. T. Mommsen (*Monumenta Germaniae Historica, Auctores antiquissimi* [Berlin, 1894]), 12: 39, no. 43: "non est maius meritum quam gratiam invenisse regnantium, nam quibus fas est de cinctis optimos quaerere, videntur semper meritos elegisse."

165. The allusion to the carnal temptations of St. Paul derived from 2 Corinthians 12: 7. The legend of the martyrdom of St. Andrew in imitation of Christ's crucifixion provided the basis for that allusion. For the Latin text that Giovanni might have known, see F. Blatt, ed., *Die lateinischen Bearbeitungen der Acta Andreae et Matthiae* (Giessen and Copenhagen, 1930), p. 85.

166. 1 Corinthians 9: 25.

167. Terence, *Adelphoe* 867–68: "duxi uxorem; quam ibi miseriam vidi! Nati filii: alia cura."

168. 1 Corinthians 7: 32–34.

169. 1 Corinthians 7: 35.

170. 1 Corinthians 7: 29–31.

171. Cf. Hebrews 6: 4 ff.

172. Tommaso da Frignano was Giovanni's much-admired uncle, who became a cardinal of the Church in 1378. Giovanni's characterization of him accords well with modern judgments. See G. B. Tondini, *Delle memorie istoriche concernenti la vita del cardinal Tommaso da Frignano* (Macerata, 1782), and G. Pistoni, "Un modenese amico del Petrarca, il cardinale Tommaso Frignano," *Atti e Memorie dell'Accademia di scienze, lettere ed arti di Modena*, 5th ser. 12 (1954): 82–96.

Selected Bibliography

Dalla Santa, G., and Bertanza, E., eds. *Maestri, scuole e scolari in Venezia fino al 1500*. Venice, 1907.

Gatari, Galeazzo; Gatari, Bartolomeo; and Gatari, Andrea. *Cronaca carrarese*, edited by Antonio Medin and Guido Tolomei. *Rerum Italicarum Scriptores*, n. ed. 17, pt. 1. Città di Castello-Bologna, 1909–1932.

Gesta Magnifica Domus Carrariensis, edited by R. Cessi. *Rerum Italicarum Scriptores,* n. ed., appendix and pt. 3. Bologna, 1942–1965.

Pastorello, Ester, ed. *Il copialettere marciano della cancellaria carrarese (gennaio 1402–gennaio 1403).* Venice, 1915.

Petrarca, Francesco. *Qualis esse debeat qui rem publicam regit,* edited by V. Ussani. Padua, 1922.

Polenton, Sicco. *Scriptorum illustrium latinae linguae libri XVIII,* edited by B. L. Ullman. Rome, 1928.

Salutati, Coluccio. *Epistolario.* Edited by F. Novati. 4 vols. Rome, 1891–1911.

Vergerio, Pier Paolo. *Epistolario.* Edited by L. Smith. Rome, 1934.

Zabarella, Francesco. *De Felicitate tres libri.* Padua, 1655.

STUDIES

Baron, H. *Crisis of the Early Italian Renaissance,* n. ed. Princeton, 1966.

Bernicoli, S. "Maestri e scuole letterarie in Ravenna nel sec. XIV" *Felix Ravenna* 32 (1927): 61–69.

Biasuz, G. "Giovanni Conversino da Ravenna, maestro di grammatica a Belluno." *Archivio storico di Belluno, Feltre e Cadore* 25 (1954): 37–9.

Billanovich, G. *Petrarca letterato.* Rome, 1947.

Bueno de Mesquita, D. M. *Giangaleazzo Visconti, Duke of Milan (1351–1402).* Cambridge, England, 1941.

Casini, T. "Tre nuovi rimatori del Trecento" *Il Propugnatore,* n.s. 1 (1888): 313–66.

Cremaschi, G. "Testi umanistici in codici della Biblioteca Civica di Bergamo" *Aevum* 33 (1959): 266–73.

Foresti, A. *Aneddoti della vita di Francesco Petrarca.* Brescia, 1928. See especially pp. 425–57.

Gargan, L. "Giovanni Conversini e la cultura letteraria a Treviso nella seconda metà del Trecento." *Italia Medioevale e Umanistica* 8 (1965): 85–159.

Gloria, Andrea. *Monumenti della Università di Padova, 1318–1405.* 2 vols. Padua, 1888.

Klette, Th. *Beiträge zur Geschichte und Litteratur des italienischen Gelehrterenaissance. Vol. I. Johannes Conversinus und Johannes Malpaghini von Ravenna.* Greifswald, 1888.

Kniewald, Dragutin. "Ioannes Concversini de Ravenna dubrovacki notar, 1384–1387." *Glas srpske akademije nauka i umetnosti* 229, Odeljenje literature i jezika 3 (1957) : 39–160.

Kohl, B. G. "Government and Society in Renaissance Padua." *Journal of Medieval and Renaissance Studies* 2 (1972) : 205–21.

———. "Mourners of Petrarch." In *Francis Petrarch, Six Centuries Later, a Symposium,* edited by A. Scaglione. Chapel Hill and Chicago, 1975, pp. 339–52.

———. "Political Attitudes of North Italian Humanists in the Late *Trecento." Studies in Medieval Culture* 4 (1974) : 418–27.

———. "The Works of Giovanni di Conversino da Ravenna : A Catalogue of Manuscripts and Editions." *Tradiaio* 31 (1975) : 349–67.

———, and Day, J. "Giovanni Conversini's *Consolatio ad Donatum* on the Death of Petrarch." *Studies in the Renaissance* 21 21 (1974) : 9–30.

Korelin, M. *Rannii ital'ianskii Gumanizm i ego istorigrafiia.* 4 vols. St. Petersburg, 1914. Vol. 4.

Lane, F. C. *Venice, A Maritime Republic.* Baltimore, 1973. Chap. 14.

Novati, F. "Donato degli Albanzani alla corte estense." *Archivio Storico Italiano,* ser. 5, 6 (1890) : 365–84.

Pastorello, Ester. *Nuove ricerche sulla storia di Padova e dei principi da Carrara al tempo di Gian Galeazzo Visconti.* Padua, 1908.

Rački, F. "Ivan Ravenjanin." *Rad Jugoslavenske Akademije znanosti i umjetnosti* 74 (1885) : 135–91.

Raulich, Italo. *La caduta dei Carraresi di Padova.* Padua, 1890.

Sabbadini, R. *Giovanni da Ravenna, insigne figura d'umanista (1343–1408).* Como, 1924.

———. *Il metodo degli umanisti.* Florence, 1920.

———. *Le scoperte dei codici latini e greci ne' secoli XIV e XV.* Edited by E. Garin, 2 vols. Florence, 1967.

Ullman, B. L. *The Humanism of Salutati.* Padua, 1963.

———. *Studies in the Italian Renaissance.* Rome, 1955.

Voigt, G. *Die Wiederbelegung des classischen Alterthums.* 3d ed. 2 vols. Berlin, 1893. 1 : 212–19.

Weiss, R.. "Il codice oxoniense e altri codici delle opere di Giovanni da Ravenna." *Giornale storico della letteratura italiana* 125 (1946) : 133–48.

Witt, Ronald. "The Rebirth of the Concept of Republican Liberty in Italy." In *Renaissance Studies in Honor of Hans Baron,*

edited by A. Molho and J. A. Tedeschi. Florence, 1971. Pp. 173–99.

Zaccaria, V. "Il *Memorandarum rerum liber* di Giovanni Conversino da Ravenna." *Atti dell'Istituto Veneto* 106, pt. 2 (1947–48): 221–50.

Zimmermann, T. C. Price. "Confession and Autobiography in the Early Renaissance." In *Renaissance Studies in Honor of Hans Baron,* edited by A. Molho and J. A. Tedeschi. Florence, 1971. Pp. 119–40.

Index

Abu Ma'shar, 18
Albanzani, Donato, 14, 17
Albertus Magnus, 24
Alcibiades, 213
Alessio, Nicoletto d', 23
Alexander the Great, 163
Anaxagoras, 187
Andrew, Saint, 265
Antisthenes, 221
Apuleius, 24
Aquileia, 225
Aquinas, Saint Thomas, 24
Aristotle, 24;
    quoted, 93, 119, 181, 189
Arsendi, Arsendino, 21
Augustine, Saint, 14, 18, 159
Augustus Caesar, 115, 127, 255

Barbaro, Francesco, 24, 28, 39
Barbiano, Alberico da, 26
Baron, Hans, 35, 45
Barone, Pietro da, 16
Belluno, 17-18, 20
Benasuda (Giovanni's second wife), 17
Bentivoglio, Giovanni, 26
Bernard of Clairvaux, Saint, 18, 203
Bible, 33, 36, 37, 38, 125, 221;
    quoted, 91, 97, 105, 125, 135, 141, 149, 151, 161, 169, 245, 247, 251, 259, 265, 269
Boccaccio, Giovanni, 24-25, 115
Boethius, 14; quoted, 151
Bologna, 13-16, 26, 131, 139; University of, 13, 15
Bombossolo, Giovanni, 89, 275-76
Bonandrea, Giovanni di, 15
Boniface IX (pope), 26
Boschetti, Niccolò, 15
Bottigari, family, 249, 251

Brescia, 59, 199, 201
Bruni, Leonardo, 31, 39
Buda (Hungary), 13

Caelius, Rufus, M., 85
Calvi, Zilio, 28, 34
Carrara, Conte da, 26
Carrara court, 20-22, 24-26, 28, 32, 34, 67-83 passim
Carrara, family, 20, 23, 27, 31, 34, 39, 67
Carrara, Francesco il Vecchio da, 20-22, 26, 27, 34-35, 67, 69, 81, 87, 89, 109, 125, 129, 211, 255
Carrara, Francesco Novello da, 23, 25-28, 32, 34-35, 51, 59, 61, 63, 65, 75, 81, 89, 157, 167, 199, 201
Carrara, Giacomo II da, 115
Carrara, Landolfo da, 31
Carrara, Rudolfo da, 27
Cassiodorus, 263
Cephisodotus, 221
Chelli, Antonio, 24
Cicero, 24, 38; pseudo-, 15-16, 24
Claudian, 24
Colonna, Aegidius, 24
Conegliano, 16

Dandolo, Fantin, 29
Dante, 20
Dialogue: forms of, 31-32; as used by Giovanni, 18-20, 34-35. *See also* Dragmalogia
Diocletian, 171, 255
Dragmalogia, discussed, 18, 20, 22, 30, 31-39; composition of, 27-29; summary of, 32-33; manuscripts of, 39-41

289

290   Index

Elizabeth (queen of Hungary), 21
Este, family, 25
Este, Niccolò II d', 15, 89, 115, 129, 211, 277
Euripides, quoted, 107

Feltre, Vittorino da, 23, 29
Ferrara, 14, 15, 25, 131, 211
Fiano, Francesco da, 20
Florence, 14, 16, 24, 26, 30, 38, 53, 55, 57, 107; University of, 16
Fortune, 18-19, 30, 61
Frignano, Bonetto da (Giovanni's uncle), 13
Frignano, Conversino da (Giovanni's father), 13, 18, 19, 23
Frignano, Tommaso da (Giovanni's uncle), 13-14, 17-20, 31, 38, 269, 271
Furlan, Margherita (Giovanni's first wife), 14, 16

Gallo, Enrico, 28, 69, 79
Galmarelli, Carlo, 20
Germanicus, 24
Giustinian, Leonardo di Bernardo, 28, 39
Giustinian, Marco di Bernardo, 28, 39
Giustinian, Marco di Pietro, 21-22
Gonzaga, Francesco I, 55, 209
Gozzadini, Gozzadino, 161
Gozzadini, Nanni, 26
Gregory the Great, Saint, 20, 24, 261, 263
Guelphs and Ghibellines, 59, 199, 201

Hanville, Jean de, 24
Horace, 20, 26, 38, 115; quoted, 171, 263

Innocent VII (pope), 28-29

Jerome, Saint, 20
Jesus Christ, 149, 151, 159, 205, 241, 247, 259
John the Evangelist, 27
Jugurtha, 109
Julius Caesar, 107
Juno, 157
Justinian, 115
Justinus, 149

Knights Templar, 157
Korelin, M., 45
Kristeller, P. O., 44

Legnano, Giovanni da, 103, 251
Liberty, 33, 37-38, 133, 245-57 passim
Life, active and contemplative, 19-20, 32, 35-36, 141-65 passim
Life, country and city, 20, 29-30, 32, 35-37, 169-195 passim, 225, 237
Livy, 25
Lottini, Giovanni, 24
Louis (king of Hungary), 13, 19, 127, 129, 171
Lucretia, 25

Maecenas, 20
Malatesta, Galeotto, 103
Medici, Michele di Lapo de', 14
Meneghino, Antonio, 87
Milan, 59
Minerva, 157
Modena, 13
Modena, Antonio da, 215
Moglio, Pietro da, 15
Monaci, Lorenzo de', 24
Monarchy, 25, 32-33, 35-36, 107-41 passim, 145; sanctioned by God, 133-137. *See also* republic
Montorso, Montorso di, 89, 97, 99, 276
Moses, 207
Muggia (Istria), 28-29

Ockham, William, 37
Ovid, 115

Padua, 15, 20-23, 25-28, 33-34, 40, 57, 59, 129, 181, 183, 211, 231, 243
Patronage, value of, 20, 34-36, 65, 115, 117, 121, 131, 229
Paul, Saint, 19, 167, 197, 245, 247, 265, 267, 269
Paula, Saint, 19
Perugia, 26
Peter of Mantua, 24
Petrarca, Francesco, 17, 21, 30, 38, 115
Phineas, 207
Plato, 24
Plautus, 24
Pliny, quoted, 77, 79
Polenta, Bernardino da, 115
Polenta, Guido II da, 16, 20, 115
Polenta, Guido III da, 89, 275
Polenton, Sicco, 23, 29
Prudentius, 14

Index

Queens, ancient, 125, 127
Quintilian, 24

Rabatta, Michele da, 69, 79
Ragusa (the modern Dubrovnik), 21-22
Ravenna, 13-15
Ravenna, Conversino di Giovanni da (Giovanni's elder son), 14-16, 22-23
Ravenna, Gerundino da, 89, 275-76
Ravenna, Giovanni di Conversino da: life of, 13-30; library of, 23-24; early works of, 17-20; works at Ragusa, 21-22; works at Padua, 25, 27; late works, 28-30; Dragmalogia, 31-39; as the Ravennate in the Dragmalogia, 34, 67-87, 95, 99, 165, 181, 223, 225, 255, 265
Ravenna, Israele di Giovanni da (Giovanni's younger son), 17, 21-22, 27
Ravenna, Luigi da (Giovanni's kinsman), 16-17, 213, 215
Religious vocation, 19-20, 33, 38, 159, 257-71 passim
Republic, 33, 35-36, 107-41 passim. *See also* monarchy
Robert (king of Naples), 36, 115
Rome, 20, 26, 29; ancient, 38, 109, 119, 207
Rugolo, Paolo, 15-16, 18, 22, 25, 27, 30
Rupert of Habsburg, 35, 55, 57, 133

Sabbadini, Remigio, 27, 42
Sallust: pseudo-, 24
Saltarelli, Simone, 28-29
Salutati, Coluccio, 24, 38-39
Santasofia, Marsilio da, 20
Scala, Guglielmo della, 27
Seneca, 20; quoted, 73, 85, 255
Sermeola (Paduan suburb), 21, 71
Seta, Lombardo della, 21, 71
Siena, University of, 13

Sins, seven deadly, 33, 37-38, 46, 171, 195-225 passim. *See also* vices
Statuti, Simone degli, 181, 281
Steno, Lanfranco, 181, 183
Strasbourg, 133

Terence, quoted, 85, 91, 141, 267
Themistocles, 207
Trevisan, Marco, 18
Treviso, 15-16, 30
Troy, 157, 213

Ubaldis, Baldus de, 21
Udine, 23, 26, 81
Urban VI (pope), 19

Valerius Maximus, 15, 30, 38
Venice, 17, 21-23, 27-28, 30, 33-34, 40, 107, 125, 129, 215; criticism of, 225-43 passim
Vergerio, Pier Paolo, 23, 28-29, 39
Vergil, 16, 36, 38, 115, 165; quoted, 95, 179
Verona, 61, 103
Verona, Guarino da, 23, 39
Vices: pride, 37, 205; envy, 37, 205, 207; anger, 207, 209; sloth, 37, 209, 211; lust, 211, 213, 215; gluttony, 217, 219; greed, 37, 217, 221. *See also* sins, seven deadly
Virgin Mary, 27, 154
Visconti, Bernabò, 89
Visconti, Caterina, 27
Visconti, Giangaleazzo, 23, 27, 53, 59, 65, 115, 131

War of Chioggia, 143, 243
War of Eight Saints, 38, 243
Warfare, condemned, 50-67 passim, 185, 201, 209, 243
Witte, Jacobus, 41

Zabarella, Francesco, 24
Zagrabia, Michele da, 14